Dennis Ted Beest
March, 1988

PREACHING THE NEW COMMON LECTIONARY

PREACHING THE NEW COMMON LECTIONARY

Year B

Lent, Holy Week, Easter

Commentary by:

Fred B. Craddock
John H. Hayes
Carl R. Holladay
Gene M. Tucker

ABINGDON PRESS
Nashville

Preaching the New Common Lectionary
Year B Lent, Holy Week, Easter

Fourth Printing 1988

This book is printed on acid-free paper.

Library of Congress Cataloging in Publication Data

Main entry under title:
Preaching the new common lectionary. Year B,
Lent, Holy Week, Easter.
Includes index.
1. Bible—Homiletical use. 2. Bible—Liturgical
lessons, English. I. Craddock, Fred B.
BS534.5.P73 1984 251 84-11118

ISBN 0-687-33846-8

MANUFACTURED BY THE PARTHENON PRESS AT
NASHVILLE, TENNESSEE, UNITED STATES OF AMERICA

Contents

Lent

Holy Week

Easter

Special Day

Introduction

It might be helpful to the reader if we make a few remarks about our understanding of our task and what we have sought to accomplish in this volume. The following comments will touch on four topics.

The Scripture in Preaching

There is no substitute for direct exposure to the biblical text, both for the preacher in preparation and for the listener in worship. The Scriptures are therefore not only studied privately but read aloud as an act of worship in and of itself and not solely as prelude to a sermon. The sermon is an interpretation of Scripture in the sense that the preacher seeks to bring the text forward into the present in order to effect a new hearing of the Word. In this sense the text has its future and its fulfillment in preaching. In fact, the Bible itself is the record of the continual rehearing and reinterpreting of its own traditions in new settings and for new generations of believers. New settings and new circumstances are properly as well as inescapably integral to a hearing of God's Word in and through the text. Whatever else may be said to characterize God's Word, it is always appropriate to the hearers. But the desire to be immediately relevant should not abbreviate study of the text or divorce the sermon from the biblical tradition. Such sermons are orphaned, released without memory into the world. It is the task of the preacher and teacher to see that the principle of fidelity to Scripture is not abandoned in the life and worship of the church. The endeavor to understand a text in its historical, literary, and theological contexts does create, to be sure, a sense of distance between the Bible and the congregation. The preacher may grow impatient during this period of feeling a long way from a sermon. But this time of study can be most fruitful. By holding text and parishioners apart for a while, the preacher can hear each more clearly and exegete each more honestly. Then, when the two intersect in the sermon, neither the text nor the congregation is consumed by the other. Because the Bible is an ancient book, it invites the preacher back into its world in order to understand; because the Bible is the church's Scripture, it moves forward into our world and addresses us here and now.

The Lectionary and Preaching

Ever increasing numbers of preachers are using a lectionary as a guide for preaching and worship. The intent of lectionaries is to provide for the church over a given period of time (usually three years) large units of Scripture that have been selected because they carry the central message of the Bible and that have been arranged according to the seasons of the Christian year. Lectionaries are not designed to limit one's message or restrict the freedom of the pulpit. On the contrary, churches that use a lectionary usually hear more Scripture in worship than those that do not. And ministers who preach from the lectionary find themselves stretched into areas of the canon into which they would not have gone had they kept to the path of personal preference. Other values of the lectionary are well known: the readings provide a common ground for discussions in ministerial peer groups; family worship can more easily join public worship through shared readings; ministers and worship committees can work with common biblical texts to prepare services that have movement and integrity; and the lectionary encourages more disciplined study and advance preparation. All these and other values are increased if the different churches share a common lectionary. A common lectionary could conceivably generate a community-wide Christian conversation.

This Book and Preaching

This volume is not designed as a substitute for work with the biblical text; on the contrary, its intent is to encourage such work. Neither is it our desire to relieve the preacher of regular visits to concordances, lexicons, and commentaries, but it is our hope that the comments on the texts here will be sufficiently germinal to give direction and purpose to those visits to major reference works. Our commentaries are efforts to be faithful to the text and to begin moving the text toward the pulpit. There are no sermons as such here, nor could there be. No one can preach long distance. Only the one who preaches can do an exegesis of the listeners and mix into sermon preparation enough local soil so as to effect an indigenous hearing of the Word. But we hope we have contributed to that end. The reader will also notice that, while each of us has been aware of the other readings for each service, there has been no attempt to offer a collaborated commentary on all texts or a homogenized interpretation as though there were not four texts but one. We have tried to respect the integrity of each biblical passage and remain within the limits of our own areas of knowledge. It is assumed that the season of the year, the needs of the listeners, the preacher's own abilities, as well as the overall unity of the message of the Scriptures will prompt the preacher to find among the four readings the word for the day. Sometimes the four texts will join arm in arm, sometimes they will debate with one another, sometimes one will lead while the others follow, albeit at times reluctantly. Such is the wealth of the biblical witness.

A final word about our comments. The lections from the Psalter have been treated in the same manner as the other readings even though some Protestant churches often omit the reading of the Psalm or replace it with a hymn. We have chosen to regard the Psalm as an equal among the texts, primarily for three reasons: (1) there is growing interest in the use of Psalms in public worship and comments on them may help make that use more informed; (2) the Psalms were a major source for worship and preaching in the early church and continue to inspire and inform Christian witness; and (3) comments on the Psalms may make this volume helpful to Roman Catholic preachers who have maintained the long tradition of using the Psalms in Christian services.

This Season and Preaching

This volume treats the readings for Lent, Holy Week, and Easter, the events and seasons central to the entire Christian year.

Of all the seasons of the Christian's pilgrimage, Lent has probably been most abused. It has in certain times and places become a period of excessive introspection, empty abstinence from tidbits of affluence, and the enjoyment of the gloom of self-denial. Correction of such excesses and distortions does not lie, however, in non-observance of Lent, but rather in the recovery of its rich tradition. The image of forty days as a period of engagement with God, of repentance and prayer is deeply imbedded in Scripture. In the early church, Lent became a time of preparation for baptism, and among the baptized, a time for reflection upon one's baptism and renewal of vows. And in all times and places, Lent looks toward God's act in the resurrection. Sober awareness of sin is appropriate, to be sure, but so is profound joy.

Holy Week is a time of reflection upon the suffering and death of Christ. A major theological task of the early disciples was to understand and accept the death of Jesus as an event transcending tragedy. How did Jesus' passion relate to the purpose of God, to Jesus' own ministry, and to his followers' hopes? In the Passover traditions, in the Suffering Servant of Isaiah, and in the Jewish interpretations of sacrifice, the disciples were able not only to interpret Jesus as "our Passover" (I Cor. 5:7-8) but also to understand in a new way their own sufferings. The preacher will find the Old Testament resources not only enriching during this week but also helpful as a guard against any residue of anti-Semitism which may darken unduly the biblical reports of Jesus' death.

Easter is not one day but a season. It is silence; what does one say when running from an empty tomb? It is a shout, "He is risen!" It is a question, Where do we go from here? When Easter morning fades into late afternoon and some disciples begin to say, "I am going fishing," the church prays and waits for Pentecost.

Gene M. Tucker (Old Testament)
John H. Hayes (Psalms)
Carl R. Holladay (Epistles)
Fred B. Craddock (Gospels)

Ash Wednesday

Joel 2:1-2, 12-17a; Psalm 51:1-12; II Corinthians 5:20b–6:2 (3-10); Matthew 6:1-6, 16-21

Joel 2:1-2, 12-17*a*

The Book of Joel is the most liturgically oriented of all the prophetical books. Concern with cultic affairs and the use of cultic language and formulations all point to the fact that Joel was probably a cultic prophet or that the book which bears his name was originally composed and used within the cult.

A central feature in the book is the call for fasting and repentance in light of an approaching or present disaster. The calamity is depicted as the onslaught of a locust plague (1:4), an agricultural failure (1:17-18), or foreign invasion (2:20). All of these may be ways of speaking about a single phenomenon described under a variety of images. As in many cultures, calamities and disasters in ancient Israel could be portrayed in very metaphorical terminology. The use of such metaphorical and pictorial language, like modern cartoons, allowed for the exaggeration of features and characteristics that could highlight the traumatic character of the threat and at the same time verbalize the feelings of those threatened. The purpose of many laments was to allow the worshiper or worshipers to provide a depiction of the threat and in so doing at least to gain a certain control over it. Description and identification aid in taking steps to overcome. Sometimes, of course, such depictions were also intended to awaken the audience or reader to the seriousness of the threat and thus to convince them that a particular course of action was most appropriate.

The selection of this text from Joel for Ash Wednesday is based on two features: the text proclaims the coming of the day of the Lord and also summons the people to repentance and preparation for the day that includes fasting and services of public penitence.

The entire Book of Joel is rather complicated in form and structure, and this is the case even with the few verses of today's lesson. Verses 1-2 call for the sounding of an alarm (the blowing of the shofar) in light of the distress and disaster which has overtaken the land. Verses 12-13*a* contain God's call to return and repent, stipulating some of the personal features of the penitential ritual. Verses 13*b*-14 are the prophet's parallel call to return and to repent. Verses 15-17*a* are the prophetic directions for carrying out the communal aspects associated with the general assembly of the people as an embodiment of their return to God. The text, of course, continues with the plea of the people followed by a favorable oracle of response from the Deity, but these lie outside today's lection.

Verses 1-2 describe the coming distress to which the fasting ritual should be a prelude or response. It is frequently difficult to know in some prophetical texts whether the event described is already existing and present or yet to come. Verses 1-2, for example, seem to imply the future coming of the calamity whereas verse 3 suggests the opposite. Whatever the calamity, it was viewed as an act of God, a day of Yahweh's judgment.

The oracle of God (verses 12-13*a*) presents some of the characteristic personal acts of penitence. Both external and internal acts are emphasized, thus indicating the necessity of involving the totality of the person. The external acts are fasting, weeping, and mourning; the internal acts focus on the heart which should be torn like a garment. Rituals of penitence not only represent a break in the normal pattern of life but also partially simulate the conditions that penitence seeks to avoid. In such rituals, the normal course of life is given up so that the abnormal state won't become normal. One weeps, mourns, and goes without food not only to demonstrate the total contriteness of heart but also to help avoid making these features the characteristics of life by appealing to God for intervention. Both the external and internal features of penitence should be stressed and given expression in Ash Wednesday services.

The prophet's plea for the people to return (verses 13*b*-14) is based on theological arguments. There is first the appeal to the character and nature of God. Since God is "gracious and merciful, slow to anger, abounding in steadfast love, and repents of evil," then there is certainly the hope that he can be trusted to give a sympathetic and sensitive hearing. Second, the summons to penitence is based on the expected future, namely that God would respond favorably and repent and leave behind a blessing. (This seems the general sense of verse 14 although who is being talked about is a little unclear.)

The seriousness and the totality of the fast is illustrated in the prophet's reiteration of the summons and description of some of the cultic activities associated with the public service of penitence in verses 15-16. The people are called on to fast and to assemble at the sanctuary, and the priests are commanded to weep and offer intercessory prayers. The assembly involves the total community from the elders to the nursing infants since all are threatened by God's judgment. The sanctification of the communal fast involved desisting from food, work, and sexual intercourse. Thus the joy of the bridal couple and the consummation of their marriage must be interrupted.

Ancient Israelite cultic practices creatively combined many features of external and internal religious matters. These texts from Joel demonstrate how both emphases were present, as they always should be in religious observations. Although the activities of Ash Wednesday are not performed to ward off a coming disaster, they nonetheless inaugurate a period that calls for both internal and external signs of penitence.

Psalm 51:1-12

Psalm 51 is probably the best known of the classical seven penitential psalms (6, 32, 38, 51, 102, 130, 143). The heading, perhaps supplied by the collectors of the Psalter, associated this psalm with David's contrition after being confronted by the prophet Nathan following the Bathsheba affair (see II Sam. 12:1-23). This association probably represents a late way of exegeting the psalm by defining a precise historical situation which might have given it birth. That is, the collectors of the Psalms felt that this was the type of prayer for forgiveness that David might have prayed after being reproached by Nathan.

The psalm opens with a plea for God to have mercy, to forgive, and to cleanse the one praying (verses 1-2). The worshiper does not claim any special status or any moral worth but can only cast him/herself upon the love and mercy of God. Three terms are used for the person's wrongdoing—transgressions (rebellion against authority), iniquity (a perverse action or straying), and sin (missing the mark)—and three terms are employed for removing the sin—blot out, wash, and cleanse. The piling up of terms suggests a strong recognition of sin and a passionate need for its removal. It is possible to develop the picture suggested by these terms although the author may not be consciously speaking of three different types of sin but only seeking to emphasize an extreme sense of wrongdoing and thus separation from God. "To blot out" suggests the idea of a book in which one's activities were recorded (see Neh. 13:13; Dan. 7:10). "To wash" suggests a stain that has become ingrained. "To cleanse" suggests that sin has contaminated and rendered one culticly impure and thus unfit for full participation in the worship of the temple.

The opening plea of the psalm is followed by a confession of sin (verses 3-5). Three elements in this confession are noteworthy: (1) The matter of sin is depicted as primarily a matter between the worshiper and God. No particular sin is mentioned. Stress is laid instead on the disruption of the divine-human relationship. The same sentiment is found in II Samuel 12 where David acknowledges that he has sinned against God (verse 13) although his actions had led to Uriah's death. Since the ordering of the world and the giving of laws were acts of the divine, infringement of these could be seen as sins against God as well as crimes against others. (2) The psalmist is quite contrite about the acknowledgment of sin. There is no attempt to escape the reality and consequences of sin or to leave the issue merely at the level of shame about sin.

Thus the psalmist can affirm that "thou [God] art justified in thy sentence and blameless in thy judgment" (verse 4*b*). (3) The psalmist acknowledges that his/her entire life, that is, the psalmist's very nature, is sinful in orientation. This is expressed in the affirmation, "I was brought forth in iniquity, and in sin did my mother conceive me" (verse 5). This assertion is about as close to a doctrine of original sin as there is to be found in the Old Testament.

After the confession of sin, the psalm reading continues with a plea or petition (verses 6-12) which not only requests the forgiveness of sin but also the restoration of the worshiper's relationship to the Deity and the total transformation of the person. Both the positive and the negative aspects of penitence and forgiveness are emphasized. In verse 6, for example, there is the request for internal changes at the depth of being and willing, while verse 7 emphasizes the external purgation and ritual washing used in the cult to symbolize spiritual purification. A similar polarity or balance is found in verses 8 and 9 where verse 8 contains a prayer for positive restoration and verse 9 for the more negative aspects of sin's removal.

The pinnacle of the prayer occurs in verses 10-12 where the psalmist requests renewal and re-creation, that is, to become, in Pauline terms (see II Cor. 5:17), a new creation with a new inner life and spirit resting on the constant presence and a close association with the Deity. The prayer that the divine Holy Spirit remain with the worshiper is perhaps equal here to the prayer that God's presence remain with the worshiper. (For the other Old Testament occurrence of the phrase Holy Spirit, see Isa. 63:10-11.) Such a presence restores the joy of divine salvation. Finally, the psalmist asks that God continue to uphold him/her, implying the recognition that forgiveness and restoration must be accompanied by the continuing support of the Deity, otherwise the future would be only the repetition of the past.

This psalm, more than any other, exposes the true nature and depth of penitence—a central theme of Lent—and at the same time recognizes what is required to become a radically changed person, a new creation.

II Corinthians 5:20*b*–6:2 (3-10)

"We beseech you on behalf of Christ, be reconciled to God" (verse 20*b*). It may seem odd that Paul urges the Christians at Corinth to accept God's reconciling act. Some commentators, in fact, have suggested that his remarks have a missionary flavor and were aimed primarily toward those who were not yet Christians. But this is to misunderstand Paul's theology of reconciliation. Far from being a once-for-all act fully experienced or achieved at the time of one's conversion, reconciliation should be seen as an ongoing process in which the Christian participates. A part of the eschatological work of God who is at work in the world to bring about righteousness, reconciliation involves not only the individual's relationship with God in a personal sense but also the individual's relationship with humanity as a whole, indeed with the whole cosmos. Paul elsewhere makes clear that the cosmos as a whole is undergoing transformation "in Christ" (Rom. 8), and the one who has been incorporated into Christ participates in this process. Through the work of Christ, God has initiated a process at work in the world in which death gives way to life. To be sure, the Christian who experiences baptism reenacts the death and resurrection of Christ in a single act, but not as if this becomes a single moment in the past which grows increasingly distant as one grows older. It is rather a reenactment that initiates a way of life which is itself typified by dying and rising. Even "in Christ" one continues to die to the world even as one experiences the power of the resurrected Christ. Thus within each individual Christian in whom the Spirit of Christ works to bring about filial obedience there occurs the eschatological renewing, triggered by the Christ-event and continued by the ongoing work of God in the world—God's reconciling work.

It is only natural that Christians be charged to "be reconciled to God" (verse 20*b*), that is, to accept the reconciliation God offers (Barrett). To do so requires penitence which, of course, is the note on which the Lenten Season begins. Ash Wednesday, in particular, as an expression of public penitence on the part of the individual Christians and Christian communities, becomes an appropriate occasion to hear this injunction of Paul. A cross etched with ashes on the forehead provides a vivid symbol for all to see how the cross of Christ continues to serve as the means of bringing humanity into reconciliation with God and the world.

It should also be noted that Paul makes this appeal "on behalf of Christ." This phrase recalls his earlier statement in verse 20 where he says that "we are ambassadors for Christ," that is, "on behalf of Christ." The Christian is here viewed as the emissary, or the legate, of Christ through whom an official appeal is made. If these remarks are more directly applicable to the Christian minister, they suggest the sacramental dimension of the minister's work, both the work of preaching and pastoring. There is the clear sense that God's work and word through Christ is continued through the work and word of those who are "in Christ." This is stressed even more in the language of 6:1, where Paul quite audaciously suggests that we are actually God's co-workers in the work of reconciliation.

Another way of understanding reconciliation is to see it as accepting "the grace of God," and this too is obviously ongoing for the Christian. The Old Testament quotation (Isa. 49:8) underscores the divine initiative: God has extended an open ear and has offered help "on the day of salvation." Paul insists, however, that the "acceptable time" and the "day of salvation" are now. Through the Christ-event, the future has invaded the present, so that the God who stands at the end of time summons hearers to receive the gift of salvation through the preached Word.

True penitence begins when we recognize that Christ became sin (5:21) in our stead. Through the crucifixion, he became sinner (Gal. 3:13) even though he was sinless, i.e., innocent. In a similar fashion, our salvation is paradoxical; in the crucifixion Christ took on a status that was not rightfully his; so too, through God's reconciling act, we acquire a status that is not rightfully ours.

Matthew 6:1-6, 16-21

Today is Ash Wednesday, the beginning of Lent, a day of profound meaning for some, a day only casually marked by others, and a day viewed with suspicion among those Christians who feel the key to genuine spirituality is the minimizing of all rites and ceremonies. It is appropriate to look to Matthew for instruction at this time, for he knew as well as anyone in the New Testament both the depth and the emptiness of what he calls "practicing your piety" (6:1). He understood and felt keenly the difference between altars that served as stations on one's pilgrimage and cold stones that stood along the road to nowhere.

Our lesson today consists of an introductory warning about practicing piety (6:1) followed by instruction in the practice of true piety in these areas: alms (verses 2-4), prayer (verses 5-6), and fasting (verses 16-21). The warning does not concern whether or not these acts are to be done but before whom—human spectators or God. The instructions in these acts of devotions are catechetical and formulaic, certain phrases being repeated in each case: "when you give alms" (pray, fast); "not be like the hypocrites"; "be seen by men"; "your Father who sees in secret"; "they have received their reward"; "your Father . . . will reward you." The passage assumes that these three acts are well-established practices in Matthew's church and that they have been observed long enough to become, for some, empty and void of meaning except as displays of religion.

In three very clear ways the church reflected in Matthew 6 is in continuity with Judaism.

First, both communities (church and synagogue) held in high regard these three acts of devotion. Jewish writings speak of alms, prayer, and fasting as indications that one has grown beyond the minimal requirements of the law, as acts of special merit and of such favor in God's eyes as to atone for other breaches of the law.

Second, both communities contained practitioners who missed the point of the acts but did see benefit for themselves in public displays of religion. It was a practice in some synagogues to announce in the assembly the names of donors to the alms box and the amounts given. Some Christians will recognize parallels in their own churches. All the possibilities for competition, improper motivation, and the dehumanization of the recipients are too obvious to require comment.

And third, both communities had prophetic calls for reform. Jesus' voice here joins those of Isaiah 58:5 ff., Jeremiah 14:12, Zechariah 7:5 ff., and Joel 2:12 in seeking to keep alive in the community of faith the faculty and voice of self-criticism. Without it hypocrisy and idolatry move in quickly. It is important to see these parallels in the two faith communities lest one be seduced into making false contrasts and false dichotomies. For example, one certainly wants to avoid giving the impression that Judaism as a whole was hypocritical while Christianity was as a whole genuine, or that Judaism was an "outward" religion while Christianity was "inward." On the contrary, the text presents Jesus instructing his church on precisely these same "outward" rites: alms, prayer, fasting.

Students of this text do not agree on the immediate background for these sayings of Jesus. Did the synagogue practices in Matthew's community involve trumpets, masked faces, and playing to the crowds or has Matthew portrayed those and all such public displays of religion in the language and images of the Greco-Roman theatre of that time? Since "hypocrite" means "actor," one can easily see how trumpets, masked or disfigured faces, and applauding audiences could have been drawn from the analogy of theatrics.

Whatever the source of Matthew's analogy, the point being made in these sayings of Jesus is clear: God is the proper audience for all our acts of devotion. And since God is in secret and sees in secret, no display is necessary. In the final analysis it is God with whom we deal in all our work and worship. If the clear assurance that God sees is not in itself payment in full, then our piety will go in search of additional recognition, with occasional applause. Again, it should be understood that the call for correction of abuses is not a call for the cessation of these acts of devotion. Sometimes a sincere but simplistic call for reform would cure hypocrisy by passivity. But it is a flawed logic that says if we do not attend worship service we are the true worshipers, if we do not pray our spirits are in tune with God, if we do not fast we honestly care, and if we do not give any money we have sincerely given our hearts. Is there not, after all, such a thing as reverse hypocrisy?

First Sunday of Lent

Genesis 9:8-17; Psalm 25:1-10; I Peter 3:18-22; Mark 1:9-15

Genesis 9:8-17

The Old Testament readings for the Second through the Fifth Sundays of Lent provide a survey of much of the Old Testament story and might form the basis for a series of sermons. With one exception, the texts concern covenants, beginning this week with the covenant with Noah and next week the one with Abraham. Then follows Exodus 20:1-17, the Decalogue which is at the heart of the covenant at Sinai. The reading from Second Chronicles on the Fourth Sunday of Lent is the report of the destruction of the temple in Jerusalem by the Babylonians, and that is followed by Jeremiah's promise of a new covenant, written on the heart.

This Old Testament text is doubtless assigned for reading on this day because of the reference to the flood story in the Epistle, which in turn follows the Gospel reading concerning the baptism of Jesus. First Peter 3:18-22 is one of the rare New Testament references to the flood, and it emphasizes the parallel between the saving power of the water of baptism and that of the flood. Close examination of Genesis 9:8-17 in its context reveals that the affinities among the texts for this day run even deeper than that parallel suggests.

Genesis 9:8-17 presents the conclusion to the story of the flood and spells out the results of the events which begin in Genesis 6:5. It will be remembered that the flood story is part of the primeval or pre-patriarchal narrative in Genesis 1–11. The flood is the next-to-last event in a history which—after the initial acts of creation—is an account of the origin and spread of human sin. The last event in this sequence is the story of the tower of Babel in Genesis 11.

The present account of the flood is the combination of two sources, the Yahwist (J) and the Priestly Writer (P). When the sources are separated two virtually complete stories emerge, each with its distinctive emphasis. Our reading comes from the Priestly Writer and resumes some of the important themes in that document's account of creation in Genesis 1. In this version of the flood, the "floodgates of heaven" had been opened to allow the waters of chaos to return, the same waters which God had separated and pushed back in order to establish the world.

The Priestly Writer, who was also interested in genealogy and chronology, viewed human history in terms of a series of covenants. Each era was marked by a covenant with particular stipulations; thus the passage before us spells out the covenant for the era following the flood. The differences between the era before and that after the flood had been spelled out in the paragraph that immediately precedes our reading (Gen. 9:1-7). The command to be fruitful and multiply is reiterated, as is the stipulation that human beings are to be over other creatures. But there are significant changes. The rest of creation will fear the human beings, who now are allowed to eat not only plants but also animals, provided they do not eat flesh with the blood. Furthermore, murder is specifically prohibited. All this indicates that the new age acknowledges the existence of human violence and sinfulness.

Apart from the introductory formulas in verses 8 and 17, the entire passage is presented as a divine speech. Until the last verse God addresses both Noah and his sons, thus emphasizing the validity of what is said for all future generations, and for Gentiles as well as Jews. Two things transpire in the speech: (1) in solemn, almost juridical language God establishes a covenant; and (2) God designates the rainbow as a sign of that covenant.

It seems clear that our writer was aware of the older Babylonian flood story, and that he depended upon older oral and perhaps even written traditions when he composed the account. Evidence for this is seen in several duplicates in the passage. Several matters are mentioned twice: the covenant promise (verses 9 and 11), the sign of the covenant (verses 12 and 17), and God's seeing the bow and remembering the covenant (verses 14 and 16). In the present form of the story such repetitions serve to emphasize the most important points.

Clearly the most important message of this text concerns the covenant. In the Old Testament, covenants are sworn agreements, either among human beings or between God and people. Both in form and content they are different from contracts, which are legal agreements attested by witnesses and enforced by law. Covenants have two basic elements, the promissory oath or conditional self-curse, and the contents or stipulations. Parties solemnly promise something concerning their future relationships. Most covenants are between two unequal partners, both of whom swear to stipulations. The central and decisive Old Testament covenant is the one made between God and Israel at Mt. Sinai, which often was summarized in a short divine speech: "I will be your God and you will be my people."

The covenant in Genesis 9:8-17 is dramatically distinctive in several ways: (1) it is made between God and all future generations, and not just with Israel; (2) it is made not only with human beings but also with all creatures of the earth; its scope is thus cosmic and universal; and (3), most dramatic of all, only one party to the agreement—God—speaks at all. No response on the part of Noah and his sons is called for or given, not even their acknowledgment of acceptance. The covenant with Noah, then, is an act of a free and gracious God on behalf of a world that did not have to ask for it or earn it, or even respond to it.

The content of the covenant is underscored in the recurring refrain, "never again" (twice in verse 11 and in verse 15). God promises not to destroy the earth and its creatures by water again. The earth is the Lord's, and God has decided that it will remain. All creatures can count on the stability of nature. The sign of that covenant promise is the rainbow. Covenants often had signs, such as the pile of stones which Jacob and Laban erected to remind them of their agreement (Gen. 31:43-50). Most readers of Genesis 9 have assumed that the rainbow sign is a reminder to human beings of the divine promise. Certainly that is one effect of the account. However, the text makes it clear more than once that the rainbow is for God, to keep him aware of the covenant made with Noah and all his descendants.

So the story, like both the Gospel and Epistle readings, has to do with God's response to the human condition, understood realistically. The sinful nature of the human creature is taken for granted. God's response here is to take the initiative, to make a covenant, and to provide the stable conditions for all life on the earth. The alternative to chaos is God's covenant.

Psalm 25:1-10

This psalm, in keeping with the interests of the Lenten Season, gives expression to the sense of sinfulness, to waiting upon God, to trusting in the divine, and to the expectation of a life lived according to God's way and truth.

Two factors should be noted about the psalm as a whole. There is, first of all, the movement back and forth between prayer and proclamation. Verses 1-7 are addressed directly to the Deity and thus clearly take the form of a prayer. Verses 16-22 are similar in form. Verses 8-10 and 12-14, however, are not addressed to the Deity but to some human audience. (Note that in these verses, the Deity is spoken of in the third person.) They are proclamation or preaching. How might we explain this alternation between prayer and proclamation in the psalm? One might imagine the worshiper moving from prayer to proclamation during the course of worship. Both the Deity and a human audience are addressed by the worshiper. If this were the case, verses 8-10 and 12-14 could be seen as the worshiper's statements of confidence. Or, and perhaps more likely, the praying worshiper recited verses 1-7 and 16-21 asking for forgiveness, deliverance, and guidance while verses 8-10 and 12-14 were part of a homily or sermon addressed to the worshiper by the official or priest participating in the service. Verses 11 and 15 would then represent the worshiper's confessional responses to the priestly preaching or instruction. Thus one can see this psalm as originally part of a ritual in which a worshiper and a worship leader (priest) participated in a service of personal prayer and priestly proclamation. Exploring the psalm in light of such a ritual can greatly elucidate the content of the psalm as well as allow the members of the congregation to picture themselves as participants in such a ritual and to experience the sentiments of the psalm.

A second factor is the alphabetic character of the psalm. That is, the psalm was written so that the first line began with the first letter of the Hebrew alphabet, the second line with the second letter, and so on right through the entire alphabet. (One or two letters are now missing from the psalm probably having been accidentally omitted when the psalm was copied in antiquity. In addition, verse 22 is not part of the alphabetic poem.) Three suggestions have been made to explain why this and other psalms (9–10; 34; 37; 111; 112; 119; 145) were written in an alphabetic form: (1) the practice may reflect the great poetic skill of the author and thus be seen as an artistic device; (2) the use of the alphabetic structure may have been an aid to memory; in reciting the psalm a person would move through the alphabet; and (3) others see the alphabetic pattern as a means for expressing completeness. As we would say, the alphabetic poem is inclusive from "A to Z." In spite of all suggestions the exact reason for such alphabetic or acrostic compositions, which one finds also in the Book of Lamentations, cannot be finally determined.

The ten verses of today's lesson from the Psalter fall naturally in two parts: verses 1-7 which are a lament prayed to God and verses 8-10 which speak of God and the divine ways. The prayer reflects the attitudes of the worshiper—trust, waiting, a desire to learn—as well as a request that earlier sins might no longer be remembered. The worshiper speaks of enemies (verse 2) but these are not further defined. In verses 2-3 we encounter a common pattern found in the psalms, a pattern which may be called a "double wish." The worshiper asks not to be put to shame (the positive wish) and requests that the treacherous (the enemies?) should be made to be ashamed (the negative wish). People in ancient Israel were quite willing to pray, "Save me [us]" and "Destroy my [our] enemy."

Much of the worshiper's petitions request knowledge of God's ways and guidance in the truth (verses 4-5). Thus they are focused on the future and request not only enlightenment and knowledge but also divine leadership to keep one on the right path and ways. Knowledge of the way must be undergirded by continuous divine aid. The psalm also expresses a deep sense of sin. In verse 7, God is asked to remember not (that is, to forget) the past sins (of youth) and present transgressions (see verse 11).

The word "remember" occurs three times in verses 6-7 (translated as "be mindful" in verse 6) and could provide the structure for preaching on this text. God is asked to remember his mercy and steadfast love, not to remember one's sins, but to remember me (the person). The one praying does not ask, "God remember me," but, "God remember me according to your steadfast love." Between the worshiper and the divine lies the passion of God's love.

The proclamation in verses 8-10 seeks to assure the worshiper that God can be relied on, that God does do what the petitions in verses 4-5 request. God instructs, leads, and teaches because the Lord is good and upright. Those who obey God's will, manifested in covenant and testimony, can rest assured that the paths of the Lord are love and faithfulness.

I Peter 3:18-22

At the beginning of Lent, Christians begin to focus their attention on the suffering of Christ. Today's epistolary lection is especially fitting in shaping our reflections concerning the Lord's passion, for it opens with the statement: "For Christ also died [literally, *suffered*] for sins once for all." It should be noted that the example of Christ is introduced at this point in the Epistle to reassure Christians who themselves were suffering for the sake of Christ (1:6; 3:14; 5:9-10). Earlier in the Epistle, the readers were introduced to the example of the suffering Christ (2:21-25).

Today's text reminds us (1) that Christ's death was sacrificial and atoning ("for sins," cf. Gal. 1-4; Heb. 9:28); (2) that this preeminent sacrifice had ultimate finality ("once for all," cf. Heb. 9:12, 26); (3) that his suffering and death were vicarious ("the righteous for the unrighteous"); (4) that Christ's death has a reconciling effect ("brings us to God," cf. Eph. 2:18; 3:12; Heb. 4:16; 7:25; 10:22; 12:22); (5) that his death was transcended by resurrection life ("being put to death in the flesh but made alive in the spirit," cf. John 6:63; I Cor. 15:44); and finally (6) that its effects were far-reaching: it had retroactive power in that Christ was able even to rescue the wicked who had suffered destruction in the flood (verses 19-20, cf. 4:6).

Much of the language in verses 18-19 is traditional. For this reason, it has been suggested that these verses should be regarded as a baptismal hymn, possibly extending through verse 22. They are not printed strophically, however, in RSV, NEB, or JB, and for this reason they should probably be read and treated homiletically as straight prose. Even so, the preacher does well to note that virtually every phrase, especially in verses 18-19 and 22, is rich in meaning and association. For example, the emphasis on Christ as "the Righteous One" who died as an innocent martyr is deeply embedded in the substructure of early Christian preaching (cf. Matt. 27:19; Luke 23:47; Acts 3:14; 7:52; 22:14; I John 2:1). We are dealing with a text, then, rich with possibilities for Christian reflection and devotion.

The presence of baptismal imagery within the passage should also be noted. Historically, Lent served as a time for preparing catechumens for baptism at Easter. Thus, as the church thought about the passion and death of Christ, it became natural during this period of meditation, prayer, and fasting to instruct potential converts in the meaning and significance of their ritual reenactment of Christ's death and resurrection. Used and understood in this catechetical setting, this text reminds soon-to-be Christians that baptism is no mere bath ("not as a removal of dirt from the body"), but "an appeal to God for a clear conscience" (verse 21). Their formal entry to the Christian faith marks an inward renewal of the human spirit empowered by the resurrection of Christ. To be sure, the connection between Noah's household being "saved through water" (verse 20) and Christian baptism appears somewhat stretched. But both are acts of divine redemption. It is at this point that the Old Testament reading

(Gen. 9:8-17) which speaks of God's covenant with humanity after the flood relates directly to the epistolary text.

Seeing these connections between today's epistolary lection and the church's practice of preparing catechumens for baptism during the time of Lent may provide a homiletical point of departure. If baptism is seen as the ritual and symbolic reenactment of Christ's own passion and death, the beginning of Lent becomes an appropriate point to reflect on one's point of formal entry into the Christian faith. This text at least reminds us that "suffering and death" are part and parcel of Christian life and thought, even as it already introduces Easter themes in verses 21*b*-22: "through the resurrection of Jesus Christ, who has gone into heaven and is at the right hand of God, with angels, authorities, and powers subject to him." While it may be premature to exploit this strong Easter affirmation this early in Lent, there is nonetheless a strong note of reassurance which should not be pushed to the periphery of Christian reflection.

Mark 1:9-15

Mark 1:9-15 records three episodes in the beginning of Jesus' public life: his baptism (verses 9-11), his temptation (verses 12-13), and his first preaching in Galilee (verses 14-15). Because verses 9-11 were treated during Epiphany on the Sunday of our Lord's baptism and verses 14-15 were discussed for the Third Sunday After Epiphany, we shall here attend only to verses 12-13, the temptation in the wilderness. One can hardly think of a more appropriate consideration for the First Sunday of Lent.

Speaking of temptation, the preacher will need to be on guard against gravitating toward Matthew or Luke in preparing the message. Not only are the longer temptation narratives of Matthew and Luke more familiar but Mark's brevity may seem at first inadequate as source and substance for a sermon. But full attention on Mark will yield more than enough for the day.

Mark ties Jesus' temptation directly to his baptism. Apparently the theme of a new exodus, developed in the portrayal of John's ministry in 1:1-8, is being continued here.

As Israel experienced God in passing through the waters of the Red Sea only to encounter trials and tests in the wilderness, so Jesus, still wet from the Jordan, is plunged into the wilderness. (In I Cor. 10:1-13 Paul compares Israel's baptism and temptation to the experience of Christians.) The forty days is also reminiscent of significant periods in Israel's relation to God. The intensity of the experience for Jesus is underscored in Mark both by the brevity of the account and by the vigor of the language: drove him out (literally, threw or cast him out); tempted (tested, put through trials); Satan (the adversary, the opposing one); wild beasts (wild animals and demons were in the wilderness, Isa. 34:8-14. Some believed demons dwelt in wild beasts); angels ministered to him (not after the temptation but during it, over against Satan).

One has to be impressed and affected by the reality of Jesus' experience in the wilderness. Not even protests that we no longer subscribe to driving spirits, demon-possessed animals, Satan, and ministering angels can obscure the clear resonance of our own experiences with that which Mark describes. If there is any reticence to accept the temptation account, the reason probably lies not in the highly symbolic nature of the description but in the fact that it is happening to Jesus. Many Christians wish to protect Jesus from trials and temptations and other difficulties common to humankind for fear that convictions about his uniqueness will be eroded by such experiences. When faced with assertions such as, "For we have not a high priest who is unable to sympathize with our weaknesses, but one who in every respect has been tempted as we are, yet without sin" (Heb. 4:15), some would respond that Jesus was not really tempted but was setting examples for us. Such a view of Jesus seems blind to the fact that anyone who walks through experiences that are not personally engaging or demanding just to set an example is not setting an example. Such approaches, however sincere, rob Jesus, the Scriptures, the gospel, and life itself of reality.

Mark's record is straightforward and clear. Jesus fully identifies with the people of God who were, and are, tested in the wilderness. For Israel the wilderness symbolized some extraordinary experiences of God (Exod. 19; Hos. 2:14), and they recalled those bittersweet days annually with the Feast of Tents. But there was a darker side to the wilderness, for there they had often failed the test (temptation), rebelled against God, and suffered God's wrath (Ps. 78; Ezek. 20:13-22). Jesus, then, has not withdrawn into pensive retreat, but Spirit-driven, he endures testing appropriate to his person, his powers, and his relation to God. In other words, the greater one's abilities, power, and influence, the greater one's temptations. Although Mark gives no details concerning the nature of Jesus' testing, we can be sure it was strong and ingeniously deceptive, given Jesus' relation to God, the many needs of the people about him, the several paths of ministry available, and the military, political, and religious forces ready to counter him. Jesus' temptation, then, is a preview of the struggle and victory yet to come. It is natural, when reading this brief account, to look ahead to Gethsemane. Gethsemane was a garden, but for one night it, too, was a wilderness.

Second Sunday of Lent

Genesis 17:1-10, 15-19; Psalm 105:1-11; Romans 4:16-25; Mark 8:31-38 or *Mark 9:1-9*

Genesis 17:1-10, 15-19

Like the Old Testament reading for the previous week, this text is assigned because of its link with the reading from the Epistle, Romans 4:16-25. The psalm also carries forward the theme of the covenant with Abraham and the blessings it offers for future generations. It is not easy to recognize a traditional or thematic connection between these three readings and the Gospel lections, unless Abraham's obedience and circumcision are taken as the denial of self called for in Mark 8:31-38.

As the reading for the previous week concerned the covenant with Noah, this one concerns the covenant with Abraham. The biblical context is the stories of the patriarchs, which began with the call of Abraham in Genesis 12:1 ff. Like Genesis 9:8-17, Genesis 17 comes from the hand of the Priestly Writer and carries forward his interpretation of human history as a series of covenants, each progressively narrower until the covenant at Sinai (Exod. 19–Num. 10) between the Lord and the people of Israel under the leadership of Moses. Finally at Sinai the detailed laws for Israel were revealed, but before that there were covenants which included not only Israel but other peoples as well. Abraham, as this chapter explicitly points out, was "the father of nations," and therefore Muslims as well as Jews legitimately claim him as their ancestor.

Viewed as a whole, the patriarchal narratives have an overarching theme, that of God's promise concerning land and progeny. To be sure, not every individual story develops that theme, but it is central in Genesis 17. Moreover, the major sources in Genesis, J and P, treat the theme quite differently. It is the Yahwist who speaks quite directly of the promise, as in Genesis 12:1-3. When the Lord calls Abraham to leave his country and go out, he promises to make of the patriarch a great nation, to make his name great, so that he will be a blessing to all the families of the earth. At other points the Yahwist reports the promise that the descendants of the patriarchs will possess the land of Canaan, in which they themselves were only resident aliens. Similar words are uttered to Isaac and to Jacob. The Priestly Writer communicates the content of similar promises, as in our text, in the context of covenants with the ancestors.

All of the patriarchal stories in Genesis 12–50, with the exception of Genesis 14, are family stories. That is, they concern not public, historical events but matters that take place in the household between husbands and wives, parents and children, brothers and sisters. Public figures such as kings and pharaohs appear on the scene occasionally, but they are important only in so far as they have a bearing on the successive generations of this great family.

These accounts of how the promise came down through the families are recounted from the perspective of later generations. In the case of the Yahwist, the perspective is that of a people who have experienced the fulfillment of the promise. He wrote probably during the era of Solomon or soon thereafter, at the height of Israel's glory and power. The Priestly Writer, on the other hand, viewed the events from the perspective of a people who had experienced loss of the land and nationhood through the Babylonian Exile. He insists, however, that the ancient covenant is still valid, and that the people of God will once again see the promises fulfilled. Moreover, when he speaks in Genesis 17 of Abraham as the father of nations and understands a covenant which extends beyond Israel, we should keep in mind that he and his contemporaries have experienced persecution and destruction at the hand of some of those nations.

The setting for the events reported in Genesis 17 is given quite briefly in the first half of verse 1. The writer considers it relevant to report of Abraham's situation only that he was ninety-nine years old and that God appeared to him. The remainder of the passage except for verses 3*a* and 17-18 is a series of divine speeches. At the end we hear that "Abraham fell on his face and laughed." He was incredulous; how could such old people as he and Sarah have children? God responds by reaffirming the promise of progeny and makes it quite specific that Sarah shall have a son whom they are to name Isaac. Moreover, God will establish a covenant with him as well (verses 19-20).

The substance of the chapter is formed by the speeches of God to Abraham. First, there is a general statement of God's intention to make a covenant, multiplying Abraham "exceedingly" (verses 1-2). Second, God spells out the contents of the covenant promise (verses 4-8). It includes the promise of progeny so that "a multitude of nations" and even kings shall come from the patriarch, the assurance that Abraham's descendants will possess the land of Canaan, and the vow of an everlasting covenant with those descendants. The granting of the covenant entails a change of names, from Abram to Abraham. Third, God calls for Abraham to "keep" the covenant by circumcising all male descendants (verses 9-14). (The lectionary tactfully omits the detailed instructions for circumcision in verses 11-14.) Fourth and finally, God addresses Abraham concerning his childless wife, changing her name from Sarai to Sarah, extending to her the promise that she would be the mother of nations and kings, indicating that the first step in the fulfillment will be a son.

The central focus of this passage is the covenant with Abraham and—to be sure—Sarah. On the meaning of covenants as promissory oaths, see the discussion of last week's Old Testament reading, Genesis 9:8-17. The initiative for the establishment of the covenant comes from God. Among the promises granted to Abraham and his descendants the divine affirmation, "I will be their God," stands out. That is not a stipulation along with the others, but states the essence of the covenant itself.

Unlike the covenant with Noah and the parallel to this text in Genesis 15:7-21, the recipient of the covenant is expected to respond with specific acts of obedience. The response is both general, "keep my covenant" (verse 9), and specific, "Every male among you shall be circumcised" (verse 10). To keep a covenant is to be faithful to its stipulations, and in this case there is only one, in perpetuity. The Priestly Writer understands that there were just a few ordinances that predated the law of Moses given at Sinai. These included observance of the sabbath, the prohibition of eating meat with the blood, and circumcision. These regulations had particular meaning for the people who had lost the temple and the land and were living in Babylon as exiles, for they were portable religious practices.

In ancient Israel circumcision was an explicitly religious observance; its meaning had nothing to do with hygiene. It was practiced also in Egypt but not in Assyria and Babylon; the Philistines are ridiculed with the epithet, "the uncircumcised." The story of Moses and Zipporah (Exod. 4:24-27) tends to suggest that it had once been a puberty rite which only later became an act performed on the eighth day after birth. At its most fundamental level, it was a sign of membership in the covenant community. (See the story of Dinah and the people of Shechem in Genesis 34.) The ritual was genuinely sacramental, an outward and visible sign of the acceptance of God's election, and parallel in meaning to the baptism of infants.

Names are of great significance in this account, as they are throughout the Bible. The initiator of the covenant identifies himself as El Shaddai, read in most translations since the Septuagint as "God Almighty." But the precise meaning is uncertain; it is simply a divine proper name, given here because it is essential that the parties to the covenant be identified. The names of the other parties are changed with the establishment of the agreement. Both "Abraham" and "Sarah" are dialectical variants of their earlier names. "Abraham" does not literally mean "father of a multitude"; the explanation in verse 5 is a popular etymology, a pun. Critical here is the understanding that the new names, like the names of the other patriarchs Isaac and Jacob/Israel, are given by God. Moreover, the new names signal transformation to a new reality. Their names confirm their destiny under the covenant with God. In a genuine sense they become what they are named; as God has promised to be their God they—and their descendants after them—have now become God's people.

Psalm 105:1-11

Psalm 105 is a thanksgiving hymn that praises God for the mighty deeds which Israel confessed as formative for its early history. The psalm in fact sounds in many ways like a poetic summary of the contents of the first six books of the Old Testament. Only references to the story of creation and the giving of the law at Mount Sinai are missing. Any use of the verses of this lection should point out how they comprise the introductory section of a larger structured poem that deals with the patriarchs of Israel (verses 12-22), the sojourn in Egypt (verses 23-25), the plagues during the days of Moses and Aaron (verses 26-36), the exodus from Egypt (verses 37-38), divine guidance in the wilderness (verses 39-43), and the taking possession of the Land of Promise (verses 44-45).

The verses of today's lection contain a call to offer thanksgiving to God (verses 1-6) and a description of God and his promise to give the land of Canaan to Israel (verses 7-11). As in most hymns, the praise is spoken about rather than to God and thus represents one of the ways the ancient Israelites had of confessing and reinforcing their faith.

The summons to worship in the opening six verses piles up a series of verbal exhortations: give thanks, call on his name, make known, sing, tell, glory, rejoice, seek, and remember. Running throughout all of this section is the emphasis on God's works and deeds, that is, the psalm focuses on what God has done rather than expounds the divine attributes of what God is in himself. This is a characteristic feature of the Old Testament where most of the material is historical or storylike in form rather than a theological discourse or systematics. It is almost as if when the Israelites were asked to confess their faith or describe their beliefs they did so by telling a story or stories. This focus on storytelling, the proclamation of Yahweh's mighty deeds, should remind us that our faith and character and that of the church are lived out in concrete, and hopefully wonderful, deeds. Faith and a person's biography and a community's history are integrally related, and offering testimony still provides a valid means to express one's beliefs.

Verses 7-11 emphasize God's fidelity to his covenant made with the patriarchs Abraham, Isaac, and Jacob to give them the Land of Promise, Canaan. (For Abraham, see Gen. 15:18; 17:1-8; 24:7; for Isaac see Gen. 26:1-5; and for Jacob see Gen. 28:13-14.) The theme of promise and fulfillment provides the external structures for this psalm. The first main section begins with reference to the promise of the land (verses 7-11) and the final lines affirm the fulfillment of the promise (verses 44-45). A similar scheme and emphasis were taken up by the early Christians who saw the career of Jesus and the life of the early church in terms of God's promise to Abraham. (See the Benediction in Luke 1:67-70 and Paul's arguments in Gal. 3:1-18.)

In speaking of God's declaration concerning the land, the psalmist uses a series of terms—covenant, promise, statute, and everlasting covenant. Such synonyms emphasize Israel's belief in God's commitment to the nation. God's covenant and promise focus on the land. In this text and throughout much of the Old Testament, the land plays a central role. As it does for no other religion, a land occupies a central place for the Hebrew faith. For outsiders, it is often difficult to appreciate the strong bond among God, people, and land which one finds in the Bible. Yet the land was and is a fundamental aspect of biblical religion, a concrete, tangible, and sensual embodiment and representation of God's promise.

Romans 4:16-25

Like the Old Testament reading from Genesis 17, as well as the reading from Psalm 105, today's epistolary lection focuses on God's covenant with Abraham. In fact, Genesis 17:5 is directly cited by Paul in Romans 4:17, and Genesis 17 along with Genesis 15 provide the basis of much of Paul's argumentation in Romans 4 (cf. verses 3, 10, 18-19). For Paul, no Old Testament character exemplified genuine faith better than Abraham, "the father of us all" (verse 16). In Romans 4, Paul moves well beyond Psalm 105 in insisting that Abraham is the prototype of faith for all who believe, both Jews and Gentiles (verses 11-13). In Abraham, Paul saw established the principle of justification by faith.

For Paul, it was crucial that in the storyline of Genesis Abraham was said to have been justified by God prior to his receiving the covenant of circumcision, and he pushed this distinction to its logical limits. This could only mean that the basis on which God's promise to Abraham—and to his seed—was sustained was "through the righteousness of faith" and not through the law (verse 13). The capacity to believe in God's promises, as incredible as those promises might appear, was prior to, and, in a real sense, transcended the principle of obeying Torah.

Today's epistolary lection, then, focuses on the kind of faith Abraham displayed. Paul insists that, qualitatively speaking, the faith of Abraham is essentially the same as the faith of the Christian. For one thing, Christian faith, for all its stress on the person and work of Christ, is fundamentally faith in the God who "gives life to the dead" (verse 17). That this is the case is seen in Paul's concluding remarks where he introduces Christ into the discussion (verses 24-25). Notice: If we "believe in him [i.e. God] who raised from the dead Jesus our Lord, who was delivered to death for our sins and raised again to secure our justification" (Phillips). It is the God who brought death to life in the womb of Sarah (verse 19) who also brought Jesus to life from the dead. What Abraham was asked to believe was as incredible as what those who heard Paul's missionary preaching were asked to believe. Yet, Abraham becomes exemplary for all those who have lived after him—Jews and Gentiles alike—precisely because he did not "waver concerning the promise of God" (verse 20). On the contrary, he was "fully convinced that God was able to do what he had promised" (verse 21).

If we ask how Abraham's faith might inform Christian life and thought during Lent, several suggestions occur. First, Abraham reminds the penitent that the God who promises forgiveness can be trusted implicitly. Genuine penitence often reopens the question of whether God does, or indeed can, forgive. To be truly meaningful and constructive, however, penitence must be predicated on the firm conviction that what God has promised, God is able to perform (verse 21). Second, today's text reminds us that justification by faith and salvation by grace go hand in hand (verse 16). To have implicit trust in a faithful God is to recognize that we are saved by a generous and uncalculated gift of divine grace. Seen this way, salvation is always gift, never reward. It is never even a reward for penitence! As the church discovered during the Reformation, even penitence can become a work looking for a reward, but salvation as Paul conceives it is no quid pro quo, extended as a reward for works of penitence. Third, our text speaks for the commonality of all who genuinely believe in God—both Jews and Gentiles. It might be worth noting that even Christians have no monopoly on the kind of faith Paul describes in Romans 4.

Mark 8:31-38

Mark is a Good Friday Gospel in the sense that the cross is central to understanding Jesus and the nature of discipleship. It is fitting then that the first prediction of the cross and cross-bearing (8:31-38) be a Lenten lesson.

Our text for today introduces a new phase in the ministry of Jesus. "And he began to teach them" (verse 31) is Mark's signal that the disciples are now to hear from Jesus a word unlike prior teaching, a word for which they are not prepared. The disciples had left boats, jobs, and families to follow Jesus. The pace of their work was hectic and exhausting, but in spite of occasions of opposition and suspicion, they had found it exciting. Sometimes they had not understood Jesus, but the fact that they were called to be disciples surely meant the work was to continue and to grow. They are not to be censured for failing to grasp the meaning of suffering, rejection, and death as the fate of their leader.

Mark 8:31-38 consists of two parts: instruction to the disciples (verses 31-33) and instruction to the multitude together with the disciples (verses 34-38). Both private and public instruction on matters difficult to understand (parables, divorce, wealth, and the kingdom) is a common pattern in Mark. Immediately preceding this passage is the account of Peter confessing and of Jesus rebuking his disciples, demanding silence on the matter (verses 27-30). These preceding verses are important for sensing the pattern of the narrative: Peter confesses and Jesus rebukes; Jesus confesses that his real mission is suffering and death and Peter rebukes. However, for Mark, and quite unlike Matthew, the confession of Peter is not central to this section. Rather, Mark's focus is upon the prediction of the passion and the fact that Jesus' passion is definitive for the life of a disciple (verses 31-38). On these twin themes there is no charge to silence, there is no mystery concealed in a parable: "he said this plainly" (verse 32). The language is intense and strong. The rebukes and counter-rebukes (verses 30, 32, 33) and the charges to silence are the same expressions used by Jesus when "shouting down" demons during an exorcism. Peter is rebuked because his rejection of Jesus' announced path of suffering represents as real a temptation as any experienced in the wilderness.

And so Jesus begins to teach his followers that the Son of man must suffer, be rejected, be killed, and be raised again. Three brief comments need to be made on verses 31-33. First, the term "Son of man" is complex with multiple uses and, unless the preacher is careful, efforts to explain it can be an endless side trip. In verse 31 it can be taken as the equivalent of "I." Matthew so understood it at this point (Matt. 16:21-23). In verse 38 "Son of man" refers clearly to an apocalyptic figure coming in judgment and salvation. Second, the rather elaborate reference to suffering, rejection, and death in contrast to the very brief mention of resurrection is significant. This same proportion holds at the end of this Gospel. Clearly Mark does not want his church to use Easter to escape Lent and Good Friday. Third, at the heart of the passion prediction is rejection by the religious establishment, both lay and clergy. That may have been the sharpest pain of all. Whether the cross-bearing Christ still suffers such fate is a judgment each one has to make. One popular preacher recently explained his approach by saying, "You cannot succeed preaching the cross. People do not want to hear that; they already have enough problems."

The second part of our text, verses 34-38, has been defined and interpreted by verses 31-33 and requires little comment.

Verse 34 makes it clear that the way of the cross was not only for the twelve but also for the multitudes. In other words, suffering and sacrifice for one's faith are not items of first-century history but are inherent in the Gospel. Verses 35-38 are a composite of four sayings, found in different contexts elsewhere (Matt. 10:33, 38-39; Luke 12:9; 14:27; 17:33). Being proverbial in nature, they are appropriate to many settings with many applications. The passage closes with an apocalyptic orientation, placing disciples in the presence of the Father, the Son, and the holy angels (I Tim. 5:21; Rev. 1:4-5). Warning against apostasy in the face of terror and threat, Mark soberly reminds his readers that decisions about the Christ described in verses 31-37 have ultimate and eternal consequences.

Mark 9:1-9

This alternate Gospel reading may seem to offer the preacher a message radically different from Mark 8:31-38, for in that lection Jesus' prediction of his passion is the central theme while here the focus is upon the Transfiguration. In fact, the Transfiguration appears at first to be an unlikely consideration for Lent. Closer examination will reveal, however, that the passage is more continuous than discontinuous with the preceding narrative.

Mark 9:1-9 consists of three parts: 9:1; 2-8; 9. Usually 9:1 is treated as falling within the unit, 8:31–9:1. The future coming of the Son of man with the holy angels was announced in 8:38, and 9:1 continues the thought, extending it with the assurance that the end shall occur soon, within the lifetime of some in the audience. The imminence of the coming of the kingdom is a common theme in Mark, even occurring at 13:30, a section otherwise instructing the reader not to be misled; the end is not yet. Our lection closes at verse 9 with Jesus instructing Peter, James, and John to be quiet about this experience until after the resurrection. The reasons probably are two: (1) it is obvious they had not understood what had occurred, so their witness would be both confused and confusing, and (2) the glory of the Son of man waits on the crucifixion. This is vital in Mark; talk of glory prior to the cross is premature and theologically inadequate. The instruction in 9:9 is in keeping with the secrecy motif elsewhere in Mark.

At the center of today's lection and governing the literary and theological territory around it is the Transfiguration (verses 2-8) of Jesus in the presence of the three who were privy to other critical moments in Jesus' life (5:37; 13:3; 14:33). The reader will recognize ways the scene is reminiscent of Moses' experience with God on the mountain. Exodus 24:15-18 contains the mountain, the clouds, the glory, and the six days, and according to Exodus 34:29-35, the experience gave to Moses a shining face because he had been talking with God. Clouds are a common feature of theophanies and Christophanies (Exod. 16:10; Mark 13:26; Acts 1:9). Elijah was widely understood to be the prophet of the end time (Mal. 4:1-6; Mark 9:11-13), but Moses, whom some believed also to have been translated (Deut. 34:6?), joined Elijah as a figure of the end of the age. The two appear together as faithful witnesses in Revelation 11:3-13.

Mark often interprets an event as much by its location in the narrative as by comments offered. Such is the case here. The Transfiguration comes at the very center of the Gospel and is the only "mountaintop" story in Mark. Only here and at his baptism does Jesus receive divine confirmation visibly and audibly. It is significant that this confirmation occurs here and not at the cross or resurrection. The absence of a resurrection appearance in Mark (assuming the text ends at 16:8) and the glorious appearance of Jesus in this scene have combined to convince some scholars that the Transfiguration is a "misplaced resurrection story." For Mark it is not misplaced; in fact, the scene is deliberately located in the narrative. Bracketed on either side by Jesus' talk of his suffering and death (8:31-38; 9:12, 30-31), the event provides the moment of recognition. The glorious coming of the Son of man which had been predicted in 8:38, and said to be imminent in 9:1, is now previewed at a time when talk of Jesus' passion is the shocking new subject of Jesus' teaching. The Transfiguration is only a preview, however. The error of

Peter and the others (verses 5-6) is their wanting to seize the moment and make present the glory which cannot be fully consummated apart from the cross.

Peter is not alone among Jesus' followers in the desire to steal from the future and bypass Golgotha.

Third Sunday of Lent

Exodus 20:1-17; Psalm 19:7-14; I Corinthians 1:22-25; John 2:13-22

Exodus 20:1-17

Specific connections between the Decalogue in Exodus 20 and the New Testament readings for the Third Sunday of Lent are difficult to discern. Psalm 19:7-14, however, is an expression of praise to God for the perfection of the law, which reveals itself in the entire creation. The Gospel lection may be taken at one level as Jesus' condemnation of the corruption of what the law had called for, and the Epistle on another level sets the Christian proclamation against what Jews and Greeks seek. In New Testament contexts in general, the Decalogue may be taken to stand for the Old Testament law as a whole.

At least two aspects of the Old Testament context of the Decalogue are important for its interpretation in Christian worship and preaching.

1. One should keep in mind the place of this law code in its narrative framework. It is part of the story of the Exodus and the wandering in the wilderness. The introductory sentence actually summarizes the story: "I am the Lord your God, who brought you out of the land of Egypt, out of the house of bondage" (verse 2). Theologically, this is of the greatest significance. The law is given to a people who have been, quite literally, saved, saved from slavery. Consequently, their salvation and election are not earned by obedience to the law: God's action comes first. Obedience to the law is the appropriate response to what God has already done.

2. The immediate context of the Decalogue is liturgical. Exodus 19ff. describes a religious ceremony, the establishment of the covenant between God and Israel. The ritual

aspects of the event, including purification, processions, the recitation of solemn words, and even a meal, would not have taken place only once, but were celebrated in various ways over the centuries. That is to say, the report in Exodus reflects actual cultic practices. The ceremony establishes and reestablishes the relationship between God and people, in which the laws, including the Decalogue, provide the stipulations.

The question of the literary source or document to which this code belongs is not very important for its interpretation. It sits loosely in the older sources, J and E, and is distinct from the Priestly legislation which follows in Exodus 25:15ff. All the sources agree that the law and the laws were given through Moses at Mount Sinai. But in any case, the laws in Exodus 20 are much more ancient than any of the Pentateuchal sources.

The individual laws in the Decalogue belong to one of the two types of Israelite law, the apodictic. The other is the casuistic, the statement of a case and its consequences in third-person style, for example, "If a man steals an ox or a sheep, and kills it or sells it, he shall pay five oxen for an ox, and four sheep for a sheep" (Exod. 22:1). Such case law was typical of ancient Near Eastern codes, such as the laws of Hammurabi. Apodictic laws, on the other hand, are short, second-person commands or prohibitions. They are not linked or restricted to any specific circumstances, but are unequivocal. They are a distinctly Israelite form of law, and are presented as the expression of the will of Israel's God.

This insight into the form of the laws becomes useful when applied to our text. It is obvious that some of the laws in Exodus 20:1-17 are much longer than others. The difference, however, is not in the length of the laws themselves, but in the commentaries on some of them. In verses 3, 13, 14, 15, and 17 we have only the laws without comment, but in all the other cases there are supplementary remarks, mainly of two kinds. Some, as in verses 4*b*-5*a*, 9-11, and 17*b*, are explanatory; that is, they spell out the meaning of the law. Others, as in verses 5*b*-6, 7*b*, and 12*b*, are more homiletical; that is, they urge that the law be observed and give reasons for obeying it. Such elements in the text indicate that the Decalogue was used in ancient Israel in teaching and preaching. As we preach on the present text, then, we are only continuing a process that began long before the Bible was completed.

That process is particularly visible when one compares this text with its parallel in Deuteronomy 5:6-21. The laws in both instances are the same. The only significant difference is in the interpretation of the sabbath ordinance. Whereas Exodus 20:9-11 bases it on the divine order of creation, Deuteronomy 5:13-15 relates it to Israel's release from Egyptian slavery. The former relates to cosmic order, the second to historical and humanitarian concerns.

In terms of formulation all but two of the laws are prohibitions, the exceptions being the fourth and fifth commandments. In terms of contents, the first four concern obligations directly to the Diety and the last six to relations among the covenant people. It would be a mistake, however, to distinguish sharply between religious or ritual laws and ethical concerns, for such a division seems not to have been made in the Old Testament. In a genuine sense, all obligations are directly related to the God of the covenant; relationships within the family and the community are to be treated as sacred.

If there is any priority among the laws it is clear that the first is the most fundamental. The prohibition against the worship of other gods is the basis for all other regulations. It is not, however, the same as monotheism; quite the contrary, it assumes that there are alternative gods to worship. But as far as the covenant people are concerned, there is to be only one God. The second commandment is a direct extension of the first, entailing polemic against those whose gods can be represented by images or likenesses. The third commandment continues the same line of thought, prohibiting magic, or the attempt to manipulate God through improper use of the divine name. The expectations expressed in these commandments should be taken with utter seriousness today, no less than in ancient Israel. But as preachers, perhaps the greatest challenge we face is to present these lines before our congregations and our world in a non-legalistic, non-moralistic fashion. One is enabled to avoid such pitfalls, first, by remembering the narrative context of the code, that God has already taken the initiative to save the people. To obey, then, is to act in grateful response, to live out one's role in a covenant. Second, the basic force of these, as well as other Old Testament laws, is to define the limits of what it means to be a covenant people. One who fails to live by these stipulations has placed himself or herself outside the covenant. Third, one would need to reflect upon some of the New Testament interpretations of the function of the law; for example, it serves to make one aware of human limitations, including sin.

Psalm 19:7-14

This lection from Psalm 19 forms an appropriate parallel to the reading of the Decalogue since much of it is concerned with the law. This psalm is generally divided in two parts and sometimes even seen as the secondary combination of two separate psalms. Verses 1-6 declare that nature and creation—especially sky and sun—proclaim the glory of God and testify to his will. Verses 7-14 praise the law (Torah) of God which has been made known in commandment, precept, and ordinance. The character of the psalm is further complicated, however, since the "law" section, verses 7-14, can be further subdivided. In verses 7-10, the law is praised and God spoken about in the third person while verses 11-14 are a prayer addressed directly to God.

In spite of its complexity, the psalm can be seen as a unity. The nature portion, verses 1-6, declares that creation, without normal words, voice, or speech points to divine will and control and thus prompts expressions of praise. The law portion, verses 7-10, focuses on the written law formulated in words that elicit attitudes of praise. Verses 11-14 are a prayer that one might be aware of sins, faults, and errors in order to live a life that is without great transgressions. The final plea, in verse 14, requests that not only the words but also the unspoken meditations of the heart be acceptable to God. Thus the psalm moves from describing the unarticulatable expressions of nature, which proclaim God's work and fill the whole expansive realm of creation, down to the inarticulated meditations of the heart. Thus the thought of the psalm moves from the outer reaches of the natural world to the inner recesses of the human personality, the human heart.

If we focus more closely on the psalm reading for this lection, only verses 7-14, we are primarily concerned with the praise and glory of the law and the worshiper's petition offered in light of the will of God manifest in nature and law. The antiphonal praise of the law, verses 7-10, knows the Torah as an object of praise and not as a burden or a yoke to be borne in grumbling servitude. Six synonymous terms are used to speak about the Torah: law, testimony, precepts, commandment, fear, ordinances. Perhaps these six terms were used to express the fullness and completeness of the known will of God. The adjectival descriptions of the Torah are extremely positive in their affirmations: perfect, sure, right, pure, clean, true, righteous. Four aspects or benefits from the Torah are noted. The Torah revives the soul: it is life-giving and sustaining. It makes wise the simple by providing them with understanding. It rejoices the heart making one glad to know the will and way of the Lord. It enlightens the eyes by providing a perspective within which to view the world and one's own life. Thus the law of God is a nobler and finer possession than gold and sweeter than honey. The law is to be more desired than the most precious of human treasures or the sweetest and most reviving of foods.

This praise of the law and its life-giving qualities was characteristic of much Israelite and Jewish thought about Torah. Christians, viewing matters from the Pauline perspective on the law as found in Galatians, frequently have difficulty affirming the value and goodness of law. Yet the positive aspects of the written Torah should be emphasized since Torah provides persons with specific directions, allows us to locate ourselves with regard to the understood will of God, and thus provides a sense of security. The law provides not only a general map for human living but also specific directions along the highway of life.

With verse 11, the focus of the psalm moves from the world of creation and the praise of the law to the sentiments and concerns of the individual worshiper. The law which like the sun is perfect, sure, and faithful also like the sun at noontime touches all so that "nothing is hid" from its preview. In light of this judging and quickening aspect of the law, the worshiper recognizes that the law not only warns but also calls into question human adequacy and constancy. Thus the psalmist prays to be kept from hidden faults, that is, those things one might do without realizing they are faults (verse 12), as well as presumptuous sins, that is, grave sins of arrogance or pride (verse 13). If one can be kept from hidden faults and presumptuous sins, then surely one is blameless, since these represent the two extreme poles.

The praise of God's glory in creation and the meditation on the law, in this psalm, led naturally to critical self-examination and to a focus on the whole range of disobedience from secret, hidden sins to overt, callous acts of open transgression. In the concluding petition, verse 14, the psalmist requests full acceptance from the words of the mouth, the external articulated word, to the meditation of the heart, the internal unarticulated thought.

I Corinthians 1:22-25

Paul was painfully aware that the message of the crucified Christ little commended itself to first-century hearers, Jews or Greeks. For Jews, the notion of a suffering Messiah was a contradiction in terms (cf. Mark 8:31-33 and parallels). To be crucified, or "hanged from a tree," was a sure sign of criminality (Deut. 21:23; 27:26), and therefore offensive to readers of Old Testament Scripture. Greek notions of heroic ideals were many and varied, but a hero who died ignominiously had little lasting appeal to them. The philosopher was a much more popular ideal for most Greeks. To be sure, for Paul to say that "Jews demand signs and Greeks seek wisdom" (verse 22) was a caricature, but like most caricatures there was a core of truth.

Paul could, however, at least speak out of his own experience of preaching the gospel, and it was his experience that the crucified Christ was a "stumbling block to Jews and folly to Gentiles" (verse 23). Even though some Jews and Gentiles had become Christians, they had done so by confronting directly the scandal of the cross. In one sense, this scandal remains even for those who have already become Christians, and who have been Christians for a long time. As one reflects on the passion of Christ, it never becomes a sensible message. In fact, the longer one lives with the Christian message the more one becomes convinced of its essential paradox. The words of today's epistolary lection stress the paradoxical nature of the Christian gospel: "The foolishness of God is wiser than men, and the weakness of God is stronger than men" (verse 25).

It is only natural for us, as human beings, to assess and scrutinize the ways of God, to employ human wisdom in trying to make sense of divine realities. As laudable as this might seem to us, for Paul it represents a fundamentally wrong way of conceiving the relationship between us and God. In verse 19 Paul cites Isaiah 29:14 as a way of reminding his readers that God's ways are beyond the scope of human wisdom. In defense of God, Paul asks rhetorically, "Where is the wise man? Where is the scribe? Where is the debater of this age" (verse 20)? For human beings to place God in the dock is but another form of human presumption.

The proper stance from which one can view the work of God is confessional. Paul recognizes that accepting the gospel is a subjective act. The gospel is the power of God to "us who are being saved" (verse 18). It is out of one's own experience of the saving work of God that one is able to recognize the crucified Christ as "the power of God and the wisdom of God" (verse 24). As Paul says, this perception is possible "to those who are called" (verse 24). One is first summoned, and in the summons one experiences the saving work of God. Then, and only then, does one possess the vantage point from which to view the work of God: from the inside.

In many respects, Paul's attitude toward human wisdom as expressed in I Corinthians 1:18-25 is difficult for many modern Christians to accept. We are, after all, children of the scientific age and have been taught to think for ourselves, and to think critically and rationally about the world around us. The phenomenal achievements of modern science are vivid testimony to scientific inquiry and the application of reason to life.

It is worth remembering, however, that Paul's remarks in First Corinthians have a specific focus and context. Some of his readers placed a high premium on wisdom and knowledge. Whether they were "Gnostics" in the technical sense is debated. Nevertheless, they seemed to have valued the intellect, and in doing so constricted their understanding of the gospel. Accordingly, Paul reminds them that "knowledge" should be balanced by "love" (I Cor. 8:1-2). He also censures them for the way in which their stress on wisdom and knowledge had created elitism within the church.

Paul's words notwithstanding, inquiring Christians still find themselves searching to understand the ways of God. Given the essential paradox of the cross, the Christian message will remain a mystery to be probed. Even if it does not "make sense" to outsiders, and possibly not even to ourselves at times, the Christian gospel does nevertheless "make sense of us" in a way that is finally redemptive.

John 2:13-22

All the lections for today dramatically curb any tendency to allow Lent to degenerate into a period of self-flagellation or efforts at self-improvement. The listener to these texts is confronted by a God of wisdom, of power and of ethical demand. It is before God and not before a mirror that the penitent stands. Our Gospel reading from John, companion to Mark in this year of the lectionary, is no less confrontive than the other lessons.

John 2:13-22 is the Fourth Evangelist's account of the cleansing of the temple. All four Gospels carry this story, but the Synoptics place it near the end of Jesus' ministry where it provides the precipitating factor in the decision to kill Jesus. But it is not so here. John removes the story from logical and chronological sequences and places it here, almost at the beginning of the Gospel, so that it may be understood in and of itself as a theological event. After all, the Evangelist is not interested in *causes* of Jesus' death, for to him Jesus' life and death were not shaped by circumstances and historical contingencies. On the contrary, no one took his life; he himself laid it down and he took it up again (10:17-18). What, then, does Jesus' cleansing the temple mean for John?

First of all, it is the Passover story (verse 13). This means that it relates to the death and resurrection of Jesus. This is the case with other Passover stories such as feeding the multitudes, which is clearly eucharistic and focuses on the body and blood of Jesus (chapter 6). The actual account of Jesus' death (19:31-37) is told in this Gospel as a Passover story. The reader of 2:13-22 is therefore alerted at the outset to the fact that the real subject here is Jesus' passion.

Second, this is a story of a conflict of values, a conflict between what Jesus Christ really means and those values espoused by the structures of religion with which Jesus contended. The writer knew that the issues at stake here were not clear to Jesus' followers at the time, but after the resurrection they remembered (verses 17, 22). The form of the narrative is the one common to the many stories in this Gospel: Jesus speaks "from above" and his auditors hear "from the earth"; Jesus speaks what is true, they hear what is apparent. "Destroy this temple, and in three days I will raise it up" (verse 19) is met with, "It has taken forty-six years to build this temple" (verse 20). Such dialogues constitute dramatic irony since the reader of the story knows what Jesus' audience does not; that is, that Jesus is speaking of his own passion. Jesus was asked for a sign and he gave the ultimate and final sign, his death and resurrection. The contrast is painfully clear. A temple, built as a witness to God and as a means of drawing persons near to God, is now an object of adoration, an end in itself. It is, therefore, ripe for destruction. But in the throes of death and in a move toward self-preservation, the temple keepers will destroy the One in whom God and humankind meet.

And finally, this is a story directed to the church. John does not relate this event as a dance over the grave of a grand institution or as an attack upon all rites, customs, and special places but upon their tendency to receive the devotion due to God and God alone. The ancient evil is tenacious, insidious, and slow to die. Who has not known persons who were apparently faithful in attention to all Christian duties but who, when there was a change in the building or minister or pattern of worship, suddenly ended all participation? It is a painful and costly lesson offered by our text; we want to be in charge of our own lives and manage all our relationships with God. Some will even kill if that control is threatened. Why is it so difficult to kneel first before God and listen and then proceed with that perspective to build our altars and frame our liturgies? Those who know that Christ is our sanctuary also know what the church building is, and is not.

Fourth Sunday of Lent

II Chronicles 36:14-23; Psalm 137:1-6; Ephesians 2:4-10; John 3:14-21

II Chronicles 36:14-23

Given the New Testament readings, the Gospel which includes John 3:16 and the Epistle which is in effect a summary of the Pauline message, it would be a bold preacher indeed who chose to focus on a text from the Book of II Chronicles. The Old Testament reading and Psalm 137 in many respects provide the dark background upon which the Good News of the New Testament readings is projected. They focus on the tragedy of the Babylonian exile as divine punishment for human sin, thus reminding us of what we forget at our peril: the essential theological prerequisite for the message of the gospel is a deep awareness of human failure and sin. Thus, especially in view of the Old Testament readings for the previous weeks—the covenants with Noah, Abraham, and with Israel at Sinai—we are taken to the low point in Israel's history.

The books of Chronicles certainly are not the best-known biblical books, so a few words of general introduction are called for here. First and Second Chronicles, Ezra, and Nehemiah probably were written by the same author, though that position has been challenged in recent years, with some attributing Ezra and Nehemiah to a different writer. The Chronicler, who had at his disposal the earlier history of Israel from the Exodus to the Babylonian exile (Deuteronomy through II Kings) as well as the Pentateuch, wrote an alternative version of the entire history beginning with Adam. He made selective use of those older books as sources, but it is clear at every turn that his is a theological history, an account of the interaction of God and people. The date of the work is very much in dispute these days, with some placing it as early as before 400 B.C. and others as late as after 200 B.C. So it is not certain whether it comes from the Persian or the Hellenistic period. It is only clear that it stems from the post-exilic era and concerns the life of the second temple.

Like the contemporary preacher, the Chronicler had before him texts which had become sacred scripture, and one of his goals was to interpret and apply them for his contemporaries. At a great many points we can compare his work with the sources and recognize that he treated those texts with a remarkable freedom. For him the historical continuity of the people of God was of great importance, as was King David to whom he attributed the establishment of the religious institutions. History was a sequence of sin and punishment, divine grace and renewal, wherein faithfulness to the Mosaic law was decisive.

In the Hebrew Bible the Book of II Chronicles is not listed with the other historical books but is the last book in the third part of the canon, the Writings. Our reading thus contains the final words of that Bible. That may explain in part why the final paragraph (verses 22-23), which repeats the good news of deliverance found in Ezra 1:1-4, concludes the book. It would not do to have the Bible end on the report of the desolation of the land noted in verse 21.

These verses summarize a considerable amount of history, from the reign of Zedekiah, which began after the first fall of Jerusalem in 597 B.C., through the destruction of the city in 587 B.C., the entire Babylonian exile, and to the edict of Cyrus in 538 which allowed the exiles to return home. At most points the Chronicler has compressed the information from his sources in II Kings 23–25, and in some cases reinterpreted the events. He also seems to have relied on some of the traditions found in Jeremiah 37–39. The Chronicler's account differs from that in Second Kings in several respects. He reports that all who were not killed were taken into exile, thus leaving the land unpopulated, whereas Second Kings reports that the poorest people were left along with a governor, Gedaliah.

More important for understanding the message of this text, however, are the distinctive interpretations of the events.

The Babylonian exile, which certainly was a life-threatening event for the chosen people, posed major problems for the faithful who survived it and for their descendants. Why did it happen? The persistent Old Testament answer, articulated even long before the fall of Jerusalem by the prophets, was that the exile was God's just punishment for a history of sin. The Chronicler agrees. The distinctive notes sounded here concern both the nature of that sin and the list of the sinners. Whereas Second Kings focuses the blame on the kings, our chapter includes "all the leading priests and the people" (verse 14). Moreover, sin is understood as unfaithfulness to the Lord and "following all the abominations of the nations" (verse 14), that is, violation of the first two commandments. Such actions entail "pollution," profaning the temple by false worship.

The Chronicler's stress on the centrality of the temple and proper ritual activity is visible here in his interpretation of the destruction of Jerusalem and of the exile. It is noteworthy that the first step in the exile was the taking of the vessels of the temple and its treasury into Babylon (verse 18). That seems here even more serious than the human tragedy. The years of the exile are also viewed as the land's "sabbaths," which had not been observed earlier. Moreover, the release of the exiles is for the purpose of building a new temple, that the name of God may be glorified. This emphasis corresponds to a stress on the radical holiness of God.

Another theme in the passage concerns the role of the prophets. Prophets in general, and Jeremiah in particular, are understood as messengers of God, sent out of divine compassion to warn the people of their evil deeds in order to avoid punishment. Not only that, the prophetic word is taken to be powerful and effective, precisely because it is the Word of God. Hence, the exile is reported to have lasted the seventy years Jeremiah said it would. The Chronicler has combined a high view of prophets with a strong priestly perspective.

Psalm 137:1-6

This lection is characterized by two sentiments: the enormous sorrow of being in exile (verses 1-4) and an unceasing devotion and loyalty to Jerusalem (verses 5-6). The final portion of the psalm, not included in the reading, is permeated with a thirst for revenge on the enemies and destroyers of Jerusalem, the Edomites and Babylonians (verses 7-9).

This psalm was composed by those who had been taken into exile following the destruction of Jerusalem by the Babylonians under King Nebuchadnezzar in 587 or 586 B.C. From this time until the edict of Cyrus, in 538 B.C., the city and its temple lay in ruins and its glory was preserved only in the memory of those who had stood within the gates.

The opening verses, 1-4, express the sorrow and heartache felt by the exiles who sat by the irrigation canals in Babylon and remembered Zion, the mount on which the temple was constructed. The time and the memories were so painful they could no longer sing or celebrate but hung their musical instruments on the trees. The captors only increased their grief by taunting the exiles by requesting that they sing one of the songs of Zion. These songs of Zion, such as Psalms 46, 48, 76, and so on, had proclaimed the greatness of Jerusalem and declared that Zion would always be protected and defended by God. Now in exile, the people were forced to recognize that Jerusalem had not been inviolable, so sacred that it could not be captured. With the faith expressed in such songs threatened by the realities of assault by Babylonian troops and overwhelmed by war machines and battering rams, it was no time for song, and especially not in a foreign land.

In these four verses, one can see and feel the sorrow and grief borne by those exiled in a strange land. We can hear the tale of sorrow, the cries of woe and anguish, and the shrieks of suffering souls. A sermon built around these verses could easily make several points.

1. Like the ancient Judeans of old, many, or perhaps all, of us live at times in a state of exile. Many are the exiles that can come our way. There is the exile of the divorced who live away from familiar surroundings and separated from family. To the unemployed, there is the exile of being without a job, of facing life without the necessary mooring. To the young adult, there is the exile of leaving home.

2. Sorrow and sadness must be given words so we can face and endure them. While there may be some value in a Stoic acceptance of sorrow—a certain nobility in the acceptance of misery—modern psychology and ageless common sense stress the need to let go with our feelings and to verbalize our pain and grief. Grief and sorrow that go unspoken may break the heart that seals them in and hugs them tight.

3. Tears are as normal a part of life as laughter and joy. When the occasion calls for tears, we should let them flow. The time to sit by the waters of Babylon and weep comes to everyone. Our prayers, when the tears flow, can renew our hope and preserve our faith.

The second part of the reading, verses 5-6, expresses the psalmist's undying loyalty to Jerusalem and the unwillingness to surrender sacred memory even in the midst of a history that seemed to defy every confidence in that loyalty. These verses address Jerusalem directly as if the city were a person. The psalmist declares his/her faithfulness by requesting to become lame and dumb if Jerusalem fades from memory or is crowded out by some other joy. Jerusalem here is of course more than just the city. It is also the symbol of better days and the embodiment of cherished memories when life was more as it should be.

In spite of, or maybe because of, the pathos of such psalms as this one, we can be thankful that the ancient Hebrews faced life and its calamities with an unfettered honesty that could give vent to the depths of affliction and torment. They could still hold to their faith and memories from the past even if that past was separated from the present by ashes of destruction, by miles of desert traversed under duress, and by the scenery of a land foreign and strange.

Ephesians 2:4-10

On the Fourth Sunday of Lent, penitential mourning gives way to joy. Its name, Laetare Sunday, derives from the opening words of the Mass text, "Laetare Jerusalem" (Rejoice, O Jerusalem). This theme of joy came to be celebrated in the ancient church in various ways, for example, by the use of a rose in connection with the liturgical celebration. This practice is attested as early as the eleventh century and seems to have derived from the Roman custom of using flowers in celebration to mark the beginning of spring. Accordingly, instead of the more somber purple vestments, rose-colored vestments could be worn on this Sunday. Also, flowers could be used as part of the worship appointments of the altar.

Today's epistolary text sounds this note of triumphant joy. Ephesians 2 opens by noting the contrast between death and life: "And you he made alive, when you were dead through the trespasses and sins in which you once walked" (verses 1-2*a*). This theme is continued into verses 5-10. Death giving way to life is vividly attested through the blooming flowers of spring, and the rose symbolism of Laetare Sunday effectively conveys this. The stress on our former state of disobedience (verses 2-3) recalls the earlier period of Lent when penitence and mourning were in the forefront. But, as this passage unfolds, there is a marked shift to the new life. In this respect, today's text shifts the attention of the reader more directly toward Easter.

On the Wednesday following the Fourth Sunday of Lent the apostolic creed was handed over to catechumens *(traditio symboli)*. They were now moving closer to the full appropriation of the paschal mystery of Christ. The baptismal imagery of today's text would thus take on additional significance.

First, we should note that God is the subject of the action described in verses 4-7. The drama of reenactment thus unfolds as one in which God is the chief actor, for God was, after all, the true administrator of baptism. The initiative of salvation is God's love: "Out of the great love with which he loved us" (verse 4). It is God who "made us alive together with Christ" and "raised us up with him" (verses 5-6).

Second, the repeated use of participatory language should be noticed, especially the preposition "with": "made us alive *together with Christ* . . . raised us up *with him* . . . made us sit *with him* in the heavenly places" (verses 5-6). The one who reenacts the death and resurrection of Christ does so not as a symbolic ritual. Instead, God may be said to reenact the death and resurrection of Christ within the baptism of each believer. God, the chief actor in the paschal drama of Christ through which death gave way to life, takes the baptized through the same sacred drama. The newly attained status of the believer is quite phenomenally depicted as sitting enthroned with the risen Christ in the heavenly places. This stands in sharp contrast with Paul's theology of baptism described in Romans 6 where the believer's full appropriation of resurrection remains unrealized in this life.

The concluding portion of this text is reminiscent of the epistolary reading for the Second Sunday of Lent. Here again is stress on salvation given through the grace of God and "not because of [human] works." The Pauline emphasis is still central here. To emphasize that salvation is "not your own doing [but] . . . the gift of God" (verse 8) is a natural extension of the thought in verses 4-7 where God is portrayed as the initiator and chief actor of the drama of salvation, both of Christ and Christians. Accordingly, the people of God are the handiwork of God—God's "workmanship" (verse 10). We are who we are as a result of the activity of God.

The readers are also reminded that this drama had its origin in primeval history (verse 10). As stated in Ephesians 1:4, it was prior to the foundation of the world that God chose us. This is in keeping with the cosmic outlook of Ephesians where the drama of salvation history is sketched from the beginning of time until the end of time as encompassing the whole universe. This provides a salient reminder to all believers, catechumens and converts alike, that the sacred drama into which we have been introduced, which we have appropriated, and in which we participate as joint-participants with Christ, extends far beyond our life and time. In appropriating the Christian story for ourselves, we become part of a historical and cosmic process that has preceded us and will succeed us, but in which we ourselves are nevertheless actively engaged.

John 3:14-21

After a first reading of the four lessons for today, two words come to mind as a summary expression of what is being said: judgment and grace. It is not uncommon to think of judgment and grace as two separate actions of God. Some texts speak of God's repeated acts of grace, when rebuffed or denied, being followed by acts of judgment. Other texts speak of God's judgment upon the people and then of God's turning toward them in favor and grace. However, in our Gospel for this Sunday one act of God is spoken of as being both judgment and grace. That act is God's sending Christ into the world.

As readers of the Gospel of John know, it is extremely difficult to divide the text into discrete units. The words of Jesus and the words of the Evangelist are interwoven and lengthy speeches close with theological summaries. In chapter 3, editors differ as to where to place the quotation marks in Jesus' conversation with Nicodemus: after verse 13, verse 15, verse 16, or verse 21? Fortunately, the meaning of verses 14-21 does not depend on the identity of the person who said it. Actually verses 14-21 consist of two distinct units: verses 14-15 and verses 16-21, neither of which is dependent on verses 1-13. Our lection is one of many theological summaries in this Gospel, placed immediately after conversations or conflicts but not materially related to them (3:31-36; 5:19-24, 25-29, 30-47 are other examples).

The first unit, verses 14-15, is a self-contained statement based on the ways in which Christ's redemptive act is analogous to the event of the brazen serpent recorded in Numbers 21:4-9. In the Numbers story, the people were suffering God's punishment for sin, but the elevation of a bronze serpent upon a pole provided relief and life for all who looked upon it. Likewise Christ is lifted up for the life of all who look to him in faith. The lifting up of Christ in this Gospel has a double meaning: it refers to the manner of his death (12:32-33) and also to his exaltation to the presence of God. Both John 3:14-15 and Numbers 21:4-9 are accounts of God's grace, God's initiative for the salvation of the people.

The second unit, verses 16-21, is a theological reflection upon the meaning of Christ coming into the world. The governing image in the passage is light, a favorite of this Gospel (1:1-9; 8:12; 11:9-10). The light metaphor is appropriate to the idea of revelation, of God being made known to us, which, according to John, is the purpose of the incarnation. No one has ever seen God but the only Son has made God known (1:18), and to know God is life eternal (17:3). But light is also a most appropriate metaphor for expressing both the judgment and the grace implicit in Christ's coming. Christ did not come to judge but his coming is a judgment in the same way that turning on a light can be the exposure and conviction of those who prefer darkness because their deeds are evil (verse 20). At the same time the light is for others a gift and the occasion for joy (verse 21). The Scriptures reveal that an act of God's love has both positive and negative effects. A stepping-stone may be for some a stumbling block; a feast may be the occasion for illnesses that result from gluttony. A saving presence can also be a disturbing presence. It is only in the make-believe world of a child that one can turn on a light without creating shadows. All who preach and live the gospel know this painful truth. To speak the Good News, to voice the love of Christ in some gatherings, is not to be unanimously received with applause and blessing. Other forces are aroused by that word of God's grace. All who would be centers of power and influence for good must live with this fact. This is what it means to *make a difference* in the world. This is what John means when he says Jesus Christ is the crisis, the difference, the judgment of the world (verse 19).

Fifth Sunday of Lent

Jeremiah 31:31-34; Psalm 51:10-17; Hebrews 5:7-10; John 12:20-33

Jeremiah 31:31-34

This reading is an unqualified announcement of salvation, containing the only explicit Old Testament reference to the New Testament, that is, new covenant. As we approach the end of a season of penitence and preparation, Jeremiah 31:31-34 anticipates a particular aspect of the good news of Easter, that God will transform human hearts. Psalm 51:10-17, the prayer for a clean heart, is preceded in verses 1-5 by one of the most powerful prayers of confession in the Bible. The link between these readings is the focus on the heart; the psalm is in effect a prayer for what is promised in Jeremiah 31:31-34. In the Gospel text Jesus announces that his glorification is near, but only through death to resurrection. Likewise in Jeremiah the new covenant comes only through and beyond suffering, in this case that of the Babylonian exile.

The context of Jeremiah 31:31-34 is important. It is part of what has been called the little book of comfort (chapters 30–31), a collection of announcements of restoration. What follows in chapter 32 is the report of something Jeremiah did during Nebuchadrezzar's siege of Jerusalem. The prophet had been imprisoned in the court of the guard for saying that the Babylonians would be victorious. While he was there, he bought a field in Anathoth from his cousin as an action symbolic of God's future for the people. Even before Jerusalem was destroyed he announced: "Houses and fields and vineyards shall again be bought in this land" (Jer. 32:15). So a powerful spiritual vision of changed lives and obedient hearts is followed by, of all things, a real estate transaction.

The point seems clear: So long as they are on this earth, even the people of the new covenant still need a place to live, actual ground for growing food, and even a marketplace where things are bought and sold.

Like so much of the Old Testament, this promise comes from a time of crisis and transition, the disaster of the Babylonian exile. When the prophet hears the Lord promise to make a new covenant with the house of Israel and the house of Judah, he has in view the situation of the exiles in Babylon. These lines respond to the most serious question on the minds of those people. Has the covenant ended? Is this blow the Lord's final word to us?

The initial words, "Behold, the days are coming," stress that this is a future hope. We see from other parts of the book that Jeremiah expected the exile to last some seventy years. Consequently, he did not expect to live to see the promises completely fulfilled.

One who speaks of a new covenant must also have in mind an old. Verse 32 spells that out directly by recalling the covenant at Mount Sinai following the Exodus and pointing out that this is the covenant that the people broke. But there were other old covenants as well, each of them new in its time. Before Mount Sinai there were the covenants with Noah, Abraham, Isaac, and Jacob. After Sinai Moses led the people in a renewal of the covenant on the plains of Moab, as did Joshua at Shechem. Later Samuel led the tribes in a covenant when kingship was established. From the perspective of Jeremiah, now there was a hope of reestablishment of the covenant under young King Josiah.

All these covenants were viewed as occurring at critical moments in the life of the community. When transitions and changes brought life and faith into doubt, it was time for a covenant. All were taken as initiated by God, and as responses to God's initiative. Moreover, all involved promise.

Notice the particularly intimate language in this text. In recalling the old broken covenant, the prophet hears the Lord saying, "I took them by the hand," like a mother leads a child, and "I was their husband." He has no problem at all with mixing the metaphors, for the message is clear. Even in the past, the Lord was as close to the people as flesh and blood. The way has been prepared for the new level of intimacy of the covenant on the heart.

The word which stands at the center of the passage is "covenant." A covenant is a special kind of relationship where parties pledge themselves to one another. Old Testament covenants generally had two parts, a promissory oath, and the stipulations or contents of what was promised. The fact that the law here is written, even on the heart, suggests that the basic reference is to the stipulations. In that respect the covenant is like the written law. Israel will not forget what they have sworn to do.

This promise of a new covenant contains one of the most ancient and persistent formulations of the covenant vows: I will be your God and you will be my people. Though the stipulations could be spelled out in lists of laws and even books of laws which defined how a covenant people behaved, this simple sentence said it all. All the people had to do to make a covenant was to say, "We will to be God's people."

It should be emphasized that the making of a covenant with God was not an individual, but a communal, act, the work of the community of faith. It was Israel's covenant with God at Mount Sinai that made them a people, the people of God, binding them not only to God but also to one another.

What then is new about the new covenant? That God initiates the covenant, that he forgives sins, and that Israel will "know" the Lord intimately had been features of older covenants. What is without precedent is the law written on the heart, the covenant at the core of one's being. The newness is a special gift, the capacity to be faithful and obedient. In the Old Testament, the heart is the seat of the will (see Jer. 29:13; 32:39; Ezek. 11:19; 36:26); consequently, the special gift here is a will with the capacity to be faithful. God thus promises to change the people from the inside out, to give them a center. This covenant will overcome the conflict between knowing or wanting one thing and doing another. In the new covenant the people will act as if they are owned by God without even reflecting upon it.

Which laws, then, are written on the heart? All the laws of Moses? Just the Decalogue? The answer is all of these things, and none of them. Just these words will suffice: "I am yours, and you are mine," says the Lord. That is the language of love and faithfulness.

Psalm 51:10-17

This selection from Psalm 51 was chosen for use with Jeremiah 31:31-34 because both speak of new life and new relationships between God and human beings. Both express the yearning of the human heart for a divine-human relationship which can withstand all challenges and which will endure through all troubles.

Verses 10-17 of this psalm are, of course, part of a larger composition, namely, the psalm as a whole. The entire psalm is a penitential composition in which there is a confession of sin, a petition for forgiveness and new life, and a pledge or vow to perform certain activities if God responds favorably. Verses 10-17 contain part of the petition (verses 10-12) and the vow (verses 13-17) made by the worshiper.

The requests of verses 10-12 must be seen as the counterpart to and further development of verses 6-9. In the latter is a prayer for forgiveness and cleansing for sins of the past. In the former, one finds the petition for positive and radical changes that will produce a new being so that the worshiper's future life will not be a repetition of the past.

The petition contains what may be viewed as three rather synonymous requests.

1. Verse 10 asks for a transformation of the person. Two terms here are of significance: heart and spirit. In Hebrew thought, the heart was the locus of the intellect and the will. (We still memorize things by heart.) Spirit is that aspect in persons which make them alive and active. Thus a request for a clean heart and a new and right spirit represents the request for a new orientation and power in life which will make possible a new type of obedience to God.

2. Verse 11 requests that God's presence and holy Spirit—the terms should be seen as synonymous—remain with the worshiper. Verse 10 is thus concerned with the

request to become a radically changed person while verse 11 asks for a continuing presence of the Deity.

3. Finally, there is the request that God restore the joy that divine salvation brings. Such joy is seen as the by-product of what has been requested earlier in the psalm. The "joy of thy salvation" is paralleled by the expression "a willing spirit." The worshiper thus requests a spontaneous inclination to obedience which correlates with the experiences of joy. Both the joy and willing spirit are referred to in such a way as to indicate that God is the source of both.

In verses 13-17 the worshiper promises to fulfill certain commitments if the earlier requests are granted. The central thrust of these verses centers on the offering of testimony and bearing witness to the experiences of salvation. Three times in verses 13-15, the worshiper refers to this offering of testimony: "I will teach," "my tongue will sing," and "my mouth shall show forth." The offering of testimony was a part of the ritual of thanksgiving when a worshiper went to the temple to offer thanks for being saved from the condition of trouble or need. Generally, a psalm of thanksgiving makes reference to the distress from which the worshiper is redeemed. It may be this thanksgiving service which the person promises to observe. The consequence of such thanksgiving is twofold: other sinners will return to God as this worshiper has and testimony and praise will be given to God.

The first part of verse 14 presents a problem for interpreters, since it is uncertain what is meant by the Hebrew term "bloodguiltness" as translated in the RSV. The Hebrew word literally means "bloods." It may refer to murder or to dying. In the former, the one praying would be kept from being a murderer and, in the latter, he would be saved from an impending death. (The last part of verse 8 may indicate sickness and thus suggest that the worshiper is praying to be saved from death.)

Finally, verses 16-17 emphasize that what God requires of the individual is a broken spirit and a contrite heart, that is, real repentance and contrition. These are contrasted with sacrifice and burnt offering. Many have seen these verses as a repudiation of the entire Israelite system of sacrifice.

Probably what the psalmist is suggesting, however, is not that all sacrifice is bad but only that sacrifices brought by the individual (rather than those offered on behalf of the community as a whole) are not as acceptable as real penitence. One can imagine even the words of verses 16-17 being spoken at the time when the worshiper offered a sacrifice in a service of lament! (Church members frequently note that it is not the gift but the giver that matters as they offer their gifts!)

Hebrews 5:7-10

The Fifth Sunday of Lent, traditionally called "Passion Sunday," originally marked the beginning of Passiontide, the final two weeks prior to Easter. The suffering of Christ received even greater emphasis during this time. Whereas the first four weeks of Lent was a time for personal reexamination and penance, the last fourteen days became a time for thinking more exclusively about the Lord's passion. It was an early custom to drape crucifixes, statues, and pictures in the churches with a purple cloth to signify that this was a period of intense mourning.

In keeping with this emphasis, today's epistolary lection focuses on the suffering of Christ. In this respect, it is typical of the Christology of the Epistle to the Hebrews with its repeated emphasis on the humanity of Christ. It is in this epistle that we find the most thoroughly and systematically developed Christology in the New Testament, and it is especially distinctive for the way it captures the human dimension of Christ. The choice of "high priest" as the overarching christological image is itself telling, because this provided Jewish readers a ready point of reference and identification. The high priests they knew were obviously human figures, and this enabled the unknown author of Hebrews a point of contact through which he could develop a systematic understanding of the work of Christ. Consequently, Hebrews especially emphasizes Christ's humanity and his ability to sympathize with human weakness (Heb. 2:17-18; 4:15; 5:2).

The passage opens by referring to the "days of his flesh" (verse 7), that is, "the days of his earthly life." The reference to Jesus' offering up "prayers and supplications, with loud cries and tears, to him who was able to save him from death" (verse 7) may recall the Gethsemane episode (Matt. 26:38-46 and parallels; cf. also John 12:27). The Gospel accounts of Gethsemane, however, do not mention "loud cries and tears." Even so, the Gospel accounts do convey the intense distress that Jesus experienced in Gethsemane. This became even more intensified in the later tradition, as seen in the clearly later textual addition to Luke 22:44 which states, "His sweat became like great drops of blood falling down upon the ground." Jesus is said to have cried out with "a loud voice" while hanging from the cross (Mark 15:34; Matt. 27:46), and this may in fact be the point of reference in Hebrews 5:7.

One puzzling feature of our passage is the statement that "he was heard for his godly fear" (verse 7). The phrasing is influenced by Psalm 22:24: "When he cried unto him, he heard" (KJV). God may have "heard" Jesus in the sense that the prayer in Gethsemane "Abba, Father" (Mark 14:36), or the prayer on the cross, "My God, my God, why hast thou forsaken me?" (Ps. 22:1*a*), came before God, but certainly not in the sense that God answered Jesus' prayer for deliverance from death. Another way of understanding the phrase is to render it: "And being heard [was set free] from fear" (Montefiore).

For the author of Hebrews, Jesus' being the Son of God did not exempt him from suffering. Here, the true significance of verse 8 should be noted. It was not simply that he was *a* son who learned obedience, for after all it is the lot of sons to learn obedience. Rather, it was that *the* Son of God should have to learn obedience. The true import is seen if we render the phrase: "Even though he was *the* Son of God . . . ." Suffering as the Son of God and learning obedience are conspicuously human experiences. Many Christians, though believing in some sense that Jesus was both human and divine, still find it difficult to believe that he shared our humanity. For them, it is difficult to see how Jesus could "learn" anything, much less obedience. Yet, this is precisely the point that our text makes—and stresses. Submitting to death on the cross became the supreme test—and example—of Jesus' filial obedience to the Father (cf. Phil. 2:8).

The text speaks of this as a perfecting process ("being made perfect," verse 9). Earlier in Hebrews 2:10, we are told that God saw fit to make Jesus "the pioneer of . . . salvation perfect through suffering" (cf. also 7:28). From our own experience, we know that suffering, rightly experienced and interpreted, has the capacity to refine our own character and make us more complete, or make us perfect in ways that we previously were not. But more is implied here. It is not simply a question of Jesus' character being refined or perfected, but that the death on the cross was the final act through which the work of Christ came to completion. Through it, the work of God in Christ was consummated. Jesus' suffering and death became the ultimate refinement of his character and also the consummate act through which his mission was completed.

In this respect, Jesus became the pioneer (cf. 2:10) for all believers, and the "source of eternal salvation to all who obey him" (verse 9). Elsewhere in the epistle, this is linked directly with Jesus' role as high priest, the note on which this passage ends (verse 10). Jesus as a high priest "after the order of Melchizedek" is developed more fully in Hebrews 7:1-28. This appropriation of an Old Testament character provides the author a way of articulating the uniqueness of Jesus' high priestly role.

John 12:20-33

"The hour has come for the Son of man to be glorified" (verse 23). The glorifying of the Son is this Gospel writer's way of referring to the death, resurrection, and exaltation to former glory of the one who became flesh and dwelt among us (11:4; 13:3; 17:1-5). By his announcement that the hour had come, Jesus is telling his disciples (and the readers) that the chain of events leading to his passion will now begin. Prior to this time, Jesus' actions and even threats against his life were "explained" with the expression "his hour had not yet come" (2:4; 7:6; 7:30; 8:20).

Jesus' comments about his impending death and what it would mean for the world were prompted by the coming of Greeks (perhaps to be understood as Greeks who had embraced Judaism) to see Jesus. The desire of non-Jews to benefit from Jesus' ministry represents the beginning of the fulfillment of two preceding passages: "He prophesied that Jesus should die for the nation, and not for the nation only, but to gather into one the children of God who are scattered abroad" (11:51*b*-52); and, "Look, the world has gone after him" (12:19). But how are the nations of the world to be blessed by Jesus Christ whose ministry was so narrowly confined in time and place? Our text is an answer to that question.

The Greeks approach Jesus indirectly through Philip and Andrew. This could be explained logically by the fact that these two were from Galilee, which had a large Gentile population, and they had Greek names. It could also be the case that at the time of the writing of the Gospel Philip and Andrew were associated with missions to the Gentiles. In our text, the Greeks are treated symbolically, representing the world seeking Jesus, for once they make their request they disappear from the story. Jesus' response, "The hour has come," means that he now must make himself available to the world. That cannot be in his present ministry in Judea, Samaria, and Galilee, but as the glorified Christ who abides through his word and through the Spirit with believers everywhere. That promised presence is a dominant theme in the farewell discourses and farewell prayer (chapters 14–17). The Johannine Church, separated by time and space from the initial events of Jesus' ministry, needed very much to hear this word of the presence and availability of Christ. They needed to be assured that living in another place in another time did not place them beyond the life giving and saving work of Christ. And we, too, need to hear that. We are not second-class disciples at a distance, born at the wrong time in the wrong place, trying desperately to survive on the thin diet of recorded memories of what it was like when Jesus was here. Christ *is* here. "And I, when I am lifted up from the earth, will draw all men to myself" (verse 32).

But this is the point: Christ's availability to believers everywhere required his death. His reflections upon his death are here offered in a threefold commentary: (1) there is a law in nature that demands death if there is to be more life (verse 24); (2) there is a principle of discipleship that demands death to self-interest in order to have life eternal (verses 25-26); and (3) is the agent of nature's creation and the master of the disciples to be exempt from this principle of death and life? Jesus responds in a word to God, "No, for this purpose I have come to this hour" (verse 27). This Gospel's Christ does not writhe in agony, does not struggle in Gethsemane, does not offer up a cry of dereliction. Rather he embraces God's will and a voice from heaven confirms his decision (verse 28). Not all heard the voice, of course; not all of us ever do.

Whatever troubling of soul Jesus experienced (11:33-35, 38; 12:27) in approaching his own death, that troubling is now over. It is as though death were a past experience. The ruler of this world has been cast out (verse 31). From this point on, the passion story in John will be without anguish and tears. As Lent moves us in quiet preparation for Jesus' Good Friday and Easter, perhaps it might also move us to prepare for our own.

Passion/Palm Sunday

Mark 11:1-11 or *John 12:12-16; Psalm 118:19-29 (for reading at the beginning of the service); Isaiah 50:4-9*a; *Psalm 31:9-16; Philippians 2:5-11; Mark 14:1–15:47* or *Mark 15:1-39*

Mark 11:1-11

Mark 11:1-11 and Psalm 118:19-29 herald the opening of the gates of worship for this special day and the days that lead to Easter. These texts are, therefore, celebrative and joyous, announcing, "This is Palm Sunday!" while the lections for the day carry the other word, "This is Passion Sunday."

The celebration described in Mark 11:1-11 has about it the abandon appropriate to the full release of tenacious hopes and ancient trust in the God who will redeem the people. A new colt is pressed into service, the owner being told the Lord needs it and will return it (verse 3). Branches cut from the fields after the manner of the celebration of the Feast of Tabernacles (Lev. 23:40) are spread on the road. Some of the crowd removed garments and placed them in the path of Jesus (verse 8). Preceding and following Jesus were the throngs of people who are so often in Mark portrayed as positive and supportive of Jesus, even though they did not understand his mission. The shout, "Hosanna," which originally meant "save us" (the term has the same root in Hebrew as the word Jesus), probably had become by this time an enthusiastic burst of praise.

The occasion Mark describes here is a Christophany, a manifestation of the Christ. But this needs to be said with the same caution that Mark has built into the account. The pilgrims sing of "the kingdom of our father David" (verse 10) but do not call Jesus the Son of David. In the preceding episode Bartimaeus who was blind gave Jesus that title (10:46-52). Later Jesus would clearly and firmly reject the Davidic image of the Messiah (12:35-37). The kingdom of which the crowds spoke was not present but "coming" (verse 10), one bit of evidence supporting A. Schweitzer's view that the people welcomed Jesus not as Messiah but as Elijah, the forerunner of the Messiah. A final word of caution which subdues Mark's record of Jesus' arrival at Jerusalem: the celebration generated by Jesus' presence occurs near the city (verse 1) but not in the city. Mark makes it clear that verses 1-10 present the festival and that Jesus does not enter Jerusalem until verse 11 (the RSV begins a new paragraph here). He is pictured entering the city and the temple alone and leaving the city with the Twelve. Jerusalem itself is not the scene of joyous reception; rather it is the place of controversy, hostility, and death. Therefore, unlike Matthew 21:4-5, Mark does not quote Zechariah 9:9, even though it lies in the background, probably because the prophet was addressing Jerusalem with a call to shout and sing.

One final look at Mark 11:1-11 prepares the reader for what is to come. The larger unit, 11:1–13:37, has about it a clear symmetry. It opens with Jesus at the Mount of Olives (verse 1). The place had messianic associations (Zech. 14:4) and closes with Jesus' apocalyptic discourse delivered from the Mount of Olives (13:3). This section opens with Jesus going to the temple (verse 11) and although he says and does nothing, two phrases project dark prospects: "when he had looked round at everything" and "it was already late" (verse 11). When the section closes, Jesus is sitting "opposite the temple" (13:3) predicting its destruction. Within 11:1–13:37 the focus is upon the cleansing of the temple and a series of controversies with religious leaders which take place in the temple. At his trial, witnesses report having heard Jesus say that he would destroy the temple and build another in three days (14:58). For Mark, the coming of Jesus means the end of the temple and the beginning of a new time and place for meeting God.

John 12:12-16

This alternate Gospel lection is John's account of Jesus' entry into Jerusalem. The Fourth Gospel has had a major influence in shaping traditional observances of this Christian festival. For example, it is this Evangelist who identifies the branches used as palm branches (verse 13), and this account has figured in calculating the day as the Sunday before Good Friday ("six days before the Passover," verse 1, and "the next day," verse 12).

However, this record of the event differs in significant ways from the Synoptic accounts. In the first place, John 12:12-16 is much briefer, even than Mark. Second, Jesus is not coming from Galilee through Jericho to Jerusalem as in the other Gospels, but he has been ministering for some time in Jerusalem. In fact, these verses are within a larger unit, 11:1–12:50, which centers in the raising of Lazarus at Bethany near Jerusalem. Six days before the Passover Jesus is in Bethany (12:1) and the next day goes into the city (verse 12). Third, the crowd present for Jesus' entry does not consist of pilgrims coming with him but rather of those who had come for the feast and went out to meet Jesus (verse 12). The crowd is large and excited because they had either witnessed or heard about the raising of Lazarus (verses 17-18). Fourth, the event is initiated by the crowd in Jerusalem (verse 13), and Jesus responds by finding a colt and riding it (verse 14). By so doing, he fulfilled Zechariah 9:9 which is here more paraphrased than quoted (verse 15). It is obvious that what Jesus does is unknown to the crowd; in fact, his own disciples do not understand until after the resurrection (verse 16).

Briefly stated, then, John 12:12-16 tells of a large crowd, excited by a sign Jesus performed (raising Lazarus), responding by proclaiming Jesus king of Israel. This sounds familiar. After the sign of feeding the five thousand, a large enthusiastic crowd sought to make Jesus king (6:15). On that occasion, the crowd misunderstood and when Jesus explained he was the true bread, available to them in his death, they forsook him. Here now in Jerusalem there is the enthusiasm spawned by a sign performed but misunderstood, for the raising of Lazarus was not only prophetic of Jesus' passion, but would, in fact, precipitate his arrest and crucifixion (11:45-50; 12:9-11). In a few days the crowd would get to see Jesus publicly heralded as king, but it would be on a placard placed by Pilate on the cross of Jesus (19:19).

Jesus *is* King, but not because the crowd elevated him or made him so. He is King by virtue of who he is. Not even faith makes Christ King; faith only recognizes that he is.

Psalm 118:19-29

This portion of Psalm 118 was selected for this point in the lectionary because it describes a victor's triumphal entry into the city or temple and thus parallels in imagery Jesus' triumphal entry into Jerusalem on Palm Sunday.

As a whole, Psalm 118 is a very complicated psalm in which many different participants and speakers were involved. In addition, portions of the psalm, especially verses 26-27, present enormous difficulties for translators. The psalm is best understood as the spoken accompaniment of a great thanksgiving ritual involving the return of a victorious king to Jerusalem and his entry into the temple accompanied by a host of followers. Verses 1-4 with their references to Israel, Aaron, and those who fear the Lord demonstrate that the psalm was used in a great public thanksgiving liturgy.

Verses 5-18 recount the distress of battle from which the principal character, the king, no doubt, was rescued and given victory over his opponents. The king describes the battle and his triumph to a human audience. Thus, like most thanksgiving psalms, this one contains a description of a former distress which has now passed and can be viewed from a position of triumph. With verse 19, the psalm becomes more complicated in terms of the speakers and addressees. The following represents one possible way of looking at the psalm in terms of an entry ritual:

verse 19—the victorious king requests entry to the temple
verse 20—priests or others respond to the request
verses 21-22—the king offers thanksgiving addressed directly to God
verses 23-24—worshipers or a choir proclaim the celebration as a consequence of God's intervention
verse 25—people, choir, or priests offer a prayer to God

verses 26-27—the king is blessed as he enters the sacred precincts of the temple and reference is made to part of the festal celebrations
verse 28—the king offers thanksgiving
verse 29—a general summons to offer thanks

Several aspects of Psalm 118:19-29 are worthy of special note: (1) the celebration that is reflected in the psalm is one of triumph, success, and victory; (2) the royal features of the ritual, that is, their connection with a ruler or king seem clearly evident; (3) the celebration is one in which a key emphasis is God's action and intervention on behalf of the triumphal figure; and (4) the triumphal figure describes himself as one who has been rejected but who has now become victorious. In verse 22, we have what was apparently a common proverb: "The stone which the builders rejected has become the head of the corner." Such a saying implies that someone or something has moved from a state of rejection to a position of prominence, in fact, to a position that is irreplaceable. "The head of the corner" would suggest either a corner or foundation stone or perhaps the keystone in an arch. The first part of the psalm refers to how the figure was threatened, challenged, and nearly defeated on the field of battle before God granted him triumph.

The numerous parallels between this psalm and Jesus' career and triumphal entry into Jerusalem, the Holy City, should be obvious although Psalm 118 should not be read as a prophetic prediction of Jesus. The analogy between the psalm and Jesus' activity is to be found in the fact that in both God worked to elevate and exalt the lowly to a place of prominence. Though in each case the lowly had to move through oppression and opposition, they were not overtaken by death, literal or otherwise (see verse 18).

Isaiah 50:4-9*a*

With the exception of the readings which open the service, the lections for this day stress its identification as Passion

Sunday rather than Palm Sunday; that is, their emphasis is not upon Jesus' triumphal entry into Jerusalem but upon anticipation of his passion and death. Psalm 31:9-16 is an individual lament that carries the theme of trouble, enemies, and suffering, but concludes on a note of trust. The epistle is a summary of the death, resurrection, and exaltation of Jesus, emphasizing his humility and obedience. The Gospel, in its long form, reports the events in the last week of Jesus. The Old Testament reading in this context becomes an expression of the obedience of Jesus through suffering and his confidence that God will vindicate him.

Isaiah 50:4-9 is the third of the Servant Songs in Deutero-Isaiah. The others are: 42:1-4; 49:1-6; 52:13–53:12. The songs stand out in their literary context because of their special personal style and content, the particular understanding of the role of the servant, and the view of suffering which they express. While some commentators have argued to the contrary, it seems most likely that the songs were composed by the author of the remainder of Isaiah 40–55, the Second Isaiah.

The original historical context, then, of this passage is the very end of the Babylonian exile, 539 B.C., and the words were first uttered in Babylon. The prophet, among the exiles, proclaims a consistent message of salvation. The Judeans who were taken captive some fifty or sixty years earlier—and their descendants—are to be set free to return to Jerusalem. This, he announces, is a "new thing" which the Lord is about to do, but it will be like the old Exodus from Egypt. God, who is Lord of the world and of history, is about to use the Persian king Cyrus to accomplish his purpose. All of this is good news, and its general relationship to the Christian Easter Season is obvious. But more immediately relevant for Passion Sunday and for the third Servant Song is the new understanding of suffering which seems to have arisen out of the painful experience of the exile. Through the darkness of the exile Second Isaiah could see a light. He and other faithful ones also realized that the suffering of some, or even of one, could benefit others, perhaps even the whole world. Suffering, when in obedience to God, can be vicarious.

The song employs the first-person singular throughout. It is as if the prophet himself is speaking, but no addressee is identified. In terms of form and themes, it is similar to some of the Psalms. Some parts (verses 5-6) echo the language of individual laments; others (verses 7-9) are like songs of confidence in the Lord's support. There are especially close parallels to Jeremiah's complaints (Jer. 11:19, 21; 18:18; 20:10).

The identification of the servant in Second Isaiah and in the Servant Songs is one of the more debated issues in biblical scholarship, primarily because it is difficult to make one figure, either corporate or individual, fit all the texts. In this case, the speaker is the servant himself, and, if he is not the prophet, his role is a prophetic one.

The song has two main parts, verses 4-6 and 7-9. The first section is confessional, almost autobiographical. Initially (verses 4-5*a*) the speaker refers to his call. The vocation concerns words and the organs of communication, the tongue and the ears. God, he confesses, constantly gives him the ability to hear and to speak a word that sustains the weary. Then (verses 5*b*-6) the servant reports that he was faithful to his duty through personal suffering. It appears, then, that he has suffered because of his vocation. The second part of the song consists of expressions of confidence and trust in God, by virtue of which the servant has been sustained. In verses 8 and 9 the language of the ancient Israelite law court is employed, as it frequently is in Second Isaiah. The Lord is the one who "vindicates" or declares innocent. The speaker invites any "adversary" who wishes a trial ("contend") to formally appear in court ("stand up"). No one can declare him guilty, for the Lord God helps him.

The suffering, indignities, and shame that the servant experienced are directly the result of his divinely ordained role. Because he was faithful he was beaten and scorned. But because he trusts in God he can see through that experience to vindication. The song may have arisen out of the prophet's own experience, that his message, while good news, was rejected and he himself persecuted. But it is not surprising that in the earliest church these words took on a new and deeper meaning. They were heard as Jesus' self-expression. The words that he spoke to the weary were given to him by

God. He suffered because of faithfulness to his role and to the end and beyond he trusted completely in God's vindication.

Psalm 31:9-16

Psalm 31 is a prayer of lament which could have been prayed by one in trouble or distress. Verses 9-16 are part of the description of the distress (verses 9-13), followed by a statement of the worshiper's confidence (verses 14-15), and a plea for redemption (verse 16).

The description of the distressful situation in verses 9-13 presents the person as one decimated by physical suffering (verses 9-10) and as a social outcast forced to endure life at the periphery of society without the benefit of friends or close acquaintances (verses 11-13).

Few psalms use such graphic descriptions to depict human misery and affliction as does Psalm 31. The descriptions are very graphic although reasonably non-specific. Thus when persons used this psalm in worship to describe their state of being, they could vent true feelings yet do so in highly stylized terms. Praying this psalm allowed persons to verbalize and express the deep-seated sense of alienation and hurt which they were feeling. The language appears to be highly metaphorical, probably using stereotypical and formulaic expressions which were highly graphic in content and emotional in nature. The labeling of one's troubles in such graphic fashion was probably therapeutic in and of itself since it allowed one to express sorrow and grief.

The expressions drawn from the arena of illness, in verses 9-10, if taken literally, suggest that the person was near death and had suffered for years in misery. The common words of suffering and affliction appear throughout these verses: distress, grief, sorrow, sighing, misery, wasting away.

In verses 11-13, the depiction of the distress uses the language of social ostracism. The descriptions here seek to present the worshiper's distress in the severest form possible. Adversaries, neighbors, acquaintances, and even the persons encountered in casual street meetings are all depicted as standing in terror and expressing disdain at the person's appearance (verse 11). Perhaps the supplicant was a person with some physical malady which rendered him or her unclean and required special isolation from general society (see Lev. 13:45-46). Job's description of his predicament, in Job 19:13-22, sounds very much like the cries of the outcast in verse 11.

The psalmist declares that he/she is like one already dead: passed out of life and even out of memory, cast aside like the shattered pieces of a broken pot: unwanted, useless, fit only for the garbage heap of the city dump (verse 12).

In fact, the psalmist describes the many out there who not only dislike him/her but who even scheme and plot to take his life (verse 13). Such language as this may sound like the ravings of a paranoid but should be seen as therapeutic language that allowed distressed persons to objectify their suffering to its most graphic, even exaggerated, level.

This psalm is not simply a recitation of a vale of sorrows. Throughout the text, there are frequent statements of a calm confidence in the Deity. Such is to be found in verses 14-15 in which the worshiper confesses trust in God and affirms that come what may the times of one's life are in the hand of God who can deliver one from the hand of enemies and persecutors.

Confidence in the Deity fades naturally into plea and petition for salvation (verses 15*b*-16). In spite of the description of the supplicant's condition in such sorrow-drawn and affliction-etched contours, confidence and calm flow through the psalm like a soothing stream. In this way it may parallel the composure of Jesus as he rode into Jerusalem—the man of sorrows but one confident of being in the hands of God.

Philippians 2:5-11

This passage opens with an exhortation (verse 5) which, in turn, introduces what many scholars regard as an early Christian hymn (verses 6-11). In spite of this emerging scholarly consensus, there is not a similar consensus among biblical translators. These verses are printed strophically in JB, but not in RSV[2] and NEB.

How the opening exhortation and the hymn that follows are related to each other is disputed. The fundamental exegetical question here is whether the Christ-hymn is quoted in order to provide the readers an example of humility and self-abnegation, or whether it rehearses the Christ-story in order to lay out the basis of the moral exhortation in the preceding verses. The Greek wording of verse 5 is obscure and may be rendered in at least two ways: "Have this mind among yourselves which was also in Christ Jesus" and "Have this mind among yourselves, which is yours [or which has been made possible] in Christ Jesus." In the former interpretation, the Christ-hymn unfolds the example of Christ to be followed. In the latter interpretation, the story of Christ's incarnation and exaltation is told to establish the basis of the ethical instruction. In this latter view, the Christ-hymn provides the "indicative" that underlies the Christian "imperative."

These two interpretive options are reflected in the various modern translations. The KJV reads: "Let this mind be in you, which was also in Christ Jesus." The RSV[2] reads: "Have this mind among yourselves, which is yours in Christ Jesus." The same two options are also reflected in the NEB. In the NEB text we read: "Let your bearing towards one another arise out of your life in Christ Jesus." The other rendering is provided in a footnote: "Have that bearing towards one another which was also found in Christ Jesus."

Although the difference of the wording in these various translations is slight, the preacher will need to be attentive to the wording of the text being used, since the various translations might point in different homiletical directions.

The chief theological difficulty is this. Although the Christ-hymn in verses 6-11 has traditionally been understood as an *imitatio Christi* passage, and in this regard has exercised great influence on Christian piety, the work of Christ unfolded in the hymn is, strictly speaking, inimitable. The descent of the Savior from heaven and his acceptance of human form in which he became obedient to death, although exemplary in its broadest sense, can only be regarded as uniquely possible for the Son of God. In what sense, realistically, could the Philippian church imitate this cosmic drama of descent and ascent?

And yet, to suggest that the drama of Christ's incarnation and exaltation is unfolded merely to show how and why the Christian exhortation in verses 1-5 is possible is not altogether convincing. The exhortation seems to call for an example, yet the example offered is not one Christians can easily identify with.

In any case, there is broad agreement that verses 6-11 contain an early Christian hymn and that it pre-dated Paul. He appears to have quoted this early hymn at this juncture, even though he makes certain editorial changes. Precisely how the hymn should be arranged into strophes and stanzas is not clear. Generally, it is arranged in two strophes consisting respectively of verses 6-8 and verses 9-11. Each of these strophes can then be subdivided into three stanzas.

The hymn unfolds a "V-shaped" Christology where the descent of Christ to earth is narrated first (verses 6-8) followed by his ascent or exaltation (verses 9-11).

The drama, of course, begins with the preexistent position of Christ (verse 6), and the language is reminiscent of wisdom traditions (cf. John 1:1-16). Christ voluntarily relinquishes his heavenly status, choosing to take the form of a slave. This language probably recalls the Suffering Servant imagery from Deutero-Isaiah (cf. Isa. 53:3, 11). His humanity is further stressed (verse 7; cf. Rom. 8:3), and the "descent" stage culminates in his obedience unto death. The phrase "even death on a cross" appears to be Paul's editorial addition to the hymn. The theme of obedience echoes that of texts treated earlier in the Lenten Season (cf. Heb. 5:7-10; 12:2).

With verse 9, there is an abrupt change ("therefore"). At this point, God becomes the subject of the action: "God has highly exalted him." This phrase includes both his resurrection and ascension. In other New Testament passages, these two stages of Christ's exaltation are kept separate (cf. Acts 2:33; 5:31). The name "above every name" (verse 9) anticipates the final acclamation in verse 11: "Jesus Christ is Lord." The submission of the whole universe to the exalted Lord is an expansion of Isaiah 45:23 (cf. also Rom. 14:11).

In one sense, the Christ-hymn might appear inappropriate as a reading for Palm Sunday since Good Friday is so thoroughly overcome by Easter and Christ's exaltation to heavenly preeminence. Even Paul seems to sense the danger of an exclusively triumphalist reading of this hymn, for he inserts "even death on a cross" in verse 8 as a salutary reminder of the centrality of the crucifixion. Philippians 3 suggests that some readers might well have begun to think that "resurrection life" was the *summum bonum* of the Christian life.

There is ample time in the Christian year to celebrate the triumph of Christ in the resurrection and ascension, and the minister's task here may be to see that the passion of Christ is not passed over too quickly.

Mark 14:1–15:47 *or* Mark 15:1-39

On this and several other occasions the lectionary offers a choice of readings. For this Sunday the choice is not between different Gospel lections but between a lengthy passage and a briefer selection from within that passage. In all such cases, the principle followed in this commentary is to discuss the larger reading on the assumption that the more inclusive one will be of more value to a larger number. Each preacher, of course, must make the decision as to the particular focus for a message drawn from that body of Gospel material. That decision, while certainly sensitive to the practical question of how much text can profitably be read in a service, will take into account a number of factors. For example, what does one wish to achieve on Passion/Palm Sunday?

One may wish to give the listeners a sense of the sweep of events contained in the passion narrative (Mark 14:1–15:47), beginning with the conspiracy to arrest Jesus and concluding with his burial. Or, a particularly critical moment in Jesus' final days or a Markan accent recurring in the narration may be deemed most appropriate for treatment in the sermon. Whatever the choice, the minister will want to think through the other services planned for Holy Week so that no subsequent message be robbed of its text by the choice for Passion Sunday. And in any case, reading through Mark

14:1–15:47 and listing the separate episodes will be immeasurably helpful, for Mark's message is not solely in the episodes but in the arrangement of events into a narrative. We will explore this characteristic of the Gospel shortly.

There are several features of Mark's passion narrative that impress themselves upon the reader.

First, there is restraint in the telling. The actual death of Jesus is quite briefly recorded (15:22-39), leading us to conclude that it was not the author's aim to use gory details to milk melancholy from the story, to create sympathetic sadness, and to draw tears from the readers. Feeling bad about it all is hardly faith and manipulating emotions is hardly preaching. According to Jesus' own statement he would suffer many things, be rejected and killed. The suffering and rejection are a major part of the story, not simply due to interest in historical reconstruction but because of the immediate need of Mark's church. What does it mean to the Christians to follow Jesus? Both internal and external evidence point to persecution; they are facing suffering, rejection, and, in some cases, death. As we know from other contexts (I Pet. 2:20-23; 3:15-17), the church drew meaning and support not only from Jesus' death but also from what he endured.

A second feature of Mark's narrative is the primacy of what happened to Jesus rather than of what Jesus did. The first half of this Gospel attends to what Jesus does, to the power of his preaching, healing, and exorcising. Jesus binds Satan and plunders his house (3:27). But it is not so in 14:1–15:47. In Mark, not even the triumphal entry is within the passion narrative (11:1-10). There is here a reference to God's power (14:36) and to the future power of the Son (14:62), but the verbs controlling the story describe what is done to, not by, Jesus: conspired against, anointed for burial, denied, betrayed, captured, tried, sentenced, mocked, crucified, buried. If the incarnation means anything, it means Jesus identified with the common human experience of not being in control. Mark's church, and ours, can find in this identification both mercy and "grace to help in time of need" (Heb. 4:16).

Third, Mark's account of the passion repeatedly recalls Jesus being abandoned by those who could have given him support and strength. Mark has in mind the Twelve. He alone among the Evangelists says that at the Last Supper they *all* drank the cup (14:23), and though all pledged loyalty till death (14:31), they *all* abandoned Jesus (14:50). The inner circle of three could not watch for an hour (14:32-42) and the betrayer of Jesus is identified three times not simply by name but as "one of the twelve" (14:10, 20, 43). And Simon's denial of Jesus is not related as an episode in itself; rather it is interwoven with Jesus' confession before the Jewish council. Once in this Gospel Jesus identifies himself as the Christ, the Son of God (14:61-62), thereby incriminating himself and drawing the death penalty. In Mark's dramatic arrangement that confession is preceded and followed by Peter's denials. Note 14:54 (Peter); 14:55-64 (Jesus); 14:66-72 (Peter). Neither the confession nor the denial could be more forcefully presented. But the Gospel is not preached if these texts release in the preacher a tirade against the Twelve. In some churches, it may be appropriate to ask if we, too, are among the Twelve. In others, the word might be found more clearly in the church's identification with Jesus the forsaken. Some messages, some decisions bring loss of public favor, members, and financial support. In fact, courage and faithfulness to the Gospel may mean experiencing at times a silent heaven. "My God, my God, why hast thou forsaken me?" (15:34).

Monday in Holy Week

Isaiah 42:1-9; Psalm 36:5-10; Hebrews 9:11-15; John 12:1-11

Isaiah 42:1-9

Among the readings for Monday in Holy Week, specific links are evident between the Old Testament reading and the epistolary text. Both have in view a covenant which will bring salvation to all peoples. In Hebrews 9:11-15 it is through the shedding of his blood that Christ has become the mediator of a new covenant. The psalm is a hymn of praise, especially for God's steadfast love and justice, paralleling some aspects of the Old Testament reading. The Gospel reports an event six days before the Passover, the day before Jesus' triumphal entry into Jerusalem.

Our Old Testament text consists of two distinct parts which probably circulated separately before they were combined in the present context. Isaiah 42:1-4 is the first of the Servant Songs, and Isaiah 42:5-9 is a distinct prophetic address. There is no serious reason to doubt that both parts stem from Second Isaiah in the last year or two before the end of the Babylonian exile (539 B.C.). As the Book of Isaiah has been handed down to us, the two sections are meant to interpret each other, but we may better understand the whole if we first look at the parts.

In this first Servant Song (verses 1-4) the Lord is the speaker throughout, and he refers to the servant in the third person. The words appear as a public proclamation, though no addressee is specified. This song appears first in the book, but it is also the first one logically, for it begins with the divine designation and election of the servant (verse 1*a*). No reasons for the selection are given except God's pleasure. In verses 1*b* the Lord announces that the servant has been given the divine spirit, and then proclaims the servant's task. While it is not possible for us to know the identity of the servant in the original context, the poem leaves no doubt about his task; it is stated three times. He will bring "justice to the nations" (verse 1); he will faithfully "bring forth justice" (verse 3); he will establish "justice in the earth" (verse 4). The meaning of justice in the prophetic tradition is clear: fairness, equity, protection of the weak, the rule of law. The unmistakably distinctive note here is that this justice will be universal, to foreign nations, to all the earth.

The remainder of the unit states how the servant is to accomplish the establishment of justice and how he will behave. The means of accomplishing the goal is stated only negatively (verses 2-3*a*), specifying only what he will not do. He will not operate by public proclamation and will not oppress those who are hurt. He will thus be gentle and sympathetic, especially to those in trouble. That he will not fail or be discouraged (verse 4*a*) suggests already that opposition is in store for him.

The understanding of the servant's role here is primarily royal; that is, messianic in the Old Testament sense. Kings were designated publicly, as in verse 1, and they were the ones responsible for seeing that justice was done. But there are also prophetic features ("my spirit upon him," verse 1*b*), and perhaps priestly ones as well, since priests were responsible for instruction in the law (verse 4*b*).

In the second unit (verses 5-9) God is also the speaker, but the divine speech is introduced by a prophetic messenger formula. Moreover, the speech, unlike verses 1-4, is a direct address that frequently employs the second person. The introductory messenger formula, "Thus says God, the Lord," is filled out with a series of three clauses defining God (verse 5). The remainder of the unit is the divine speech proper.

These verses amount to an almost systematic theological summary of the message of Second Isaiah. Both first and last, there is the statement of the nature of God. He is creator of all that is (heaven and earth), and the one who gives life to all peoples (verse 5). His name is Yahweh, the Lord, and he gives his glory to no other, especially not to graven images (verse 8). Elsewhere in the book this point is even more explicit: there is no other God. Second, the God who created the world has chosen and saved Israel (verse 6). The central message of the prophet is that God is about to set the captives in Babylon free, just as he had acted in the past to save his people. Third, Israel is chosen and saved for a purpose consistent with the faith in a single God for the whole world. They are to be "a covenant to the people, a light to the nations" (verse 6). That is, they are to bring enlightenment and unity to all peoples. Moreover, they are to open blind eyes and set prisoners free. Election, as the prophets as early as Amos had insisted, entails responsibility.

In verses 5-9 it seems clear that the servant is the people of Israel as a whole. They are the ones who have been redeemed, and their proper response is to be a light to the nations. The present context then suggests that the servant of verses 1-4 is also Israel, though when verses 1-4 are read independently other possibilities appear. There are several important contributions that this text can make in the context of the remembrance of the passion of Jesus. In particular, they call to mind the role of God's chosen servant to establish justice in all the world. Moreover, they may serve to remind all those who have been redeemed by the Lord that they may be a light to the nations.

Psalm 36:5-10

In verses 1-4 this psalm opens with a description of the wicked which takes the form of a proclamation to a human audience. One would assume that this, using a pattern like that in Psalm 1, would be followed by its counterpart, namely, a description of the righteous. Instead, what we have in verses 5-9 is hymnic praise of attributes of the Deity, addressed directly to God as if in a prayer. Verse 10 forms a petition or request addressed to God. Consciously the psalmist seems to be contrasting the life of the wicked with life under the grace of God. That is, the psalm does not describe the life of a godly man but instead talks about God and the benefits that come from him. Over against the reality of sin and the sinner, the psalmist sets God and the divine benefits.

In verses 5-6, God's love and faithfulness are extolled in terms of their immeasurable quality. In height, they extend to the heavens and up to the clouds. In constancy, they are like the mountains and the great deep beneath the earth. In breadth, God's concern to save is not limited by the boundaries of human existence but extends even to the beasts of the earth.

In verses 7-9, the poet focuses attention on the human benefits that accrue from the Divine or on what might be called the delights of enjoying God and his love. In verse 7, the neutral inclusive term "children of men" is used instead of the more customary "children of Israel." One could suppose that the psalmist here made a deliberate choice so as to universalize those included under divine favor. The image for protection in the verse—"in the shadow of thy wings"—may draw upon the protective role of the parent fowl in caring for its young. Such imagery, however, could be based on the fact that the ark, the representative symbol of God, rested in the Holy of Holies beneath the outstretched wings of the cherubim (see I Kings 8:7).

Just as verse 7 emphasizes the nature of protection offered by the Divine so verse 8 emphasizes the divine provision of food and drink. Some uncertainty exists about what "thy house" refers to. Is it a reference to the earth or the world as a whole? (See Psalm 93:5 where this appears to be the case.) Or is it a reference to the temple as the house of God? In the former, "feast on the abundance of thy house" would refer to eating the fruits and products of the earth. In the latter case, the expression would refer to the sacrificial meals consumed in the temple precincts where eating and drinking were common (see I Sam. 1:3-8). In any case, the psalm emphasizes the value and worth of the more sensual aspects of life—eating and drinking—which are seldom viewed and enjoyed in relationship to the Divine.

Two images characterize the statement in verse 9—life and light. God is seen as the source of all life and divine light as the source of human light.

Lest the blessings of God prove to be temporary, the psalmist prays that God will continue his love and salvation (verse 10). Here the bequest is hemmed in somewhat when compared with verse *7b*. In verse 10, those who know God and the upright of heart are the expected recipients of God's favor.

The association of this psalm with Holy Week can be made through its emphases on God's loving-kindness and on the divine blessings bestowed upon humanity.

Hebrews 9:11-15

As is well known, the Epistle to the Hebrews argues for the superiority of Christianity over Judaism. Today's lection occurs in a section of the epistle that shows how the sacrificial death of Christ exceeds the Mosaic sacrificial system administered by the Levitical priesthood (8:1–10:39). It opens by asserting that "Christ appeared as a high priest of the good things that have come" (verse 11). Early in the epistle, Christ is introduced as "a merciful and faithful high priest in the service of God" (2:17-18), and this christological image is repeated and elaborated as the epistle unfolds (cf. 3:1; 4:14–5:10). As high priest, Christ was able to identify with human needs and weaknesses (4:15), and he, like Aaron, was divinely appointed by God (5:1-6). As a priest "after the order of Melchizedek" (6:20), Christ is infinitely superior to his Levitical counterparts. Unlike them, he exercises his priestly function permanently (7:24). In addition, his moral qualifications far exceeded theirs; he is "holy, blameless, unstained, separated from sinners" (7:26). But, most decisively, unlike them, he was "exalted above the heavens" (7:26). Both the scope and the locus of his priesthood transcended the Levitical priesthood.

Today's lection introduces a section (9:11–10:18) which explores further the sacrifice of Christ. It should be noted that Christ is presented here not only as the high priest who officiates in the "heavenly sanctuary," but also as the sacrificial victim. He is both priest and sacrifice.

Several themes, already introduced in the epistle, converge in today's lection: (1) Christ as the high priest (verse

11); (2) heaven, or the heavenly sanctuary as the place where he officiates (verses 11-12; cf. 8:1-5); (3) the finality of Christ's sacrifice—"he entered once for all into the Holy Place" (verse 12; cf. 9:26; 10:11-12); (4) the superiority of the blood of Christ to the blood of animal sacrifices (verses 12-13; cf. 10:4-10); and (5) Christ as the mediator of a new, and therefore better, covenant (verse 15; cf. 8:6-13).

Although Christ as the high priest is developed extensively in Hebrews, Christ as the sacrifice, or the paschal lamb, is developed elsewhere in the New Testament. In I Corinthians 5:7, Paul refers to Christ as "our paschal lamb" who has been sacrificed. In Revelation, Christ is frequently referred to as the "Lamb that was slain" (Rev. 5:6, 12-13; 7:14; 12:11; 13:8). In the Fourth Gospel, Christ is understood as the paschal lamb, seen by the fact that the death of Christ is made to coincide chronologically with the slaying of the sacrificial animals on the eve of Passover.

Today's text has several problematic features with which the preacher will need to deal before moving on to proclamation.

First, there is the question, Did Christ appear as a high priest of "the good things that have come" or of "the good things to come"? Has Christ's high priesthood already achieved all the promised blessings, or does Christ preside as high priest over eschatological blessings that are still unrealized? There are strong textual grounds for adopting the latter reading (followed by JB, but not by RSV and NEB). Theologically, this offers hope for Christians and enables the celebration of Holy Week to direct their thoughts to the future which belongs to God. This eschatological theme is further reinforced in verse 15 where Christ is said to be "the mediator of a new covenant, so that those who are called may receive the promised eternal inheritance."

A second difficulty occurs in verse 11*b* in the phrase "through the greater and more perfect tent" (tabernacle), which, we are told, is "not made with hands, that is, not of this creation." Is this the "tent" of Christ's resurrected body, or does it refer to the heavenly tabernacle? If it is the former, it is an unusual way for the author to refer to Christ's risen body. If it is the latter, the following phrase in verse 12*a* ("he entered once for all into the Holy Place") appears redundant. In spite of the apparent redundancy, it appears to be the latter. In his death and resurrection, Christ was "exalted above the heavens" (7:26), and there became seated "at the right hand of the throne of the Majesty in heaven, a minister in the sanctuary and the true tent which is set up not by man but by the Lord" (8:1-2). The heavenly tabernacle is envisioned here as the place through which Christ the high priest proceeds, ultimately entering the Holy Place. But he does so with a difference. He does not offer the blood of sacrificial animals, but the blood shed in his own sacrificial death. The argumentation here becomes *a fortiori:* if the blood of sacrificial animals was effective in achieving purification, how much more effective is the blood of the ultimate sacrifice—Christ himself—in purifying our polluted consciences? In contrast to the animal sacrifices, the sacrifice of Christ was "without blemish" and occurred as "a spiritual and eternal sacrifice" (verse 14 NEB). His sacrifice is neither physical nor temporal, as were animal sacrifices; it transcended the physical and penetrated to the eternal.

From all this, it follows that Christ is the "mediator of a new covenant." His high priesthood operates in the heavenly realm where God dwells and where the Levitical priesthood was unable to penetrate. For that reason, the effects of Christ's sacrifice were retroactive, extending even to redeem those who died under the law (verse 15; cf. Heb. 11:39-40).

John 12:1-11

From Passion Sunday through Easter the Gospel lections will be drawn from the passion narratives. Because these accounts have always been regarded as containing the heart of the gospel, it is likely that the narrative of Jesus' final days, his arrest, trial, and death hardened quite early into a fixed tradition among the churches. Some scholars believe this may account for the fact that all four Evangelists relate the story with basically the same outline and with strikingly similar details. However, each Evangelist has his own purpose in writing and each church addressed has its own needs, and therefore, episodes from a common tradition are related from different perspectives. The preacher will want to be alert to this fact in order to avoid preaching from a composite of four accounts rather than from the particular text for the day.

The Gospel for today is John 12:1-11 and not the general topic, "the anointing of Jesus." All four Gospels record the event (Matt. 26:6-13; Mark 14:3-9; Luke 7:36-39) but with important differences. Matthew and Mark place the story in Bethany in the home of Simon the leper where "a woman" anoints Jesus' head. Anointing the head was in the biblical tradition the ceremony for the coronation of a king. Luke locates the act in Galilee in the home of Simon the Pharisee where a sinful woman anoints Jesus' feet with tears and with ointment. Luke, like John, knows of Jesus' visits to the home of Martha and Mary but Luke 10:38-42 and John 12:1-11 are otherwise quite different. For this message, we give our attention solely to the text before us. What would John have us hear?

1. In this Gospel the anointing at Bethany is a passion story; that is, it focuses on the death of Jesus. In this regard John is like Matthew and Mark but unlike Luke, whose anointing story is early, unrelated to Jesus' death, and is told to dramatize the nature of forgiveness. John not only locates the anointing within the passion narrative but weaves into the brief account all the dark forebodings of death. The scene is Bethany where there waits an empty and available tomb (11:38-44); at the table is Lazarus to whom Jesus gave life, an act which will now cost Jesus his (11:4; 12:9-11); the time is Passover (12:1) which in this Gospel is death time; into this pleasant circle of friends comes Judas the dark intruder who, in the time and place of this Gospel, was viewed as betrayer and as thief (12:4-6); and finally there is Mary's act, an anointing for Jesus' burial. The approaching death of Jesus is clearly the governing theme of the story.

2. This Evangelist repeats a conviction common to the entire Gospel: in relation to Jesus Christ, the words and acts of others have meanings and effects far beyond what may have been intended at the time. Caiaphas the high priest unwittingly prophesied that Jesus' death would save the world (11:49-52); the Pharisees unwittingly acknowledged

that the whole world was going to Jesus (12:19). So here, Mary performs an act of hospitality, friendship, and gratitude for a brother restored, but in that act she unwittingly prepares Jesus for burial. However, this is a message not only in John, but in the entire Bible: God uses our acts beyond our intent or capacity. Abraham was hospitable to strangers and entertained angels unawares; two disciples from Emmaus invited a fellow traveler to rest and eat, and a supper became a sacrament; Paul wrote letters to the churches and a New Testament canon had its beginnings. We never know; our task is to speak and act in a way appropriate to faith's response to the occasion and to leave the conclusions to God.

3. Mary's act will bless and plague every minister who has to counsel and evaluate similar acts of devotion and gratitude. Three hundred poinsettias announce Christmas; five hundred lilies embellish Easter; and then there are the memorial chimes, the memorial silver communion ware and the memorial window. "A gift in gratitude," says the donor; "a sinful waste," says not only Judas but everyone who has looked into hollow eyes and heard the cries of a hungry child. Sound sense and Christian duty know the need is for potatoes not perfume, and yet checking the shopping list even of the poor reveals that among flour, beans, and pork there will be candy and cologne. The appropriate word is not easily found or easily spoken.

Tuesday in Holy Week

Isaiah 49:1-7; Psalm 71:1-12; I Corinthians 1:18-31; John 12:20-36

Isaiah 49:1-7

The readings for this day continue the preparation of the community of faith for the crucifixion and resurrection of Jesus. The psalm is an individual lament similar in some ways to Psalm 22; it combines cries for help with expressions of confidence in God. The epistolary text interprets the meaning of the cross, and the Gospel reports events in Jesus' last week, especially a number of his sayings that anticipate the crucifixion and resurrection. In this context, although the Old Testament reading expresses especially the feeling that the work of God's servant has been in vain, it also proclaims that his mission is to bring salvation to all the earth.

Isaiah 49:1-6 is the second of the Servant Songs in Deutero-Isaiah. The speaker in these verses is the servant, the one designated by God in the first Servant Song, Isaiah 42:1-4 (for discussion see the comments on the texts for Monday in Holy Week). The unit is introduced and structured as a prophetic address, beginning with a summons to attention (verse 1*a*) and presenting a message from God (verse 6). It is important to keep in mind that the addressees of the speech are the "coastlands," the "peoples from afar" (verse 1*a*); that is, the servant's message is not for Israel but for the world at large, the Gentiles in particular.

After the summons to attention, the servant reports how he was called and equipped for his task (verses 1*b*-3). Like Jeremiah he was designated before birth (Jer. 1:5) and identified by name (see also Isa. 43:1). He uses metaphorical language ("sword," "polished arrow") to describe his equipment for his duty, which entailed communication ("mouth"). God, he reports, formally declared him to be his servant (verse 3). At this point the poem clearly indicates that the servant is Israel.

The next movement in the poem is the servant's account of his response to his task (verse 4). He reports on the one hand that he thought his work had been in vain, and on the other hand that he is confident that he is approved by God. Frequently in their reports of their vocations the prophets indicate a deep sense of unworthiness (Isa.6:5; Jer. 1:6). But the account here does not seem to belong to the call report as such. It expresses not unworthiness when called but frustration with the results of the work. He was called and equipped for the mission, but felt that he had failed.

The next element in the poem is a very expansive messenger formula (verse 5) which introduces the divine speech in the next verse. The formula, "And now the Lord says," is filled out by subordinate clauses that describe the Lord and his reason for calling the servant. The Lord is the one who formed the servant in order to bring back Israel from exile, the one who honors the servant, and the one who is the strength of the servant.

The last element of the song is the divine message (verse 6). From the first verse it was clear that this word is addressed to the foreign nations. Now it appears that the message that the nations are to hear is something that God says to the servant. The servant is, as already indicated, to raise up and restore Israel. But more than that, he is given as a light to the nations in order that God's salvation "may reach to the end of the earth." That is a message of the universal reign of the Lord of Israel, parallel to the purpose for the servant's designation in the first place, that is, to establish justice in all the earth (Isa. 42:1-4).

Verse 7 is distinct from the poem as a prophetic announcement of salvation concerning the Lord's chosen. In that verse the servant clearly is understood as Israel, once despised and abhorred by nations, but eventually vindicated.

In the Servant Song itself, as it now stands, it is also obvious that the servant is Israel. Some commentators, however, have argued that "Israel" in verse 3 is a secondary addition. More substantial objections to the easy identification of the servant as the people are the highly individualistic and personal language and the fact that the servant has a mission to and for Israel. This second point has led some to see the servant as ideal Israel or a group within Israel. The identity is so elusive that one is tempted to conclude that it is intentionally ambiguous.

Far more important than the identity of the servant in the original historical context at the end of the Babylonian exile is the understanding of the mission of the servant of God. On this point the text is quite clear. There are two tasks: (1) the servant has a role in the return and restoration of Israel; and (2), and dominant in this passage, is the universal mission, all the more dramatic when seen in the era of the Babylonian exile when the first hearers of this text were subjects of foreign powers. The servant is to be a light to all nations, that the Lord's salvation may reach to the ends of the earth. As the Gospel reading has it, Jesus is that light (John 12:35-36). When he is lifted up he will draw all people to himself (John 12:32).

Psalm 71:1-12

The fabric and texture of Psalm 71 are the products of heartfelt supplication and lament interwoven with statements of great trust and confidence in God and interspersed with petitions and appeals to the Deity.

All of the basic components of a lament are to be found in this psalm. The passage selected for this lection contains an opening address to the Deity (verse 1), an appeal pleading for help (verses 2-4), a statement of the worshiper's confidence in God (verses 5-8), a description of the distress (verses 9-11), and a second appeal (verse 12).

We can examine the salient features of this psalm in terms of (1) the nature of the distress, (2) the worshiper's statements of confidence, and (3) the nature of the help requested from God.

1. The troubles undergone by the worshiper are related primarily to his enemies. The gallery of opponents are described as "the wicked," "the unjust and cruel man," and

"enemies" who seek the worshiper's life. (Reference is made to accusers in verse 13.) The bitterest opponents appear to be those enemies who consider the person forsaken by God and thus without help and support (verses 10-11). One might assume that the malady or problem the person had was taken as a sign that God had forsaken or was no longer supporting the one praying.

2. This psalm is permeated by a strong sense of trust and confidence. As the person looks back to the past, he or she affirms that God has been his/her trust from youth. God is even seen as the one who like a midwife took him/her from the mother's womb (verse 6). Looking to the future, the psalmist prays that the trust in and association with God, which was begun as a child, will continue into "old age and gray hairs" (verses 9, 18). A common theme throughout the psalm is that God is a refuge. The worshiper confesses that God is a refuge and at the same time prays that God will be a refuge (compare verses 1 and 7 with verse 3). The concept of a refuge is further explicated with reference to God as a strong fortress and a rock—all expressive of both stability and protection.

An interesting feature of the psalm's statements of confidence is the reference to the special role the person has for making known or proclaiming God not only to the contemporaries of the day but also to generations yet to come (verses 7-8, 18). This would suggest that the psalm was not originally composed for an ordinary Israelite but was probably written for the king who had a special responsibility for proclaiming the nation's God.

3. The petitions and appeals made to God for help focus primarily on the requests that God not forsake the worshiper (verses 9-10) or let the person be put to shame (verse 1). Shame plays both a positive and a negative function in the psalm. The worshiper asks to be preserved from shame (verse 1) and at the same time prays that the accusers be put to shame and consumed (verse 13). Shame, of course, meant being put in a humiliating situation, and at the same time having to accept the identity that the situation imposed.

This psalm can be exegeted and preached in the context of Holy Week since it expresses many of the factors that we think of in terms of Jesus' suffering: the opposition of enemies who do not believe God is his supporter, the trust and confidence of the worshiper, and a message to be proclaimed and made known to generations yet to come.

I Corinthians 1:18-31

Paul's exposition of the "word of the cross," that is, preaching "Christ and him crucified" (I Cor. 2:2), begins in 1:18 and extends through 2:5. For this reason, the limits of this passage should be extended to include the next paragraph (I Cor. 2:1-5). In this passage, we get close to the center of Paul's gospel, and in doing so, find ourselves more fully drawn into the passion of Christ as we move through Holy Week.

The overall structure of this passage should be noted. First, the essential paradox of the cross is stated: God has chosen weakness through which to display power. What humans regard as inexplicably foolish is, in fact, a display of divine wisdom. In this standoff between human wisdom and divine wisdom, the ways of God transcend human ways. When judged by human standards, God comes up short. This turns out to be an indictment, not of God, but of humanity itself. For human beings to presume to subject God to human standards of judgment is to misconceive both who we are and who God is. Sitting in judgment on God stems from human presumption, or "boasting" (1:31).

To counter this attitude of human presumption, Paul develops two lines of argument.

First, he appeals to the example of the Corinthians themselves (1:26-31). On any showing, they were an unimpressive lot, relatively speaking: few of them were wise, powerful, or well-bred (1:26). In their own right they had nothing to commend themselves before God. Yet, they existed as a community of God's people, a position, incidentally, from which they presumed to sit in judgment on God. With three emphatic declarations, Paul reminds them that they are who they are because of God's initiative and action: (1) God chose what is foolish in the world (the

Corinthians) to shame the wise; (2) God chose what is weak in the world (the Corinthians) to shame the strong; and (3) God chose "what is low and despised in the world [the Corinthians] . . . to bring to nothing things that are," that is, to shatter all pretensions. The Corinthians are vivid testimony of the paradoxical work of God. How can they "boast in the presence of God" (1:29)? If their existence as a people of God can be explained only as an act of God, as an act of divine creation and power, how can they be presumptuous before God? They are not the source of their own existence. They are reminded therefore that God is the "source" of their life in Christ Jesus (1:30*a*). They are not self-generated. They are instead generated by a miracle of divine power in which they were transformed from "nothing" into "something." Their own conversion and continued existence as a community of God's people serve as the most vivid testimony of God's strength, power, and wisdom.

Second, Paul adduces the example of his own preaching (2:1-5). Here he insists that what he preached and how he preached ("my speech and my message," 2:4) did not derive its strength and power from human eloquence or wisdom (2:1). His preaching occurred instead "in demonstration of the Spirit and of power" (2:4). The preaching through which God called them into existence was no pure and simple human effort. Its content was "Christ and him crucified" (2:2). The heart of his message was foolish and senseless and ran against the grain of human wisdom. In no way, then, could their response to the gospel be a "rational response," one that met the approval of human judgment. Consequently, their faith could in no way "rest in the wisdom of men" (2:5). The source of their faith was the power of God.

In summary, neither the preaching which they originally heard nor their form of existence as a community of God's people could not have been humanly conceived or humanly executed. In both cases, God was at work in and through them to display his strength and wisdom. If it appears to them that God's ways are weak and foolish, this is their own self-indictment.

John 12:20-36

For a discussion of this Gospel lection the reader is referred to the commentary on John 12:20-33 for the Fifth Sunday of Lent. Even if this text provided the message for that Sunday, the emphasis on God's love and grace toward all nations will be no less appropriate here. All the readings for today carry that theme which, in a time of international suspicion, fear, and violence, must not be neglected. The importance of the issue overrides the preacher's fear of repetition.

It should be noticed that today's lection extends beyond that of the Fifth Sunday of Lent (12:20-33) to verse 36. These additional verses do not, however, alter the central thrust of the passage. The Evangelist is simply following a pattern familiar in this Gospel, that of concluding with a brief theological summary, not just of the preceding speech but of the whole Gospel. Here in verses 34-36 that summary is framed on the favorite metaphor of light and darkness.

Wednesday in Holy Week

*Isaiah 50:4-9*a*; Psalm 70; Hebrews 12:1-3; John 13:21-30*

Isaiah 50:4-9*a*

The Old Testament reading for Wednesday in Holy Week is the same one assigned for Passion/Palm Sunday, and has been commented on there. Linked as it is on this day with the report that one of the disciples will betray Jesus (John 13:21), Isaiah 50:4-9*a* will emphasize the obedience of God's servant through suffering and humiliation. Both the psalm and the epistle likewise carry the theme of response to persecution and suffering.

Psalm 70

This entire psalm is practically identical in form to Psalm 40:13-17. In Psalm 40, this material comprises part of a ritual text which was probably used by the king in worship before battle. What now appears as Psalm 70 is the lament or supplication portion that requests God's help in a coming crisis.

Psalm 70:1-3 provides a good example of what has been called the double wish of the lament psalms, because the request to be saved is balanced by a request for the destruction of one's enemies or opponents. Frequently the calamity that is requested to befall one's enemy is very similar to the condition that the one praying faced. Thus numerous psalms reflect something of that attitude, so widely felt, namely, that those who plan evil should have a corresponding evil beset them. Christians often shy away in horror from the prayers in the psalms which request a destruction or a calamity to fall on one's enemies. Such sentiments seem contrary to the teaching and life of Jesus. We must, however, understand that the psalms sought to give full and appropriate outlets for people to express their true feelings and sentiments. It may be that only by verbalizing such sentiments and expressions can they be overcome or transcended. Expressions of one's truest and deepest feelings may be necessary before that person can release them and replace them with better feelings. In many ways, some of the psalms probably allowed persons to vent their anger and hostility to such a degree of animosity and with such a degree of revenge that the mere recital of such cursing wishes relieved the anxiety and pent-up emotions of the worshiper (for example Ps. 109).

The opening verse of Psalm 70, with its plea for God to hasten and to deliver, is followed by two verses asking that the enemies be put to shame and turned back; that is, make their plans go awry, so they will end up being shamed. If the prayer was originally offered by the king, then the adversaries could be foreign powers or nations who were threatening hostile military action.

Verse 4 is an intercessory prayer, although the worshiper is included in the group being prayed for. The intercessor requests that all those who seek God and love his salvation rejoice and proclaim forever that God is great. This is obviously a prayer asking that the king and his subjects be victorious over the enemy or that they be spared a possible impending conflict.

In the final verse, the worshiper reverts to an appeal on his/her own behalf. The fact that the one praying is described as poor and needy does not mean that the person was destitute and in poverty. Such expressions are metaphorical statements characterizing the person in the most sharply drawn and the humblest terms in order to evoke God's aid.

The association of this psalm with Holy Week can be made in two ways: (1) like Jesus, the psalmist was challenged by enemies who sought his death and destruction; and (2) like Jesus, the psalmist prayed and made intercessory requests on behalf of others.

Hebrews 12:1-3

These verses form a fitting conclusion to the well-known eleventh chapter of Hebrews in which various Old Testament figures are presented as exemplifying the life of faith (*pistis*). They should be read as words of exhortation addressed to fainthearted Christians and designed to bolster their faith and confidence (cf. 5:11-12; 10:25, 35; 12:12-13; 13:17). It should be remembered that the entire epistle is a "word of exhortation" (13:22) written with the same general purpose.

Today's passage resembles many other passages in the epistle that are hortatory in nature. Especially frequent are exhortations introduced with the words "let us . . ." (cf. 4:1, 11, 14, 16; 6:1; 10:22, 24; 12:28; 13:13). These hortatory subjunctives function as gentle words of encouragement. They are less direct than outright imperatives and derive from the author's sensitive pastoral concern. Clearly, the author senses that some of his readers are in danger of falling "away from the living God" (3:12).

In this exhortation, the author employs an athletic metaphor (cf. I Cor. 9:24-27; Phil. 1:27-28; 3:14; I Tim. 6:12; II Tim. 2:5; 4:7-8; Jude 3). The image is that of the footrace in a stadium full of spectators. The Old Testament heroes of faith are envisioned as "so great a cloud of witnesses" (verse 1), the host of spectators assembled to watch the race. The participants are surrounded by a crowd who are not merely spectators, but who themselves have already run the race and presumably have won. It is as if those who are surrounding the track have finished their race, passed on the baton, and have gathered to shout for their teammates running the final leg of the race. This is indicated by the use of the word "witnesses" (*martures*) which no longer connotes merely "those who watch or testify" but has already begun to move in the direction of its later sense "martyrs" (cf. 11:39-40; also Acts 22:20; Rev. 2:13; 17:6).

The readers are urged to "lay aside every weight" and "run with perseverance the race that is set before us" (verse 1). The former phrase doubtless refers to the final disrobing that precedes the start of the race. The "sin which clings so closely" suggests the image of a robe or garment which would obviously hinder running. Given the prominence of "faith" in the previous chapter, it is likely that the "sin" referred to here is the sin of unbelief, or the inability to persevere in the life of faith. The image of removing clothing to symbolize the removal of sin became a frequent metaphor in early Christian teaching (cf. Rom. 13:12; Eph. 4:22, 25; Col. 3:8; I Pet. 2:1; also James 1:21).

It goes without saying that athletic contests involve "perseverance" (*hupomonē*), or endurance. In the teaching of Jesus, endurance was seen as a prerequisite to the life of faith (Luke 8:15; 21:19). Paul also stressed that "suffering produces endurance, and endurance produces character" (Rom. 5:3-4), and several times indicated the need for Christians to have endurance, or steadfastness (cf. Rom. 8:25; 15:4-5; II Cor. 6:4; 12:12). Quite obviously, in contexts of suffering, Christians are called upon to "endure" (I Thess. 1:3; James 1:3-4; 5:11; Rev. 2:2-3, 19; 13:10; 14:12). As the following verse (verse 3) shows, the readers are encouraged not to "grow weary or fainthearted," the temptation of every athlete, particularly in the final moments of the contest.

To this point, it is those who have preceded us in the life of faith that serve as the models of steadfastness and endurance. Now, however, another model of endurance is introduced: "Jesus the pioneer and perfecter of our faith" (verse 2). He too is envisioned as having previously run the race and won. But he is not merely one of the many spectators in the gallery of Old Testament witnesses. He is instead singled out for his unique capacity for faithful endurance (5:8-9). In this respect, he was also regarded as the patriarchs' motivation for endurance (11:25-26). The connecting link between the previously employed athletic metaphor and the example of Jesus is "endurance," for it was he who "endured the cross" (verse 2). It was precisely in this sense that he "paved the way," becoming the "pioneer" (*archēgos*) and "perfecter" (*teleiōtēs*) of our faith. Not merely endurance, however, commended the example of Christ, since the cross carried with it "shame" (cf. Gal. 3:13). Yet, he was motivated by the "joy that was set before him." This may refer either to the "joy which was still in the future" (JB, also NEB), that is, his final joyous exaltation with the Father, or the "joy that was open to him" in his preexistent state (cf. NEB, note). If the latter, it should be rendered "who, in place of the joy that was open to him, endured the cross" (cf. Phil. 2:6-11; II Cor. 8:9).

Christ serves as the model of endurance: "Consider him who endured from sinners such hostility against himself" (verse 3). This final verse brings into focus even more sharply the example of Christ's endurance in the face of enmity and hostility.

It should not be difficult to see how this passage can be utilized during Holy Week. After all, it brings Christian readers, particularly those who are fainthearted and lack confidence, face-to-face with the host of our ancestors in the faith, and especially with Christ himself. To believe is often to despair, especially in the face of hostility and suffering. Believers are confronted with many reasons and experiences that tempt them to "fall away from the living God." The challenge to persevere is constant, even for believers, or perhaps especially for believers.

John 13:21-30

Since the Gospel lections for today and tomorrow are from John 13, let us take a moment to familiarize ourselves with this portion of the Gospel.

In John's Gospel the ministry of Jesus as the revealer of God on earth is presented in chapters 1–12. That ministry is one of signs and speeches in the presence of the disciples, the crowds, and the opponents. While the writer is quite aware of the reader and the reader's situation as evidenced by the way the story is told, still these twelve chapters are *about* Jesus in *his* historical context. The reader overhears and observes. However, beginning in chapter 13, the reader (that is, the church) is more directly addressed. The crowds, the opponents, and the public scenes are gone and Jesus turns to prepare the church for betrayal, death, departure, and the coming of the Spirit as "another Counselor" (14:16). Chapters 13–20 could well be entitled "Farewell." These chapters contain the account of the farewell of Jesus (18–20) and a rather lengthy preparation for that farewell (13–17). By prediction, promise, warning, charge, encouragement, and exemplary act Jesus prepares his followers for the first major crisis of the church, his departure and absence. It is vital that, following his return to God, Jesus' disciples remain in continuity with the historical Jesus. That continuity will be maintained by remembrance of Jesus' words, apostolic tradition, and the Holy Spirit. These chapters (13–17) make that abundantly clear.

Chapter 13 begins this section with an account of Jesus' farewell meal with his disciples. During that meal Jesus indicates his betrayer, and Judas leaves the table to attend to his dark business. The writer closes the scene (verses 21-30) with a statement more symbolic and dramatic than informative: "And it was night" (verse 30). However, it is interesting that "night" is preserved in the earliest of our traditions about the Last Supper: "The Lord Jesus on the night when he was betrayed took bread" (I Cor. 11:23).

The scene and drama presented in John 13:21-30 center on the roles of three persons: Jesus, the disciple Jesus loved, and Judas. Jesus in the characteristic Johannine portrait knows what is to happen (verse 21) and who will do it (verse 26). He also is totally in charge, commanding Judas to do quickly what he has to do (verse 27). After all, no one takes the life of the Johannine Christ; he lays it down and he takes it up again (10:18). However, the description of Jesus as "troubled in spirit" (verse 21) seems to portray a Christ more like ourselves. What does it mean? It could be in the same vein as 11:33; that is, Jesus is emotionally disturbed by the events before him, in this case betrayal by a friend. But "troubled in spirit, and *testified*" (verse 21, italics added) can also be a description of the prophetic state immediately preceding a prophecy. The preacher will have to make an exegetical decision here setting this paragraph within the portrayal of Jesus throughout this Gospel.

The second significant figure in this text is the disciple whom Jesus loved (verse 23). The commentaries will aid in attempts to guess the name of this disciple traditionally identified as John the son of Zebedee. This unnamed disciple appears in six scenes in John 13–21 (13:21-30; 18:15-18; 19:25–27; 20:1-9; 21:4-7; 21:20-24), and except for the scene at the cross with Jesus' mother (19:25-27), he is in the company of Simon Peter. This person, obviously very close to Jesus, provides the Johannine church with continuity with Jesus and gives it apostolic authority. This disciple also precedes Simon Peter in knowledge, in faith, and in relation to Jesus. If there were Johannine and Petrine circles of Christianity, then this writer is certain who lies closest to the heart and truth of the tradition about Jesus.

The third important character in 13:21-30 is Judas Iscariot (verses 26-30). Other than Jesus, Judas receives more attention in 13:1-30 than any other person. Why? Perhaps because the treason by a close associate put the heaviest burden upon those who interpreted the story for the church. Perhaps it was to assure Christians that even in betrayal and death Jesus was not a victim but the one who orchestrated the redemptive drama. Or perhaps it was a warning to that church or to any church of the real possibilities of loss of affection, of unbelief, of self-serving departures from Jesus. After all, the writer says that none of the disciples knew themselves or one another well enough to be sure. "The disciples looked at one another, uncertain of whom he spoke" (verse 22). Rather than speculating on what social, political, economic, or psychological forces created a Judas, perhaps it would be better for the church to respond as Mark says the original disciples did: "They began to be sorrowful, and to say to him one after another, 'Is it I?'" (Mark 14:19).

Holy Thursday

Exodus 24:3-8; Psalm 116:12-19; I Corinthians 10:16-17; Mark 14:12-26

Exodus 24:3-8

The Old Testament reading for Holy Thursday provides the background for the New Testament texts concerning the Lord's Supper. The lection from the epistle contains the words of institution for the eucharist: the cup as a symbol of participation in the blood of Jesus. The Markan account of the meal cites a key phrase from Exodus 24:3-8, "blood of the covenant," and the psalm speaks of "the cup of salvation." All these texts interpret the meaning of the death of Jesus in terms of the new relationship that it makes possible among the followers and between the faithful and God.

Exodus 24:3-8 is an account of the sealing of the covenant between Yahweh and the people of Israel at Mount Sinai. Its literary context is Exodus 19:1–24:18. Having arrived at Sinai, Moses and the people begin the ritual preparations for what turned out to be a covenant with the Lord who brought them out of Egypt. These preparations include consecration and purification, and are followed by a theophany (Exod. 19). Then Moses presents the laws which the Lord had set as the stipulations of the covenant (Exod. 20–23). Exodus 24 reports the solemn conclusion of the covenant, but the account is by no means a simple one. What is presented as a sequence of rituals appears to be two distinct accounts of the ceremony. Exodus 24:1-2 resumes where Exodus 19 left off, and is the introduction to Exodus 24:9-11. This event happened on the mountain, and its central feature was a ceremonial meal involving the leaders and the elders. The ceremony described in Exodus 24:3-8 took place at the foot of the mountain, involved all the people, and concluded a covenant with sacrifices, solemn words, and blood rituals.

Literary complexities such as these suggest the presence of different sources in the text. Most commonly Exodus 24:1-2, 9-11 have been attributed to the Yahwist and Exodus 24:3-8 to the Elohist, but the evidence is far from conclusive. What does seem clear—and far more important than identifying its particular source—is that Exodus 24:3-8 is a very ancient tradition concerning the establishment of the covenant; the fact that "young men" (verse 5) offer the sacrifices links it to an era before there was a formal priesthood.

While the text reports an event that happened just once at a particular time in Israel's history, the highly ritualized character of the presentation strongly suggests that the ceremony would have been reenacted on some regular basis. Moses acts as the mediator of the covenant, first reporting the "words of the Lord and all the ordinances" (verse 3*a*). Together these two would have included all the laws in Exodus 20–23, though the "words" may have meant the Decalogue. With one voice the people solemnly affirm their acceptance of the covenant stipulations (verse 3*b*). Then Moses writes the words down and gives instructions for the building of an altar, the erection of twelve stones symbolizing the twelve tribes, and the offering of sacrifices (verses 4-5). As the sacrificial animals are prepared, Moses collects the blood and divides it in two parts, splashing half of it on the altar, which represents the presence of Yahweh. Then he reads "the book of the covenant"—which presumably contains the words of the Lord that he had written down—to the people, and they again affirm their acceptance and promise to be obedient (verse 7). The covenant is concluded by a blood ritual and words of institution: Moses throws the other half of the blood on the people, declaring it to be "the blood of the covenant which the Lord has made" (verse 8).

Two features of the ceremony stand out, the "words of the Lord and all the ordinances" and the blood ritual connected with the sacrifices. Neither is explained in the text, probably because their meaning was self-evident in ancient Israel. But the meaning of the first, the words and ordinances, is not difficult to see. A covenant is in essence a sworn agreement, a solemn promise to do something or live in a certain way. The words and ordinances constitute the contents of the covenant oath; they are what the people promise to do and be. The very early tendency to codify and write down those definitions of covenant responsibilities is reflected in this account.

The meaning of the blood of the ritual, so important in the New Testament, is not so obvious. Blood and bloody actions such as animal sacrifice were very important features of many Israelite rituals, including covenant ceremonies (see Gen. 15:7-19). The Passover celebrated the last night that the Israelites were in Egypt, when the blood of the lamb was smeared on their doorposts so that their firstborn would be spared (Exod. 12:21-28). But why was blood important and efficacious? The clearest explanation, and one which is consistent with most Old Testament texts, is given in Leviticus 17:11: "For the life of the flesh is in the blood; and I have given it for you upon the altar to make atonement for your souls; for it is the blood that makes atonement, by reason of the life." Blood is life, and has the power to atone. It is sacred because God is the giver of all life. The blood ritual in Exodus 24:3-8, then, is a sacrament which establishes a bond of life between God and people, and among the people. It is comparable in the deepest sense to the sacramental participation in the blood of Jesus, which conveys forgiveness to the participants and thereby establishes a bond of life between the faithful and God, while at the same time binding the faithful to one another.

Psalm 116:12-19

These verses of Psalm 116 are the closing portions of a thanksgiving psalm and are concerned with the fulfillment of vows made earlier, probably at the time when the worshiper petitioned God for deliverance from trouble, most likely a debilitating illness. In the Judaism of Jesus' day, Psalms 113–118 were sung as part of the observance of Passover. These psalms were sung in the temple by the Levites as the Passover lambs were being slaughtered and then again in the homes as the Passover meal was consumed. Psalm 116 was most likely selected for use in the Passover ritual or Seder meal because of the reference to the cup in verse 13. Four cups of wine were ritually drunk in the Passover ritual, and Psalm 116 seems to have been used at the point in the meal when the fourth and final cup was consumed.

The selection of this psalm for use in the Holy Thursday service is, of course, based on its use in the Passover ritual which Jesus is said to have observed with his disciples on Thursday in Holy Week. Since many churches observe Communion Services on Holy Thursday, this psalm can be reused in a context comparable to its early usage in Judaism.

Psalm 116 would have been used originally in the context of a thanksgiving service at the sanctuary. Verses 3-4 describe the distress and anguish that the person had undergone during a sickness when death seemed near. After offering general thanksgiving to and praise of God for deliverance, the worshiper moves to the fulfillment of vows made earlier (see verse 18).

In rendering the vows, which would certainly have included the offering of sacrifice, the worshiper addresses a human audience (verses 12-15, 18-19) as well as the Deity (verses 16-17). We should think of such thanksgiving rituals as times of great happiness and jubilant celebration. A person whose life had been threatened, disoriented, and removed from the normal course of activity had been restored to wholeness. The life that had fallen into the grip of hell itself and had been invaded by the power of death was now free of both the illness and the anguished turmoil that the sickness brought. Now the worshiper can look back and speak of the sorrowful plight of the past which now is only a life-transforming memory. There certainly must be "scars" from such a past but they are signs of past triumphs and the residues of God's grace, to be cherished and celebrated, not embarassingly hidden. At such a celebration, friends and family of the formerly ill person would have attended worship with the redeemed. Such worship would have included not only thanksgiving in word but also feasting, drinking, and dancing. These festive symbols marked the end of a former state and the beginning of a new state of living. They were enjoyed as the sacramental signs of God's concern and care.

In verses 12-15, the worshiper addresses a human audience of friends and family. The elements of the thanksgiving spoken of included the offering of a cup of salvation, the worship of God, and the fulfillment of vows. The cup mentioned is best understood as the drink offering made as part of the thanksgiving sacrificial ritual (see Num. 28:7) or perhaps the cup of wine drunk in the thanksgiving meal (Ps. 23:5). Such a cup symbolized God's deliverance, the opposite of the cup of God's wrath (see Isa. 51:17; Jer. 25:15). The worshiper reminds the listeners that God does not wish the death of one of his faithful worshipers because for God such a death is a serious, weighty matter (verse 15).

The place of the thanksgiving celebration was the temple in Jerusalem where sacrifices could be made (verse 18-19). In such thanksgiving services, most of the animal sacrificed would have reverted to the worshiper to be cooked and eaten in the temple precincts before the next day had passed (see Lev. 6:11-18). Thus the sacrifice of Thanksgiving imposed lavish and extravagant eating and communal sharing.

Verses 16-17 would have been prayed directly to God in conjunction with offering the thanksgiving sacrifice. The worshiper thus declared his/her status before God, "I am thy servant," a status dependent upon the redemptive work of God, "Thou hast loosed my bonds."

I Corinthians 10:16-17

A central feature of the celebration of Holy Thursday is the Mass of the Lord's Supper to commemorate the Last Supper and the institution of the eucharist. The close connection between Holy Thursday and the eucharist is seen in the various ways used to refer to Thursday in Holy Week. It goes under the liturgical name "Thursday of the Lord's Supper," and in the Greek church is called the "Holy and Great Thursday of the Mystic Supper." According to the chronology of the Synoptic Gospels, the Last Supper occurred on Thursday evening. The eucharistic celebration on the evening of Holy Thursday thus becomes a celebration of the origin of the Lord's Supper. For this reason, the celebration is marked by special solemnity and the service has extraordinary significance for the believer. The symbolism of the service should also be noted: only one priest presides at the Mass on Holy Thursday and in turn administers the Sacrament to the other priests and believers. In this way, the scene of the Last Supper is more vividly reenacted.

This passage from Paul has been chosen as the epistolary lection since it is one of the two major Pauline texts that treat the Lord's Supper. The other passage, I Corinthians 11:23-26, is the epistolary lection in Year A. It forms a fitting complement to the Gospel reading which gives the Markan version of the Last Supper (Mark 14:12-16).

Paul's remarks about the eucharist in I Corinthians 10:16-17 occur in the context of his discussion concerning eating meat offered to idols. Immediately preceding these verses, he has enjoined the Corinthians to "shun the worship of idols" (verse 14). To reinforce his point he reaches into the center of their own Christian experience—the experience of worship in the eucharist—in order to make his first point: to participate in a cultic meal is to become one with the cultic figure who is worshiped. Thus, to drink of "the cup of blessing" is a "participation [*koinōnia*] in the blood of Christ." Similarly, to eat the broken bread is "a participation [*koinōnia*] in the body of Christ." The force of the Greek word *koinōnia* should be noted. It suggests that the one who eats and drinks the sacred meal actually has "communion with" (JB) or is "sharing in" (NEB) the body and blood of Christ. This is true not only in the sense that one experiences the saving effects of the sacrificial death of Christ, but also in the sense that one becomes one with Christ. This becomes especially clear in his later remarks in verses 18-22, where he insists that to drink "the cup of demons" is tantamount to becoming "partners with demons" (verses 20-21). Although Paul is making a polemical point here, he reveals something fundamentally true about the eucharist: it involves Christ and the Christian in an intimate union.

Besides emphasizing the Christian's union with Christ in the eucharist, Paul makes an additional point: participating in the Lord's Supper is a unifying act. There is both a personal and a corporate dimension. "We who are many are one body, for we all partake of the one bread" (verse 17). This corporate aspect of the sacred meal is also emphasized in I Corinthians 11:23-26, where it is clear that the actions of some Christians at the Lord's table have adversely affected the lives of others. Here, too, where Paul insists that Christians cannot simultaneously claim loyalty to "the cup of the Lord and the cup of demons" (verse 21), the point is clear. To participate in the Christian eucharist is an act of corporate consolidation. In celebrating the one Lord, Christians demonstrate their corporate solidarity, and thereby disclaim all competing loyalties. Elsewhere, Paul states that as members of the "one body in Christ," we are "individually members one of another" (Rom. 12:5). Applied to the Corinthian situation, this could only mean that one is not to "seek his own good, but the good of his neighbor" (verse 24). When seen as a corporate celebration, the eucharist becomes an expression of Christian unity when all believers are made more aware of the needs of one another and their responsibility to act selflessly toward one another.

These two themes, the Christian's union with Christ and the Christian's union with all other Christians, experienced in and symbolized by the eucharist, come to the fore in today's epistolary lection. Either, or both, can be profitably explored in the homily for the celebration of the Lord's Supper on Holy Thursday. It should also be noted that the liturgical color for this service is white, used to symbolize joy. This may be conveyed homiletically in several ways: (1) the celebration of the institution of the eucharist as an occasion of joy; (2) the possibility of the Christian's mystical union with Christ in the eucharist; or (3) the hope for Christian unity.

Mark 14:12-26

For a discussion of this text see the commentary on Mark 14:1–15:47 for Passion/Palm Sunday, page 86.

Good Friday

Isaiah 52:13–53:12; Psalm 22:1-18; Hebrews 4:14-16; 5:7-9; John 18:1–19:42 or *John 19:17-30*

Isaiah 52:13–53:12

The Fourth Servant Song in Second Isaiah has long been the traditional Old Testament reading for Good Friday, and with good reason. No other Old Testament text more clearly describes the Messiah as a Suffering Servant of God, one who was obedient to death, and one whose suffering and death were vicarious. This text, above all others in the Hebrew Bible, enabled the earliest Christians to understand and communicate to one another and to the world at large the meaning of the death of Jesus (see Acts 8:34; Rom. 5:21; I Cor. 15:4).

Psalm 22:1-18 belongs in the liturgy for Good Friday not only because its initial words were spoken by Jesus on the cross but also because its description of suffering corresponds to that of the servant in Isaiah 52:13–53:12 (see especially Ps. 22:6-8, 12-15). Moreover, Psalm 22:18 is cited in the Gospel lection (John 19:24) as a part of the report of the death of Jesus. The epistolary text, like the Old Testament reading, stresses the obedience of the Messiah through suffering and his ability to sympathize with our weaknesses.

The fourth Servant Song continues to be a powerful text not only because of what it says but also because of the way that content is expressed. Some attention to its structure and poetic characteristics will thus be of value to the interpreter. Its structure is relatively easy to recognize if one is attentive to the shifts in the speakers. The poem has three parts, and in none of them does the servant speak. At the beginning (52:13-15) God speaks to proclaim the exaltation of the servant and the astonished response of nations and kings. In the central section (53:1-11*a*) some unnamed group speaks to report on the life and death of the servant and their response to it. Finally (53:11*b*-12), God speaks again to confirm the meaning and effect of the servant's suffering; he will be exalted because he "bore the sin of many."

The passage is a genuinely distinctive poem, but it does have affinities with other Old Testament materials. The account of the servant's suffering is indebted to the cultic tradition of individual laments such as Psalm 22 and individual thanksgiving songs. However, in such psalms it is the person in trouble who gives an account of that suffering and salvation, whereas here that of a third party is described and interpreted. The body of the song includes words of confession by the unnamed speakers (especially verses 4-6), suggesting a service of penitence. Moreover, the citation of the words of God at the beginning and the end is like that in prophetic speeches. But the poem is a highly artistic creation, using a wide range of images to hammer home its message. Although it stands out dramatically in its context, it probably was composed by the same prophet who wrote Isaiah 40–55.

It seems unlikely that the question of the identity of the servant in the original historical context can be resolved decisively. Analysis of the form, however, suggests an answer to part of the eunuch's question in Acts 8:34: "About whom, pray, does the prophet say this, about himself or about some one else?" The prophet is speaking about another. It is also clear from the introduction that he is speaking of the same one introduced in the first Servant Song, Isaiah 42:1-4. But whereas the context of the first song takes the servant to be Israel as a whole, this one clearly speaks of an individual. Those commentators who interpret the servant as Israel take the personal language of Isaiah 52:13–53:12 metaphorically: Israel's suffering and humiliation through the exile were on behalf of the world, and she shall be vindicated. However, far more important than the historical identity of the servant is the meaning of his life and death.

This text is so rich in meaning that it would be a serious mistake to reduce it to a single point. Nevertheless, its major themes are unmistakable. First, and in the broadest sense, the message is stated at the outset: God will vindicate and exalt his suffering servant. That point, not only in its original context but in all others, is a reversal of expectations. God's power and authority are manifested in weakness; God acts through one whose suffering is so great as to make him repulsive to all who see him. Second, there is the poignant account of a life of innocent suffering, from youth (53:2) through a trial and death (53:7-8). Third, the servant's life of suffering and humiliation is both vicarious and efficacious. That is, it is on behalf of others, and it effectively removes their sin (53:6, 8, 12). Others do not have to pay the price because he has already paid it. Some of the language seems to allude to ritual sacrifice ("poured out," 53:12), but the song as a whole goes far beyond what one finds elsewhere in the Old Testament concerning sacrifice for sins. Finally, the servant will be vindicated before the whole world, for his suffering is on behalf of the transgressions of all ("many," 53:12).

The Christian community at worship on Good Friday, as it seeks the words to respond to the crucifixion of Jesus, could hardly find more appropriate language than the central portion of this song (53:1-11*a*). The speakers of those words, while reporting on the suffering of the servant, confessed their own sins. But at the same time, in acknowledging that his suffering is vicarious and efficacious they profess that God's servant has removed those sins.

Psalm 22:1-18

Probably no other psalm is more appropriate for use on Good Friday than Psalm 22. It expresses, in the most powerfully drawn imagery, a sense of suffering and a feeling of being abandoned by God. In addition, this psalm greatly influenced the early church's interpretation of Jesus' death as well as the way in which early Christians shaped and told the story of the passion and death of Jesus, utilizing even the words of the psalm (see Matt. 27:39, 46; Mark 15:24, 34; Luke 23:34).

This lection from the psalm interweaves descriptions of distress (verses 1-2, 6-8, 12-18), statements of confidence (verses 3-5, 9-10), and general appeal for help (verse 11; see further verses 19-21) to form a tapestry of a soul in torment. The worshiper describes the distressful situation in terms of both sickness and oppression by enemies. As frequently in the psalms, such language may be highly metaphorical and formulated to solicit the concern of God. The language is that of personal chaos, of life in complete disarray, of troubles that torment one to the breaking point.

Two themes run through the statements about the person's distress: a sense of alienation from the Deity and hostile opposition from opponents.

The theme of God's distance and correspondingly the person's sense of alienation are sounded in the opening lines. A sense of divine forsakenness pervades the words—God is so far away he cannot hear the sufferer's groanings; day and night move through their ceaseless revolutions but for the worshiper there is neither answer nor rest from God but only dismay at the divine silence and the loneliness of feeling forsaken.

The theme of human opposition parallels that of divine alienation. If God is too far distant, humans are too near. Human opposition and enmity are described in various ways. People mock, wagging their heads and making faces, ridiculing the person's dependence and seemingly futile reliance on God (verses 7-8). Powers described as bulls, lions, and dogs, a company of evildoers, assail the worshiper (verses 12-13, 16). The depiction might suggest that the speaker was a king and the enemies were foreign powers. In any case, the opponents are portrayed as menacing, life-threatening, and life-destroying. They seize the person's abandonment by God as the occasion for attack.

The consequences of the worshiper's status are described in terms suggesting low self-esteem, complete despair and disorganization, and overall desperation. The image of a person's self-designation as a worm implies a feeling of utter hopelessness and helplessness, a state of feeling horribly subhuman (verse 6). Fright and incapacitation run through the imagery of verses 14-15 and 17-18 which is extremely graphic. Life seems no longer to have legitimate boundaries and normal structures ("poured out like water"); things do not function as they should ("bones are out of joint"); fear pervades everything ("heart is like wax . . . melted"); strength has ebbed away ("dried up like a potsherd"); speech fails ("tongue cleaves to my jaws"); death seems to be the only foreseeable certainty; and emaciation exposes the body's boney structure ("count all my bones"). The enemies are pictured as already going through the postmortem ritual of dividing up the belongings of the deceased as if death had already occurred. The psalmist speaks of his own demise and the distribution of his goods in a game of fortune and luck. Although not greatly emphasized in the psalm, God appears as the real enemy of the worshiper. The last line of verse 15 declares that it is God who has already laid the supplicant in the dust of death. Behind the opposition and oppression of the enemy lies the activity of God and God becomes the real opponent.

In spite of the dismal picture which the descriptions of distress paint, the psalm is shot through with statements and confessions of great confidence in the Deity. Verses 3-5 affirm that God is holy and that in the past the faith and trust of the fathers were rewarded with divine favor. Such confidence in the worshiper was based on both the nature of God and the experience of the past, that is, the paradigm of the past functions as a source of hope for the future. The confidence in God, expressed in verses 9-10, stresses the prior intimacy that existed between the one praying and God. The psalmist seems to be implying that previously God had been his/her "father," his/her caretaker from the days of birth and youth.

The confidence in God displayed throughout the psalm moves in verses 22-31 to pride of place and suggests that the worshiper received from God some oracle or sign affirming that a reversal of fate was in store, that tears and pains would be replaced by songs and celebration. The lection for Good Friday, however, ends with the pain and tribulation not with victory and triumph.

In relating Psalm 22 to the passion of Jesus, one should not expound it as a prophetic prediction of his suffering and death in spite of the fact that the early Christians used this psalm as one of the first Old Testament texts for understanding the passion and suffering of the Messiah. Its lines and view of the suffering righteous raised to triumph and praise helped Christians overcome the scandalous execution and suffering of the Christ the deliverer.

Hebrews 4:14-16; 5:7-9

Since Hebrews 5:7-10 was treated earlier in the readings for the Fifth Sunday of Lent, here we will limit our remarks to Hebrews 4:14-16.

Again, the text focuses on the high priesthood of Jesus, a theme already introduced in the epistle (2:17; 3:1) and one that continues to be central to the Christology of the epistle (5:5, 10; 6:20; 7:26; 8:1; 9:11; 10:21). Unlike the Levitical high priest, however, Jesus has "passed through the heavens" (7:26; Eph. 4:10), and in this exalted status officiates in our behalf as the Son of God (6:6; 7:3; 10:29).

But it is not so much the exalted status of Christ that is in the forefront here. Rather, it is his complete identification with our human condition that is stressed. It is his ability to "sympathize with our weaknesses" (verse 15; also cf. 2:17-18; 5:2) that enables him to identify with us. He is "one who in every respect has been tempted as we are" (verse 15). This crucial phrase is more adequately rendered in NEB: "One who, because of his likeness [*kath' homoiotēta*] to us, has been tested every way." Earlier in the epistle we are told that Christ "had to be made like his brethren *in every respect* [*kata panta*]" (2:17 italics added). The author's insistence on Christ's likeness to us is unqualified (cf. also Rom. 8:3; Phil. 2:7). The reference to his being "tempted" may recall the Synoptic account of Jesus' temptation by Satan (Matt. 4:1-11 and parallels; also Luke 22:28). These three temptations or "tests" that occurred at the beginning of his ministry struck at the heart of his messianic vocation. They have long been regarded as representative of the ways in which filial obedience to God can be tested. As such, all children of God are able to identify with the Son of God.

But if our text asserts without qualification that Christ was tempted "in every respect . . . as we are," it is also unequivocal in asserting that he remained "without sin" (verse 15). This conviction was widely shared among early Christians and is attested in various strata of the New

Testament (cf. John 7:18; 8:46; II Cor. 5:21; Heb. 7:26; I Pet. 2:22; 3:18; I John 3:5). In this respect, of course, Christ differed from his Levitical counterparts (Heb. 7:27-28). His complete humanity enables him to identify and sympathize with our weaknesses, but his unsullied life enables him to mediate in our behalf.

We should note that our text is not merely christological reflection, but exhortation: "Let us hold fast our confession" (verse 14); "let us then with confidence draw near to the throne of grace, that we may receive mercy and find grace to help in time of need" (verse 16). It is significant that such exhortations are grounded in the Christ-event. Because of the finality of Jesus' sacrifice, the quality and degree of his humanity, the perfection of his life, we can be justifiably confident in our confession of faith. Also, we can pray to God boldly in order to "receive mercy and in his grace find timely help" (verse 16, NEB). Similar assurances are given elsewhere in the New Testament (cf. 3:6; 10:19, 22, 35; I John 3:21; Rom. 5:1-2).

We can now see why this text is joined with Hebrews 5:7-10 as the epistolary lection for Good Friday. It opens with a triumphant statement of Christ's exaltation, and then it turns to his humanity. The companion lection, however, focuses more strongly on Jesus in "the days of his flesh" (5:7), his anguish ("loud cries and tears"), probably in Gethsemane but possibly on the cross itself, his prayer for deliverance, the obedience learned through suffering, and the perfection or completion of his messianic work through his death on the cross. The theme of "weakness" in 4:15 certainly carries over into 5:7-10 and provides one direction for homiletical development. In fact, 5:7-8 serves to elaborate on 4:15, for it makes more precise the ways in which the crucified Christ identifies with our own "cries and tears."

Several themes, thus, emerge from these two texts: (1) Christ's complete identification with human weakness; (2) his sinlessness; (3) his anguish that was experienced in the "days of his flesh"; (4) his prayer to God offered in godly fear; (5) his unqualified obedience through suffering; (6) the completion or perfection of his filial vocation as *the* Son of God; (7) his deserved status as the quintessential high priest who serves as "the source of eternal salvation" to those who render similar obedience to God; and (8) his exalted and unique status as a high priest after the order of Melchizedek.

John 18:1–19:42 *or* John 19:17-30

As stated in the comments on the Gospel for Passion/Palm Sunday, on those days when the lectionary offers a choice between a longer reading and a shorter portion of that same reading, we will treat the longer in an effort to be more inclusive. Choices within the passage are left to the preacher. For Good Friday, the choice may be determined largely by the kind of services provided. If there is but one service of usual length, one may well choose to deal only with the crucifixion (19:17-30). However, if the three-hour afternoon services are scheduled, then the entirety of John 18:1–19:42 could be used.

A text of this size and significance can hardly be treated in one sermon but it can be approached, even if not too closely. One way of approaching this body of materials is to see it as a narrative in five episodes: arrest (18:1-12); interrogation by religious leaders (18:13-27); interrogation by Pilate (18:28–19:16); crucifixion (19:17-30); and burial (19:31-42). Telling the story as John tells it has its own appropriateness and power. Another approach would be to draw from the narrative the accents, the emphases that the Evangelist makes. In other words, be especially sensitive to overhear what this Gospel writer understands as the meaning of Jesus' passion. Here we will try to combine the two approaches in a necessarily brief sketch.

The arrest of Jesus (18:1-12) is related with drama, with more details than in the Synoptics, but without the emotion of the other accounts. There is no crying or beating the breast here, for John's Jesus does not agonize, neither here nor on the cross. Gethsemane is "a garden" (verse 1). This Evangelist alone says Roman soldiers (verses 3, 12) were involved in the arrest. A "band of soldiers" (verses 3, 12) was a "cohort," about six hundred men and a "captain" was a "chiliarch" (verse 12), an officer over a thousand soldiers. By mentioning their presence, along with officers of Judaism (verse 3), John says the whole unbelieving world, political and religious, joined in opposition to the Word of God. Through it all Jesus is in charge. Judas, Peter, the soldiers—all receive their directions from Jesus. Because his hour has come, he allows those who could not arrest him earlier (7:30, 44; 8:20, 59; 10:39; 12:36) to do so now.

The interrogation by religious leaders (18:13-24) is minimally related by John, the only official action being the questioning before Annas (verses 13, 19) who does not appear at all in the Synoptics. Caiaphas is mentioned four times but with sarcasm ("was high priest *that year*," italics added) and disregarded as a factor in the story. Jesus' hour had come; what power did they have in the case? Significantly, more attention is given to Peter than to Jesus' trial. After all, the trial of Jesus has been settled since 12:18 but the trial of Peter, of the disciples, and of the church continues. The writer again shows himself more preacher than historian.

The interrogation by Pontius Pilate (18:28–19:16) is, compared to the Synoptics, quite lengthy. There are seven episodes, alternating between Pilate questioning Jesus inside the praetorium and dealing with the Jews outside. The account is full of irony: Jesus the prisoner is in charge; Pilate the governor shuttles back and forth indecisively like a frightened lieutenant; the Jews, in this Gospel the epitome of "the world," have death in their hearts but refuse to enter a Gentile building lest they be ceremonially defiled (verse 28). Pilate's only success is in getting the religious leaders to make what is their real confession of faith, "Caesar is king." At Passover, on the anniversary of freedom from the pharaoh, the pharaoh is embraced. Contemporary parallels flood the mind of every preacher.

The crucifixion (19:17-30) is briefly recorded. Even Mark is more extended here. Jesus is still in control, carrying his own cross (there is no Simon of Cyrene), acting and speaking so as to fulfill Scriptures and bring the intention of Judaism to completion (verses 24, 28), making arrangements for his mother's care (verses 26-27), and giving up his spirit (verse 30). He dies as Good Shepherd and as King. As Good Shepherd he cared for his own to the end and gave his life for the sheep (10:11-18); as King, he was unwittingly enthroned by those who mocked, who unwittingly called him King of the Jews. "And I, when I am lifted up from the earth, will draw all men to myself" (12:32). Even the wrath of man serves to praise God.

The burial (19:31-42) receives as much attention as the crucifixion itself even though the story of Jesus and his disciples is now the record of a corpse and its caretakers. This passage contains two stories about the body of Jesus, verses 31-37 and 38-42. The second provides closure to the preceding events, prepares for the resurrection story, and tells how two hesitant and uncertain believers, Joseph and Nicodemus, found courage in Jesus' death which they could not find during his lifetime. The first, verses 31-37, interweaves two interpretations of Jesus' death. Jesus died as the Passover Lamb and his body was so treated (Exod. 12:2, 46; Num. 9:12). The Evangelist describes the Passover to end all Passovers, thereby proclaiming a new exodus, not from the slavery of Egypt but from bondage to sin and death (chapter 8). Related to the Passover theme is the sacramental interpretation. The church has understood the water and blood to which John calls special attention (verses 34-35) as symbolic of baptism and the eucharist. See also I John 5:6-8: "This is he who came by water and blood." The writer is thereby telling the reader that the subject is not really the corpse of Jesus but the body of Christ.

Easter Eve, Easter Vigil, or the First Service of Easter

Genesis 1:1–2:2; Psalm 33;
Genesis 7:1-5, 11-18; 8:6-18; 9:8-13; Psalm 46;
Genesis 22:1-18; Psalm 16;
Exodus 14:10–15:1; Exodus 15:1-6, 11-13, 17-18;
Isaiah 54:5-14; Psalm 30;
Isaiah 55:1-11; Isaiah 12:2-6;
Baruch 3:9-15, 32–4:4; Psalm 19;
Ezekiel 36:24-28; Psalm 42;
Ezekiel 37:1-14; Psalm 143;
Zephaniah 3:14-20; Psalm 98;
Romans 6:3-11; Psalm 114;
Mark 16:1-8

(Easter Vigil is traditionally a service of readings with little or no homily.)

Genesis 1:1–2:2

Ordinarily the Old Testament lessons for the Easter Vigil are simply read, not preached, taking the worshiping community through a summary of ancient Israel's history. Read in this order and on this occasion, these texts present a history of salvation in preparation for the death and resurrection of Jesus. The story begins with the first chapter of the Bible.

This reading contains all but a verse and a half of the Priestly Writer's account of creation. The mood of the story is solemn and measured; the repetition of phrases lends a liturgical dignity to the recital. If the account was not actually put into this form for worship, it certainly was shaped by persons with a deep interest in liturgy.

In terms of structure, the report consists of two uneven parts, Genesis 1:1-31 and Genesis 2:1-3, that is, the six days of creation and the seventh day of rest. One of the purposes of the story in its present form is to account for the sabbath rest. It was divinely ordained from the very first, and thus is taken by our writer as the most universal of laws.

Creation is not ex nihilo, out of nothing, but out of chaos. Before creation there were the primeval waters, within which God established the world. Moreover, as the Priestly account of the flood indicates (Gen. 7:11), the waters of chaos stand as the alternative to creation. If God withdraws his hand, the waters can return. In that sense, then, this chapter actually understands God as both creator and sustainer of the world.

In sharp contrast to the other account of creation which begins in Genesis 2:4*b*, God is transcendent and distant. The only actor or speaker in this chapter is God, by whose word or act all things that are come into being. Human beings certainly occupy an important place. They are created last of all, and then given stewardship over the creation. If this moving and majestic account can be said to have a major point, it is in the divine pronouncement that recurs throughout: "And God saw that it was good." The natural order is good not only because God created it, but also because God determined that it was so.

Psalm 33

This psalm, as a responsorial reading to the Priestly account of creation, stresses the role of the word of God and especially the creation of the world through the word. The description of God's creating acts are much more poetic and metaphoric in expression in the psalm than in the Genesis account; for example, God is depicted as gathering the sea as in a bottle (verse 7). In addition, the psalm stresses God's continuing interaction with and governance of the world. God's relationship to the world is not a once-for-all creation but a constant guiding and governance.

Genesis 7:1-5, 11-18; 8:6-18; 9:8-13

Like Genesis 1, the account of the flood is part of the primeval history, the story not just of Israel but of the entire human race. Between that initial chapter and Genesis 7 a great deal transpired. There was the second account of creation coupled with the story of the fall, ending with the expulsion of the original pair from the garden. Next came the story of Cain and Abel, when a brother kills a brother. Then follow genealogies along with short reports of events in the lives of the earliest generations. The immediate background of the flood story is the little account in Genesis 6:1-4 of how the "sons of God" took the "daughters of men" and gave birth to a race of giants. From the accounts of creation to the time of Noah the story is basically one of human sin and disorder, culminating in God's decision to put an end to the race, with the exception of Noah and his family.

The flood marks an important turning point in biblical history, but as the Book of Genesis is organized, it is not the most decisive one. Following the flood, the history of human sinfulness continues, with the story of the tower of Babel. The critical event is reported in Genesis 12:1 ff., the call of Abraham. To be sure, sin continues, but now, with the promise to Abraham, the direction of history is known. It becomes a history of salvation.

The verses for this reading comprise a rather full account of the flood, with the exception of the report of God's decision and his instructions to Noah. The assigned text comes mainly from the Priestly Writer, but some of it is from the Yahwist, whose name for God in most translations is LORD. It is also the Yahwist who reports that seven pairs of clean and one pair of unclean animals went into the ark; P has one pair of every kind. Moreover, in P the water comes when the floodgates of heaven are opened; the Yahwist speaks of rain. But according to both writers, God put an end to all human beings except that one family, and afterward vowed not to do it again. The reading appropriately ends with the good news that the natural order will abide and the rainbow will be a sign of God's promise.

For further comment on the conclusion of the flood story, see the notes on the Old Testament reading for the First Sunday of Lent in this volume.

Psalm 46

This psalm praises God for his divine care for his people and especially for Jerusalem, the City of God. With its emphasis on security in the midst of great turmoil and disruptions in the earth, it provides a proper response to the narrative of the flood. The worshipers confess, as Noah and his family may have, that they have nothing to fear should the mountains quake and the whole of the cosmos become chaos again.

Genesis 22:1-18

One must keep in mind the framework in which this reading is placed—both in the Book of Genesis and in the Old Testament—or important aspects of it will be missed. The context is the narrative of the patriarchs, Abraham, Isaac, Jacob, and the sons of Jacob, the leading theme of which is the promise that their descendants will become a great nation, will own their land, and will be a blessing to all the peoples of the earth (Gen. 12:1-3). The fulfillment of those promises comes first with the Exodus and then with the occupation of the land of Canaan as reported in the Book of Joshua.

The immediate prelude to this story is the report in Genesis 21:1-7 of the birth of Isaac. The promise of descendants had been repeated to Abraham and Sarah over and over. Just when it appeared that all hope was lost, they are given a son in their old age. Isaac is not simply symbolic testimony that the divine promise is trustworthy, he is also actually the first step in the fulfillment of that promise.

And then comes the account in Genesis 22:1-18 of God testing Abraham, by means of a command which threatened to take away the child of the promise. It is certainly one of the most poignant and moving stories in the Bible, and all the more so because of its restraint. Emotions are not described or analyzed, but the reader or hearer can sense the fear and grief. Even though we know how the story comes out, each time we read it we can experience the rising tension, feeling that the results may still be in doubt. Will Abraham go through with the sacrifice of Isaac? Will the angel speak up before it is too late?

The story is so meaningful and fruitful and has been told in so many ways over the centuries that it would be a serious mistake to reduce it to a single point. At one level, in the old oral tradition, it probably dealt with the question of child sacrifice. Being among cultures where child sacrifice was a genuine possibility, some early Israelites could well have asked, "Does our God require that we sacrifice our children?" The answer, through this account, is a resounding no. Our ancestor was willing, but God did not require it. The sacrifice of a ram was sufficient. In the framework of the Easter Vigil one is reminded that God gave his Son.

The leading theme of the story, as recognized through centuries of interpretation, is faith. It is, as the initial verse says, the test of Abraham's faith. What is faith? The biblical tradition answers not with a theological statement, or with a set of propositions, or with admonitions to be faithful, but with a story. It is the story of Abraham who trusted in God even when God appeared to be acting against his promise. Faith is like that. Faith in this sense is commitment, the directing of one's trust toward God. And it entails great risk, not in the sense of accepting a set of beliefs, but by acting in trust. Did Abraham know that the God he worshiped would not require the life of Isaac? We cannot know. We are told only how the patriarch acted, and how God acted.

Psalm 16

This psalm, probably originally used as a lament by an individual during a time of sickness, contains a strong statement of devotion to God and thus can be read as a theological counterpart to the narrative of Abraham whose faithfulness led him to the point of sacrificing his son Isaac. Like Abraham, the psalmist shows confidence in whatever fate or lot God might assign him. This psalm came to be understood in the early church as a prediction of the resurrection, especially Christ's resurrection, and was quoted in this regard by Peter in his sermon at Pentecost (see Acts 2:22-28).

Exodus 14:10–15:1

With this reading we come close to the heart of the Old Testament story and the Old Testament faith. In ancient Israel's faith no affirmation is more central than the confession that the Lord is the one who brought them out of Egypt. Traditions concerning the Exodus provide the fundamental language by which Israel understood both herself and her God. The basic focus of most of those traditions is upon the saving activity of the Lord; the history is a story of salvation.

The account in Exodus 14 actually follows the Exodus itself. The departure from Egypt had been reported in chapters 12 and 13; the rescue of the people at the sea happens when they are already in the wilderness. The two themes that mark the stories of the wandering in the wilderness are already present in this chapter, namely, Israel's complaints against Moses and the Lord (14:10-13), and the Lord's miraculous care (14:13-18, 30-31). The report does mark, however, Israel's final escape from the Egyptian danger, and this relates directly to the theme of the Exodus itself.

This reading, like the flood story, is the combination of at least two of the sources of the Pentateuch, those of the Priestly Writer and of the Yahwist. Two virtually complete accounts have been combined. The writers tell the story differently, with P reporting a dramatic crossing of the sea between walls of water (verse 22), and J speaking of a "strong east wind" (verse 21), and the chariots clogged in the mud as the water returns (verse 25). But a more important implication of the source division for our use of the text in the context of worship is the recognition that the sources place very different theological interpretations upon what happened. For the Priestly Writer, the emphasis is on revelation. The Lord "hardened the heart of Pharaoh" (verses 8, 17) to pursue the Israelites in order to "get glory over Pharaoh and all his host" (verse 17). That is, the Lord's purpose is for the Egyptians to "know that I am the Lord" (verse 18). For the Yahwist, the purpose is the salvation of the people (verse 13), and their consequent faith, not only in the Lord, but also in Moses (verses 30-31). In the combined report, both themes are important. God acts in order to reveal who he is and also to save his people.

Exodus 15:1-6, 11-13, 17-18

The psalm text overlaps with the Old Testament reading and continues where it left off. Moses, having led the Israelites in their escape from the Egyptians at the sea, now leads them in worship. The expression of praise is generally identified as the song of Moses, and much of it is in the first person singular, "I will sing to the Lord." But the introduction points out that it was sung by Moses and the people, and its communal, congregational character is evident throughout. While the song is not in the Psalter, it is a psalm nonetheless and probably was used in worship by faithful Israelites through the centuries. The initial lines are placed in the mouth of Miriam in Exodus 15:21, except that they are in the second person instead of the first; she calls for the people to sing to the Lord.

The song is a hymn of praise, specifically praise of the Lord for saving the people at the sea. The hymn is for the most part narrative in form; that is, it praises God by recounting the story of his mighty deeds. In one sense what emerges is another interpretation of the rescue at the sea, different in some respects from the accounts in Exodus 14. But the language is at points highly metaphorical and rich in imagery which goes beyond the immediate events.

Recollection of the Lord's saving activity at the sea evokes two leading themes in the hymn. The first concerns God's awesome power over events and nature. The specific form of that theme here stresses the image of the Lord as a warrior who triumphs over his enemies. But it also emphasizes that the God praised here is incomparable; there is none like this one (verses 11, 18). The second theme of the hymn concerns God's love and care for the people whom he has redeemed. God is strength, song, salvation (verse 2), the one who cares for his people out of steadfast love (verse 13). Moreover, his past care for the people gives rise to hope that he will continue to act on their behalf in the future (verse 17), and will reign forever (verse 18).

Isaiah 54:5-14

The central message of Second Isaiah (chapters 40–55) is the announcement that the Babylonian exile is coming to an end; the Lord will bring the people back to Jerusalem. This text incorporates that theme but goes beyond it to proclaim and characterize the new era in Israel's history with her God. In this passage, which actually begins with Isaiah 54:1, the unnamed prophet of the exile employs a wealth of metaphors to characterize the new relationship between Israel and Yahweh. He is "husband," "Redeemer," the "God of the whole earth" (verse 5). These three expressions remind the hearers that the God who created all that is and acts in historical events to save is also as close to the people as a husband is to a wife.

God speaks (verses 6-10) to assure Israel that he has forsaken her, but only for a moment. He then declares what is in effect a new covenant, like the one sworn in the days of Noah. God now vows not to be angry again and establishes a "covenant of peace" (verse 10). Israel has in no sense earned this new covenant; it is simply that the Lord has compassion on those whom he had rejected. The concluding lines (verses 11-14) are addressed to the city of Jerusalem, which will be reestablished in righteousness for an era of peace.

Psalm 30

This psalm was originally a thanksgiving psalm offered by a worshiper who had recovered from sickness. As thanksgiving, it celebrates the transition from a time of sickness and destitution to a time of celebration and joy. Just as Easter marks the transition from death to life so this psalm marks the worshiper's transition from sickness to health. Its two keynote expressions of this transition are: "Weeping may tarry for the night, but joy comes with the morning," and "Thou hast turned for me my mourning into dancing."

Isaiah 55:1-11

Again, as is so often the case in the lectionary as a whole, and especially during Easter, the words of Second Isaiah come before us. This text from the end of the Babylonian exile was a call for hope and trust and a promise of salvation to the hearers; it reiterates that same call and promise during the Easter Vigil.

The passage has two distinct parts, verses 1-5 and 6-11, which are similar in both form and content. In the first section God is the speaker throughout, addressing the people of Israel as a whole. He begins with a series of imperatives (verses 1-3*a*) which resemble on the one hand Lady Wisdom's invitation to a banquet (Prov. 9:5), and on the other hand the calls of street vendors. The invitations to come for what the Lord has to offer are both literal and metaphorical: God offers actual food, and "food" which enables one to live the abundant life ("that your soul may live," verse 3*a*). What the people are invited to "come, buy and eat" is the proclamation of salvation which follows in verses 3*b*-5. God announces that the ancient covenant with David (II Sam. 7) now applies to the people as a whole. Again, Israel has in no sense earned this new covenant; it is a free act of God's grace. Moreover, as the Lord made David a witness to the nations, now all nations will come to the people of Israel. The proclamation of salvation, then, is ultimately directed toward all peoples.

The second section (verses 6-11) also begins with imperatives, calls to "seek the Lord" and to "call upon him." The "wicked" and "unrighteous" are invited to change their ways and "return to the Lord." These invitations, while addressed to the human heart, are quite concrete. To "seek" and "call upon" the Lord refer to acts of prayer and worship. For the wicked to "forsake his way" is to change behavior. The foundation for the imperatives is stated at the end of verse 7, "for he will abundantly pardon." The remainder of the section (verses 8-11) gives the basis for responding to God's call. God's plan for the world ("ways," "thoughts") is in sharp contrast to human designs. That plan is the announcement of salvation which the prophet has presented throughout the book, the redemption and renewal of the people. The will of God is effected by the word of God, another theme found throughout Isaiah 40–55. That word is the one uttered at creation (Gen. 1:3 ff.), and it is the divine announcement of the future through the prophets. In its emphasis on the word of God and its contrast between human and divine wisdom this concluding section of Second Isaiah alludes to the beginning of the work (Isa. 40:1-11).

Isaiah 12:2-6

Not all Old Testament psalms are found in the Psalter. Isaiah 12 actually includes two, along with traces of the liturgical instructions (verses 1*a*, 4*a*). The songs conclude the first section of the Book of Isaiah and suggest that the prophetic book was used in worship even before an official canon of scripture was established. Both psalms are songs of thanksgiving. The first (verses 1-3) celebrates and gives thanks for deliverance from trouble. In verse 2 it echoes the vocabulary of the Song of Moses (Exod. 15:2), moving from thanks for a specific divine act to generalizations about the nature of God as the one who saves and who is the strength, song, and salvation of the worshiper. The second psalm (verses 4-6) consists almost entirely of calls to give thanks and praise (verse 4). God is praised especially for his mighty deeds. Because God, the Holy One of Israel, is great, all the earth should know, and those who live in the shadow of the temple in Zion should sing for joy.

Baruch 3:9-15, 32–4:4

This passage, often characterized as a hymn to wisdom, is not actually a song of praise such as those in the Book of Psalms. While it does characterize and praise wisdom, it is basically an admonition to the people of Israel to listen to and learn from wisdom.

The book of Baruch is attributed to Jeremiah's scribe and placed in the Babylonian exile, but it actually stems from a later time. The section from which this reading comes is like other late wisdom literature such as the Wisdom of Solomon and Ecclesiasticus. It identifies wisdom with the law of Moses, "the commandments of life" (3:9), and "the way of God" (3:13; see also 4:1). Behind that answer stands a question that became prominent in the so-called intertestamental period, Is there a conflict between the truth which can be discerned by human reflection and that which is revealed in the law?

Our text alludes to the Babylonian exile (3:10-13), but it is characterized as a spiritual situation of separation from God rather than the actual exile. The verses not included in the reading (3:16-31) also contain somewhat spiritualized allusions to the history of Israel. The reading finds its place in the Easter Vigil, first because of the references to death and its alternative. Israel, growing old in a foreign land, is as good as dead (3:10-11), because the people have forsaken "the fountain of wisdom" (3:12). If they will attend to wisdom they will gain strength, understanding, life, and peace (3:14). All who hold fast to wisdom will live, and those who forsake her will die (4:1). The second reason for the use of this passage in the Easter Vigil is its theme of wisdom as the gift of God which reveals the divine will to human beings. This is quite explicit in 3:37, which is echoed in John 1:14, and has been taken as a reference to the coming of Jesus.

Psalm 19

This psalm of hymnic praise of God declares that God has communicated his will and himself through nature—verses 1-6—and through the law or Torah—verses 7-13. Without speech, God's voice is heard in the world of nature, and his communication, like the light of the sun, falls everywhere and nothing can hide it. In the Torah, God's will is embodied in commandment and precept and offers its blessings to those whose ways it directs and guards.

Ezekiel 36:24-28

This reading is the central section of a passage in which Ezekiel presents the divine announcement of a new Israel. God, through the prophet (see verses 22, 32) is the speaker. This dramatic announcement of good news presupposes that the people of God are in trouble. The description of that trouble is given in the context (verses 16-21) and alluded to in our reading. Israel is in exile, away from the sacred land, but the trouble is even deeper. Separation from the land corresponds to separation from their God. They are in exile because of their sin, their disobedience which led to uncleanness. Now God is about to act, not because Israel deserves it, but for the sake of his "holy name" (verse 22).

There are two aspects to the coming work of salvation, one external and one internal, corresponding to Israel's present plight. First, the Lord will gather up the people and return them to their land (verse 24). But if they are to remain there (verse 26), a major transformation must occur. That is the second aspect of the good news, the establishment of a new covenant (see Isa. 54:10; 55:3) with a new Israel. This transformation is spelled out in terms of three distinct steps: (1) the Lord will sprinkle (cf. Exod. 24:6) the people with water, purifying them from their uncleanness; (2) he will give them a new heart and a new spirit, replacing their heart of stone with one of flesh (cf. Jer. 31:31); and (3) God will put his own "spirit" within them. "Spirit" here represents both the willingness and the ability to act in obedience. The promise is summarized by the reiteration of the ancient covenant formula, "You shall be my people, and I will be your God" (verse 28). The radical difference between this new covenant and the old one is that the Lord himself will enable the people to be faithful.

Psalm 42

This psalm can be closely associated with the sentiments of Ezekiel 36:24-28, the Old Testament lesson to which it is a response. Ezekiel predicts the coming rescue of God's people from exile and the transformation of the human personality and will. The psalm, originally used as an individual lament, early became associated with the Easter Vigil because it expressed the people's longing for redemption and their lamenting over being absent from the sanctuary. The psalm presupposes that the speaker is living away from the Sacred City. The psalmist's thought about former days when the worshiper went on a pilgrimage to Jerusalem only intensifies the depression and despair that accompany living in a foreign and hostile land and heightens the desire to be at home again in the temple.

Ezekiel 37:1-14

Ezekiel's vision of the valley of dry bones, like so many other Old Testament readings for this season, stems from the era of the Babylonian exile. That it is a vision report is indicated by the introductory formula, "The hand of the Lord was upon me," which the prophet uses elsewhere to begin reports of ecstatic experiences (Ezek. 3:22). The report is in the first person and, like most prophetic vision reports, consists of two parts, the description of what was revealed (verses 1-10) and the interpretation (verses 11-14). Throughout there is dialogue between Yahweh and Ezekiel.

The message from the Lord communicated through the report is the response to the problem stated in verse 11. The people of Israel are saying, "Our bones are dried up, and our hope is lost; we are clean cut off." Ezekiel sees himself carried by the spirit of Yahweh to a valley full of bones, like the scene of an ancient battle. When the Lord asks if the bones can live again, Ezekiel gives the only possible answer, "O Lord God, thou knowest" (verse 3). While the nuance of the response is not immediately plain, it becomes clear in the context; the God of Israel can indeed bring life in the midst of death. When the prophet obeys the command to prophesy to the bones a distinct sequence of events transpires: bones to bones, sinews to bones, flesh on the bones, and then skin covering them. The importance of the next step is emphasized by a further divine instruction. The prophet calls for breath to come into the corpses and they live. The view of human life as physical matter animated by the breath that comes from God is found throughout the Old Testament (cf. Gen. 2:7).

The interpretation (verses 11-14) emphasizes that the vision is a promise of national resurrection addressed to the hopeless exiles. In no sense is the seriousness of their plight denied. They are as good as dead, and death in all possible forms is acknowledged as a reality. But the word of God in the face of and in the midst of death brings to the people of God a new reality, life. It is a free, unconditional, and unmerited gift. When read on the eve of Easter, this text is a strong reminder that God is the Lord of all realms, including that of death. Moreover, the promise of life is addressed to the people of God, and resurrection is a symbol not only for a life beyond the grave but also for the abundant life of the community of faith this side of physical death.

Psalm 143

Originally used as an individual lament by worshipers suffering from illness, this psalm prays for God's intervention and rescue. The condition of the worshiper's distress is described in terms of death, of going down to the pit. Such depictions fit well with the description of the exile as a graveyard in Ezekiel 37. Like those awaiting Easter morning, the psalmist asks to "hear in the morning of [God's] steadfast love."

Zephaniah 3:14-20

The last of the Old Testament readings for the Easter Vigil is a shout of joy and an announcement of salvation to Jerusalem. The passage begins with a series of imperatives addressed to the Holy City, calling for celebration (verse 14). The remainder of the unit in effect gives the reasons for celebration. These reasons include the announcement that the Lord has acted on behalf of the city and is now in its midst as king (verse 15) and a series of promises concerning the renewal of the city and the return of its people (verses 16-20). Both the mood and contents of the text anticipate the celebration of Easter.

Our unit is the fourth and last section in the Book of Zephaniah and stands in sharp contrast to the remainder of the book. The section which immediately precedes this one (Zeph. 3:1-13) had announced a purging punishment upon the city and its people. But now darkness has become light; fear and terror have become hope and celebration.

The prophet Zephaniah was active in the seventh century, not long before 621 B.C. He was concerned with the coming judgment upon his people, particularly because of their pagan religious practices. It is possible that this concluding section of the book was added in a later age, perhaps during the Babylonian exile (cf. 3:19-20), by those who had actually been through the fires of destruction and who looked forward to celebrating God's forgiveness, which the return from exile represented. But in any case the theological interpretation presented by the structure of the book in its final form is quite clear: The celebration of God's salvation follows the dark night of judgment and suffering.

Psalm 98

Like Zephaniah 3:14-20, this psalm is an exuberant affirmation of divine triumph and success. This affirmation is noted by the word "victory" in each of the first three verses. The psalm proclaims the victory of God and calls upon the whole world to break forth into song and the sound of musical instruments. As part of the Easter Vigil, this psalm contributes its call for a celebration of salvation and for the recognition of God as king.

Romans 6:3-11

The liturgy of the Easter Vigil consists of four parts: (1) the service of light, (2) the liturgy of the Word, (3) the liturgy of baptism, and (4) the celebration of the Eucharist. The time for the celebration of this service has fluctuated through the ages. Originally, it lasted through the night, but gradually through the centuries this Roman liturgy was moved to Saturday. Eventually, it was restored as a night celebration, beginning after nightfall and ending at dawn.

When celebrated as a night service, the Easter Vigil provided the occasion for the baptism of those who had been properly prepared through teaching and fasting. This was done at midnight when the celebrants gathered at the baptismal font and the candidates were presented to the community. Several features accompanied the liturgy of baptism: (1) the consecration of the baptismal water, (2) a homily by the priest addressed to the catechumens, (3) the candidates' divesting themselves of ornaments and jewelry before entering the water, (4) the candidates' renunciation of Satan and their profession of faith, (5) the anointing of the newly baptized, and (6) the clothing of the newly baptized in the white garments to be worn through the duration of Easter Week.

The use of Romans 6:3-11 in the Easter Vigil service provides a direct link with the liturgy of baptism. It is obviously an excellent text for a homily addressed to catechumens. In this text, Paul unfolds his own theology of baptism, showing how the believer in baptism dies and rises with Christ. Equally important is his insistence on the ethical implications that follow (verse 11, also verses 12-14). But we would miss the point were we to regard the text as only for catechumens on the verge of being initiated into the Christian faith. After all, Paul addresses these words to those who are already Christians. He couches his remarks in the first person plural, thus including himself with those whom he addresses. This is worth noting, since some Christians apparently misunderstood his teachings concerning salvation by grace. They seem to have concluded that being saved by grace meant that they could sin even more abundantly, since this would simply provide a greater occasion for the grace of God to work (cf. verse 1). Paul's remarks on baptism in Romans 6 are designed to show that salvation by grace, far from encouraging sin, actually signals the death of sin and its hold on the one who is in Christ.

The symbolism of this text read at this time should not be missed. This is, after all, the night in which Jesus lies in the tomb, enclosed as it were in the bonds of death. Those who have been baptized into Christ have been baptized into his death (verse 3), that is, those who have been incorporated into Christ through baptism have actually been plunged into "death." Being immersed in the baptismal waters, as the early Christians were, became their symbolic entry into the tomb. They were thereby "walled in by death." Paul thus can speak of their baptism as being "buried . . . with him" (verse 4). Even though we already know how the story ends, we still do well to relive Jesus' entombment on this night prior to the resurrection.

For all its emphasis on the believer's co-participation in the death of Christ, this text brims with anticipation: it speaks not only of death, but also of resurrection. During the Easter

Vigil, as night approaches dawn, there is a noticeable shift in mood from despair to hope, from grief to joy. Already in the service of light, there is the celebration of the transition from darkness to light, from death to life. In today's passage, Paul also stresses that the one who is baptized shares in Christ's resurrection. There is a difference, however, in the way Paul conceives both sides of the antithesis. Consistently, when he discusses the believer's death, he understands it as something already achieved. By contrast, the believer's union with him in the resurrection (verse 5) is consistently kept in the future tense: it is still to be realized. As he says in verse 8, "We believe that we *shall* also *live* with him" (italics added). This is not to say that the believers' resurrection life is postponed entirely until the eschaton, for in this life, through our death and resurrection with Christ, we can consider ourselves "alive to God in Christ Jesus" (verse 11). Resurrection life begins here, but does not end here. The Easter Vigil, then, directs our attention toward Easter morning and the resurrection hope; it also directs us ultimately toward Christ's Second Coming when our life with him is experienced fully.

Psalm 114

This psalm, read as a response to Paul's discussion of the association of Christian baptism with the death of Jesus, is a celebration of the Exodus from Egyptian bondage and of the entry into the Promised Land. Typologically, one might say that the Exodus, like Christ's death, symbolizes the end of an old state of life and the dawning of a new state. The entry into the Promised Land, like Christian baptism, was a time when the benefits of redemption became real. In this psalm, Exodus from Egypt and entrance into the Promised Land are closely joined so that parallel events are seen as characteristic of the two episodes. At the Exodus, the sea fled and the "mountains skipped like rams"; at the Jordan, the river rolled back and the hills skipped like lambs (verses 3-4). The address to the sea and river, the mountains and hills in verses 5-6 which is continued in the address to the earth in verses 7-8 serves as the means for making contemporary the Exodus and entrance events. Thus the users of the psalm, which was always read at the celebration of Passover, "became" participants in the past events of salvation as the Christian in baptism becomes contemporary with the death of Jesus.

Mark 16:1-8

The mood and content of this service depends primarily on whether it is held Saturday evening or early Sunday; that is, whether despair or hope dominates. If it is a Saturday service, then worshipers will be led to place themselves between Good Friday and Easter or that cold, silent and empty day when the darkest sentence imaginable is pronounced: Jesus is dead. If Jesus lives again it will be by an act of God. We do not vaguely believe in immortality; we believe in resurrection from the dead. In the meantime, there is a death in the family, people want to help but there is nothing for them to do. No one goes to work; no one goes to school. There is too much food, and no one is hungry. Time drags itself along. But on the other hand if this is to be an early Easter service, everyone will be excited as they run from the empty tomb!

Mark 16:1-8 is, in either case, the proper text, because its mood and content are on the border between Saturday and Sunday; that is, if verse 8 is accepted as the conclusion of Mark, as the most ancient and respected manuscripts indicate. Of course, "and they said nothing to any one, for they were afraid" is an unusual way to end a Gospel. There is no shout of victory, only astonished silence; no leap for joy, only running in fear. It is understandable that both Matthew and Luke end their accounts with resurrection appearances, reunion with the eleven, and a commission to preach. It is understandable that some scholars have theorized that the scroll of Mark had become worn and the end frayed and the last lines were lost. It is understandable that in the second century longer, and "more appropriate," endings were added, the more familiar being what we now have as verses 9-20. And it is also understandable that editors of English-language New Testaments have difficulty deciding what to do: close at verse 8 and put verses 9-20 in a footnote

(RSV, 1946), put verses 9-20 in the text and explain in a footnote (RSV, 1971), or add both the shorter and longer additions to 16:1-8 in the text with explanations in footnotes (NEB). Whatever conclusion is reached by the reader, our lection for today is 16:1-8. In this writer's opinion, this is Mark's conclusion. Mark's accent, central focus, and climax is the cross. Mark, of course, believed in the resurrection (9:9; 14:28), but he did not include any dramatic resurrection appearances that would transcend and, in a sense, reduce the centrality of the cross as the definition of Messiahship and of discipleship. For Mark, the resurrection served the cross; Easter did not eradicate but vindicated Good Friday. And if worshipers do not experience Jesus as dead, they can hardly experience him as resurrected.

Mark 16:1-8 completes the strange conclusion of this Gospel in which insiders become outsiders and outsiders do their work. A Roman centurion, not a disciple, confessed faith at the cross (15:39). The disciples fled (14:50), and their places are taken by the women who saw the crucifixion from afar (15:40), observed the burial (15:47), and then anointed the body (16:1). The burial was handled not by the disciples but by Joseph of Arimathea, a member of the council that had condemned Jesus to death (15:43-46).

What the women find early on the first day of the week is the stone rolled away, the tomb empty, and a young man in a white robe (an angel with the appearance of lightning, Matt. 28:2-3; two men in "dazzling apparel," Luke 24:4). As evidence of the resurrection the young man indicates the empty tomb and tells the women that Jesus has risen. He sends them out to tell the disciples to meet Jesus in Galilee where Jesus said he would be after he was raised up (14:28). The women ran, amazed, afraid, and silent.

Whether the meeting in Galilee was to be for a resurrection appearance, as Matthew understood it (Matt. 28:16-20), or was an intimation of Galilee as the site of the return of Christ, as some scholars hold, the reader has to decide first of all whether Mark 16:1-8 ends or begins a story. It certainly contains that word of grace, that offer of renewal necessary for a new beginning. To the fearful disciples who abandoned Jesus and to Peter who denied him, the word from the Risen

Christ is, "I will meet you again in Galilee." And even the reader is drawn into the story by its open-endedness. Perhaps the women's fear and flight place them in the same unfavorable light as the disciples (14:50). Even so, astonishment, trembling, fear, and silence do not seem inappropriate for Easter morning. They will find their tongues and they will witness, but early in the morning is no time to be glib and chatty about an empty tomb and a Risen Lord.

Easter Day or the Resurrection of the Lord or the Second Service of Easter

Acts 10:34-43 or *Isaiah 25:6-9; Psalm 118:1-2, 14-24;*
I Corinthians 15:1-11 or *Acts 10:34-43;*
John 20:1-18 or *Mark 16:1-8*

(If the first lesson is from the Old Testament, the reading from Acts should be the second lesson.)

Acts 10:34-43

The Cornelius episode is decisive in the Acts narrative, as seen by its location in the second stage of mission to the region of Samaria. The amount of space devoted to it is also significant (chapters 10–11). It represents the moment of revelation for Peter as well as for the Jerusalem church as a whole, both of whom recognize that it was God's will for the Gentiles to receive full admission to the messianic community. In one sense, these two chapters record two conversions—that of Cornelius and that of Peter himself as he comes to know that Christian salvation is devoid of ethnic barriers.

The abbreviated summary of Peter's sermon to the Roman centurion is remarkable in several respects. Though similar to other statements of the early Christian kerygma, it shows distinctive Lukan formulations, and should be interpreted in the light of Luke's overall theological and literary purpose. The opening declaration of God's impartiality relates the sermon directly to the preceding narrative which has vividly depicted Peter's own "conversion" from religious and ethnic exclusivism. God as an impartial judge who does not discriminate between nations in dealing with them is also an important Pauline theme (Rom. 2:11; Gal. 2:6; Eph. 6:9; Col. 3:25; cf. I Pet. 1:17), with Old Testament roots (Deut. 10:17). Placed here on the lips of Peter, it reflects his own changed outlook that resulted from the heavenly vision. Having been censured by God for his narrow vision of humanity, he now more fully recognizes that he should "call any man common or unclean" (Acts 10:28). The terms of God's acceptance turned out to be more broadly defined than he imagined: fearing God and doing what is right are the terms for acceptance by God. What is more, these two admission requirements—one attitudinal, the other behavioral—know no racial boundaries; those "in every nation" who fear God and do what is right find acceptance with God.

As Paul insists elsewhere, the impartiality of God is a corollary of belief in the one God (Rom. 3:30). The one God does not have separate means of justifying humanity: both Jews and Gentiles are justified before God in the same way—by faith. This theological claim is also reinforced by the christological claim that Jesus Christ is "Lord of all"—not of some. One group, no matter how keenly they feel elected, cannot lay exclusive claim to God or to Christ. Even though God first sent the "word"—the Christian message of salvation—to Israel, the "good news of peace by Jesus Christ" extends to all humanity. Obviously, Luke tackles the serious theological question with which he and the early church struggled—how and why salvation first came to Israel. Because of the unversality of Christ's Lordship, "every one who believes in him receives forgiveness of sins through his name" (Acts 10:43). Logically extended, this would preclude the existence of separate Jewish and Gentile churches, each relating to God through Christ in different ways and on different terms. Luke's inclusion of the Jerusalem Conference (Acts 15) finally resolves this difficulty.

The similarity of Peter's sermon with the broad outline of the Gospel of Mark has often been noted: the Gospel story begins with John the Baptist—no infancy stories—the baptism of Jesus, and Jesus' works of benevolence and healing. The geographical transition from Galilee to Judaea is also similar, as is the passion the climax of the kerygma. The references to appearances, however, are Lukan (cf. Luke 24).

Typical of the Gospels, the sermon climaxes in the declaration of Christ's death and resurrection. The Easter faith is boldly and simply proclaimed. The Risen Lord was not revealed to all but to those "chosen by God as witnesses, who ate and drank with him after he rose from the dead." This recalls Luke 24 as well, with its eucharistic overtones. There the Easter faith dawns in the context of the sacral meal where genuine enlightenment and communion with the Risen Lord are most intimately experienced. The elevation of Jesus to the status of eschatological Lord is a role uniquely his, since he alone has died and lived. Elsewhere, his eschatological Lordship receives its underpinnings from his resurrection (Acts 17:31).

Isaiah 25:6-9

This passage from Isaiah, one of the very rare Old Testament texts containing an explicit promise of the abolition of death (verse 8), is placed on Easter Day among the classical New Testament resurrection texts. Both the epistolary reading and the speech of Peter in Acts 10 contain creedal summaries of the meaning of the life, death, and resurrection of Jesus; the Gospel texts give accounts of the discovery of the empty tomb.

The literary context of Isaiah 25:6-9 is the collection of late and mainly eschatologically oriented materials generally called the Isaiah Apocalypse (Isa. 24–27). While this section is not apocalyptic in the narrow sense of the term, it contains numerous motifs and ideas that appear in apocalyptic literature. Above all, these chapters express the confident view that, beyond a day of judgment, the reign of God will be established.

In terms of form Isaiah 25:6-9 is an announcement of salvation with strong eschatological overtones. That is, unlike earlier prophetic announcements which saw the intervention of God in terms of historical events such as military defeat or return from exile, this one sees a radical transformation of the human situation. The main focus is upon a banquet which the Lord will prepare on Mount Zion ("this mountain," verse 6). The meal will include the richest possible food, and "all peoples" will participate. In the background of this promise stand cultic meals (Exod. 19; 24:9-11) which symbolize the intimate relationship between Yahweh and Israel, and perhaps also the sharing of sacrifices. One day, the visionary says, all peoples shall come to the holy place for communion with one another and with the one God.

But there is more. God will inaugurate with the eschatological banquet a new age of joy and peace. The "covering that is cast over all peoples, the veil that is spread over all nations" (verse 7) must refer to the attire for mourning, for God "will wipe away tears from all faces" (verse 8). Mourning cannot be ended as long as there is death, consequently, "He will swallow up death for ever" (verse 8). This language seems to be indebted to Canaanite mythology which tells of the defeat of the god Mot (Death), but it has a very different construction here. Death is not another deity, but a human reality, and its defeat does not recur but is a single act of God when the new age begins. The Apostle Paul cites the verse in his account of the nature of the resurrection (I Cor. 15:54).

One of the most important features of this passage should not be overlooked on Easter Day. The announcement of the new age of joy and peace extends to all peoples.

Psalm 118:1-2, 14-24

Portions of Psalm 118 formed one of the lections of Passion/Palm Sunday and at that point in the lectionary commentary we sought to show how the ancient psalm used on the occasion of a king's trumphal reentry into Jerusalem for a service of thanksgiving parallels the experience of Jesus' entry into the Holy City. As part of the scripture readings for Easter Day, the verses selected for today's reading focus on victory and triumph, God's redemption of the one threatened.

Verses 1-2 form part of the call to offer thanksgiving to God; verses 14-18 are hymnic praise of God for the victory given the ruler in battle (see verses 10-13), and verses 19-24 are part of the litany of entry into the temple.

Psalm 118 is a community psalm of thanksgiving and the call to offer thanks in verses 1-4 includes all of ancient Israel—the lay and the clergy. Thanksgiving is to be offered by declaring that God's steadfast love endures for ever. Thus the opening words of the psalm clearly proclaim and anticipate the note of victory that follows, a victory already anticipated in the reference to the character of God and his love.

In verses 14-18, the triumphant leader returning from victorious battle, affirms and proclaims the deliverance worked by God, even deliverance from death itself. The description of the struggle and battle in the field has given way to praise and thanksgiving. Like Moses of old, the ruler and the victorious proclaim a triumph wrought by the right hand of God (see Exod. 15).

The experience of battle and the triumph of victory are described in terms of a life and death struggle in verses 17-18. The distress and trouble of battle are declared to be the chastening of God, yet God is not surrendering the king to the power of death. These verses are thus very similar or analogous to what Christians proclaimed about Jesus: both his suffering and his triumph over death were the work of God. In both, misfortune and humiliation as well as victory and triumph are seen as components in divine activity.

With verse 19, we move to the entry litany itself which was discussed in conjunction with the lesson for Passion/Palm Sunday. Insofar as Easter Sunday is concerned, the choral response in verses 23-24 (following the royal thanksgiving in verses 21-22) is the text to be highlighted. The choir proclaims that what has taken place and is now celebrated has been the work of God and thus it is marvelous (beyond belief, transcending the normal). It is the day in which God has acted and made the rejected stone the cornerstone (verse 22). The response to such activity should be rejoicing and celebration because the sound of battle and the presence of death have been replaced with songs of victory and the gift of life.

In early Judaism, at the time of the origin of the church, Psalm 118 formed the concluding psalm sung in the Passover celebration. It was used both in the temple and in home observances. As such, it marked and celebrated the triumph of God which had brought the Hebrews out of slavery and bondage in Egypt and toward freedom and service of God in the Promised Land. Thus it is fitting that such a psalm play a role in the Christian celebration of Easter which affirms the triumph of God in Christ as the triumph of life over death.

I Corinthians 15:1-11

This is the earliest tradition of the resurrection of Christ preserved in the New Testament. As it stands, the text is set in First Corinthians which was written in the early fifties, and thus precedes by several decades Mark, the earliest Gospel written. The wording used by Paul makes it even clearer that his gospel of Christ's death and resurrection preceded him. He says, "I delivered to you . . . what I also received" (verse 3). The terms "delivered" *(paredōka)* and "received" *(parelabon)* are technical terms used by both Jewish and Graeco-Roman authors to describe the transmission of ancient sacred traditions. Paul, thus, "received" this tradition of Christ's death and resurrection from those Christian witnesses who preceded him, and he passes it along as a faithful witness with impeccable credentials (cf. II Tim. 2:1-2). When we celebrate the Easter faith, we may be assured that it represents one of the very earliest strata of Christian preaching and that it is a sacred message traceable to the very dawn of the Christian church.

The heart of this tradition of early Christian preaching occurs in verses 3-4. The language is traditional, suggesting that this formulation of the message is pre-Pauline. In its present form, the gospel is summarized in a four-part scheme, but this is likely already an expansion of an earlier two-part scheme. Quite likely, early summaries of the gospel message were two-pronged: the Christ who (1) died has also been (2) raised (cf. Rom. 10:9). Here, however, we see an expansion of this two-part kerygma:

(1) Christ died
for our sins
according to the Scriptures

(1*a*) he was buried

(2) he was raised
on the third day
according to the Scriptures

(2*a*) he appeared
to Cephas
then to the Twelve
then . . . to more than five hundred brethren
then to James
then to all the apostles
he appeared also to me

Here we see that (1) and (2) represent the original points of early Christian proclamation. In each case, the element of proclamation is buttressed by a formulaic expression. "For our sins" gives the purpose of his otherwise inexplicable death, suggesting that it was vicarious. The language is reminiscent of Isaiah 53:5-6, "he was wounded for our transgressions, he was bruised for our iniquities." (Cf. also Isa. 53:8-9, 12.) By interpreting his death in light of this, and other Old Testament passages, early Christians were able to proclaim that his death had occurred "according to the Scriptures."

With regard to the second main element of proclamation, Christ's resurrection, we also find two formulaic expressions to buttress this claim. The first is "on the third day," which again recalls Old Testament language (cf. Hos. 6:2; Jon. 2:1). That Jesus arose on the third day became part and parcel of early Christian preaching (cf. John 2:19; Matt. 16:21). As was the case with the first element, so here, the Old Testament enabled Christians to interpret Christ's resurrection. They thus proclaimed the Easter faith as having occurred "according to the Scriptures."

Although we cannot be certain, (1*a*) and (2*a*) appear to have entered the tradition at a later point and served to anchor the primary elements of proclamation. If Christ died, it should have been self-evident that he was buried. But, early on, rumors circulated that his body had been stolen (cf. Matt. 27:62-66). At a later period, some Gnostic teachers claimed that Christ had not in fact literally died, but only appeared to have done so. In either case, the tradition of his burial served to anchor the preaching in history.

Similarly, the appeal to appearances by the Risen Lord served to buttress the proclamation of his resurrection. What's interesting about the list of appearances in this text is that, unlike the Gospel accounts, women are omitted. It is also obviously longer. We can see not only that the tradition of appearances is quite early, with Peter and the Twelve occupying conspicuous places of importance, but also that Paul places himself in the company of those to whom the Lord appeared. To be sure, his was an exceptional case (verse 8), but valid nonetheless.

We should notice that this "elementary" Christian tradition is introduced for the benefit of those who are already Christians. They are being "reminded" of that with which they are already familiar (cf. verse 1). As the remainder of chapter 15 shows, there was misunderstanding concerning the final resurrection. Since the latter was predicated on the truth of Christ's resurrection, Paul begins the discussion with this elemental statement of the Christian gospel. The gospel he preached, which they received, provided them with a place to "stand" (verse 1; cf. also I Cor. 10:12; 16:13; II Cor. 1:24; I Thess. 3:8). This suggests that "death and resurrection" provide the existential basis for Christian life, both in the sense that it forms the center of gravity for Christian existence and it creates the perspective from which Christians view life. As Paul's life showed, "dying and rising" became more than a message he preached; it was a life-style through which the gospel itself became heralded (cf. II Cor. 4:7-12).

Also important to notice is his insistence that by this gospel, they were "saved" (verse 2). The NEB correctly renders this phrase, capturing its continuing dimension: "which is now bringing you salvation." The message of Christ's death and resurrection must be appropriated by Christians continually, for in doing so the saving work of God continues to transform their lives. The annual celebration of Easter is but one way in which the Easter faith exerts its ongoing power to shape and transform our existence through our own experience of the Risen Lord.

John 20:1-18 *or* Mark 16:1-8

We will devote our attention here to John 20:1-18 since Mark 16:1-8 was the Gospel lesson for Easter Vigil. Before looking at John 20:1-18 in particular, two observations need to be made about resurrection materials in general and one about the Johannine shape of those materials.

1. We need to remind ourselves that the New Testament offers no account of the resurrection of Jesus. What we have are reports of an empty tomb and appearances of the Risen Christ. The various accounts in the Gospels and in I Corinthians 15:3-8 reflect different sources and different purposes.

2. We should appreciate how restrained are the uses of resurrection stories in the New Testament. Unlike some non-canonical accounts which have the Risen Christ appear to passersby—the disinterested and unbelieving—in order to overwhelm and coerce faith, in the canonical Gospels Jesus appears to believers to vindicate and confirm the faith of his followers.

3. And more directly to our present consideration, in the Fourth Gospel the resurrection materials are shaped into a carefully constructed piece of literature consisting of two stories (20:1-18; 20:19-29). Chapter 21 has a resurrection appearance but it is clearly an epilogue to the body of the Gospel itself. Each of the two stories contains two parts and all four episodes are said to have occurred on Sunday (20:1, 19, 26); perhaps they existed once as separate stories for use in Christian worship. As they now stand in the Gospel, the two principal stories center on the responses of some of the original disciples to the resurrection, each focusing upon the experience of a particular person. In the first narrative (20:1-18) that person is Mary Magdalene; in the second (20:19-29) it is Thomas.

In John 20:1-18, the response of Mary Magdalene is interwoven with that of Simon Peter and "the beloved disciple." In these two related episodes the writer is able to show how faith in Christ's resurrection was generated in different ways. In the case of Peter and the disciple Jesus loved, as we have now come to expect (13:22-25; 18:15-16), the disciple Jesus loved is first, first to the tomb and first to believe. Peter arrived second but entered the tomb first, looked around, saw everything and yet nothing, and left. The beloved disciple entered and "he saw and believed" (verse 8). Even though they did not yet understand the Scriptures concerning the resurrection (verse 9), this disciple believed. With no evidence but an empty tomb and grave cloths, this disciple was so close to Jesus that his faith did not need the scaffolding of vision and voice.

Mary Magdalene, on the other hand, represents faith formed another way. The empty tomb, rather than even hinting resurrection, saddened Mary with the thought of Jesus' body being stolen. So far from faith is she that even the appearance of two angels (verse 12) does not break her sorrow. In fact, the voice and the appearance of Jesus do not at first stir her to belief (verse 14). Only when he speaks her name (he knows his own, calls them by name and they know his voice, 10:3-4) does she believe (verse 16). Unlike the beloved disciple, Mary comes to faith through the word of Christ and by that word she must be sustained. Mary Magdalene cannot resume her old relationship with her Lord. This is Jesus to be sure; the Risen Christ is none other than the crucified Jesus, but the ministry of the historical Jesus is over. Now begins the ministry of the glorified Christ who relates to his followers by giving them the Spirit who will abide with them forever (14:16). Therefore Jesus says to Mary, "Do not hold me" (verse 17). She and the disciples and the church are not to long for the way it was or wish to return to some past relationship with Jesus Christ. Rather they, and we, are to believe his word: it is best for you that I go away (16:7); "if I do not go away, the Counselor [Spirit] will not come to you" (16:7); the Spirit will not leave as I am leaving but will live with you for ever (14:16); because I go away to the Father, greater works than I have done you will do (14:12).

Not everyone takes the same path to faith in the Risen Christ, and the preacher will not want to give the impression that one way is normative. Some respond to a word, others to evidence, and others to a relationship. But whatever the path, and whether sudden or slow, faith removes the distance between the first Easter and our own.

Easter Evening

Acts 5:29-32 or *Daniel 12:1-3; Psalm 150;*
I Corinthians 5:6-8 or *Acts 5:29-32; Luke 24:13-49*
(If the first lesson is from the Old Testament, the reading from Acts should be the second lesson.)

Acts 5:29-32

Brought before the Sanhedrin, Peter and the apostles are censured by the high priest for filling Jerusalem with their teaching (5:27-28). Luke records their response in summary form in verses 29-32, and in doing so provides us with an early summary of the Christian kerygma.

The proclamation begins with a reference to "the God of our fathers," a phrase reminiscent of the Old Testament (Exod. 3:15; Dan. 2:23). The opening assertion is that God raised Jesus, the central claim of early Christian preaching (Acts 2:24; 3:15; 4:10; 10:40; 13:30, 37). Since this element is in the forefront here, this text becomes especially suitable for an Easter evening service.

The Jewish authorities are directly accused: "Whom you killed by hanging him on a tree" (verse 30*b*). The phrase, again, is reminiscent of the Old Testament (Deut. 21:22) and was applied by Christians to the crucifixion (Acts 10:39; Gal. 3:13).

The emphasis then shifts again to Christ's exaltation: "this very one God exalted him at his right hand as Leader *[archēgos]* and Savior *[sotēr]*" (verse 31). Exaltation to the right hand of God becomes a fixed part of early Christian preaching (Acts 2:33) and worship (Phil. 2:9). Earlier, Christ is proclaimed as the "Author *[archēgos]* of life" (3:15), and the term translated by RSV, NEB, and JB as "Leader" might appropriately be rendered "Author," "Source," even "pioneer" (cf. Heb. 2:10; 12:2). As one who passed through death to life, the exalted Christ is now the very source of life, the one who mediates resurrection life. This single christological title might well serve as the point of departure for the homily on Easter evening.

In spite of their rejection of Christ as God's Messiah, Israel is now extended the offer of "repentance and forgiveness of sins." Later Gentiles are also granted repentance (Acts 11:18; 26:20). It was a standard feature of early Christian preaching to stress the "forgiveness of sins" offered by God through Christ (Acts 2:38; 10:43; 13:38; cf. Luke 24:47).

The apostolic testimony rested on their unique status as "witnesses of these things" (Luke 24:48; Acts 1:8, 22; 2:32; 3:15; 4:33; 10:41; 13:31; I Cor. 15:5-9, 15). What they had seen and heard, they bore witness to (Acts 4:20). Especially remarkable, however, is the double witness mentioned here. Not only the apostles, but the Holy Spirit as well bears witness to the Easter faith (cf. John 15:26-27).

Convinced of the truth of this proclamation, the apostles boldly asserted, "We must obey God rather than men" (verse 29; also cf. 4:19). Luke's portrayal of this scene allows us to see the apostles confronted by the authorities in a life-and-death standoff (cf. verse 33). Yet, the conviction of the Easter faith gave them confidence to defy human authority and obey the God who vindicated Christ. This scene has motivated many Christians to stand firm in their faith when intimidated by authorities both civil and ecclesiastical. It vividly depicts the kind of confidence engendered by the "Author of life."

Daniel 12:1-3

The readings for Easter Evening continue the celebration of the resurrection of Jesus (I Cor. 5:6-8; Ps. 150). The Old Testament text which contributes to that celebration is one of its two clear expressions of a belief in the resurrection from the dead. The other is found in Isaiah 26:19 which, like Daniel 12:1-3, is quite late.

It could be misleading to read Daniel 12:1-3 apart from its context. It is part of the fourth vision report in the book,

Daniel 10:1–12:13. Like the three which precede it, this is the report of an apocalyptic vision in which God reveals to the visionary the course of history and its ultimate destiny. History is summarized in terms of a series of eras, the final one being an age of tribulation for God's elect. History culminates in the establishment of the reign of God. Our reading comes precisely at the point of climax, when God intervenes just as times become most difficult. God, acting through the angel Michael, will act to deliver his people. Moreover, at that time there will be a resurrection of the dead, "some to everlasting life, and some to shame and everlasting contempt" (verse 2).

Texts like this one, which deal with such important matters as the end of history and the resurrection of the dead, often become the foundation for full doctrinal statements on their subjects. While this text alone cannot bear such weight, it does contribute several important points to the Christian community's reflections at Easter.

1. Belief in the resurrection from the dead is intimately connected to apocalyptic eschatology; that is, it is one element in the belief that God will transform history and the cosmos, establishing his kingdom. In both Old and New Testaments the nature and even the location of that kingdom are understood variously, so one should be cautious about spelling out the details. In Daniel 12:3, those who are raised to everlasting life "shall shine like the brightness of the firmament"; that is, in the new age they will be transformed.

2. It is God who brings in this new age. While there are only a handful of Old Testament texts that express a hope for life beyond the grave, the foundation for that belief has long been in the affirmation that there is no limit to God's power, not even death.

3. There is a moral dimension to the hope for the reign of God. That is expressed here in the expectation of a twofold resurrection, some to eternal life and some to eternal shame. Note, however, that there is no description of a heaven or a hell.

4. It is important to emphasize that Daniel 12:1-3, like the dominant New Testament message, speaks not of immortality of the soul but of the resurrection of the dead. In the New

Testament era the Hellenistic view of the immortality of the soul was widespread, but the fundamental biblical perspective is quite different. It acknowledges the reality of human death—Jesus also really died—and bases hope not on some innate human characteristic such as a soul, but upon the power and grace of God. The life of the resurrection is understood as eternal, but God is the one who raises persons from the dead.

Psalm 150

This final psalm in the Psalter concludes the book with a great and universal call to praise God. As such, it may be seen not only as the fitting conclusion to the book as a whole but also as a statement of faith and confidence in the future. How different the book of Psalms would have been had it concluded with a moaning and depressing lament!

The tenfold repetition of the call to praise in the body of the psalm is the most characteristic feature of this psalm. Like other examples of ten in the Bible, the number was probably deliberately chosen both as a memory device (note that we have ten fingers) and as an affirmation of completeness or fullness. The two hallelujahs ("Praise the Lord") at the beginning and end are opening and closing liturgical statements which bring the number to twelve.

Three factors in the praise of God are noted: the places of praising (verse 1), the reasons for praising (verse 2), and the means of praise (verses 3-5).

The places of praising are the temple, which was considered the center point of the universe in late Jewish thought, and the firmament, which was considered the dome or heavens encircling the universe. Praise should thus extend from the center outward to the whole of creation and include every living thing (see verse 6).

The reasons for praise are both what God does ("his mighty deeds") and what he is ("his exceeding greatness"). Thus both divine action and divine being are stressed.

The means of praise are multiple musical instruments of all types. This call to orchestrated adulation suggests something of what went on in festive worship services in the temple.

The one medium of praising God that is noted, which is not a musical instrument, is the dance. Throughout the Bible, dancing is associated with celebration and joy (see Exod. 15:19-21; Ps. 30:11) and probably played a significant role in Israelite worship.

The appropriateness of this psalm for the Easter Evening service is based on its call to and emphasis on praise since Easter is the central day of celebration and praise in the Christian year.

I Corinthians 5:6-8

In this text, Paul asserts that "Christ, our paschal lamb, has been sacrificed" (verse 7). It is quite a remarkable assertion, since it is the only time in all of his writings that he refers to Christ in this manner. In this respect, his understanding of the sacrificial death of Christ is close to that of the Fourth Gospel in which the death of Christ occurs at the time of the slaying of the paschal lamb prior to the Passover meal (cf. John 19:14; also John 1:29, 36).

This christological claim occurs within the context of moral instruction. As the previous verses show, not only did the Corinthians tolerate gross immorality within their midst, they actually boasted about it (cf. 5:2, 6). Paul's concern is to bring them to their senses and to remind them of the moral character required of a community of Christians. He seizes on the metaphor "leaven" because of its close association with that which is impure and corrupt. Its use as a fermenting agent meant that it was a contaminating substance and was regarded as ritually unclean (cf. Lev. 2:11). Thus, in preparation for the Passover, Israelites were instructed to remove all leaven from the house (Exod. 12:15; 13:7). Only unleavened bread was to be used during the Passover meal (Exod. 12:8). The order here should be noted: first, all leaven was to be removed from the house, then the paschal lamb was to be slain. Those wishing to participate in the Passover feast had to eliminate all leaven from their midst.

By adopting this metaphor and engaging in allegorical exegesis, Paul reminds the Corinthian church that their corporate conduct, which not only allows but fosters gross immorality, does not conform properly to the sacrifice of Christ, the paschal lamb. As a community of faith for whom Christ was sacrificed, they should eliminate all corruption and impurity from their midst. Only when they have so prepared themselves and have made themselves "unleavened" can they "celebrate the festival" (verse 8). He thus charges them to "cleanse out the old leaven" so that they can become what they actually are—"unleavened" (verse 7).

What is worth noting about this passage is that our celebration of the death and resurrection of Christ has moral implications not only for the community as a whole, but for individuals as well. The ethical instruction is grounded in the Christ-event itself. The church is expected to behave in a manner appropriate to the sacrifice of Christ. Corporate responsibility is also in view here. As Paul insists, "a little leaven leavens the whole lump" (verse 6). The presence of "leaven" within the community of faith has a contaminating effect, and each celebration of Easter should serve as an occasion to remove "the old leaven, the leaven of malice and evil," and to celebrate with the "unleavened bread of sincerity and truth" (verse 8). So understood, Easter becomes more than celebration. It also becomes an occasion for moral renewal.

Luke 24:13-49

Sometimes the lectionary offerings are too rich; neither preacher nor congregation can dine without surfeiting. Such is the case for this service. Easter Evening worship should not ask too much of us; it is a time for reflection. For that reason and two others we will here confine ourselves to Luke 24:13-35. Since Luke 24:35-48 will be our Gospel for the Third Sunday of Easter and Luke 24:46-53 for Ascension Day, the decision to conclude at verse 35 is not one of deletion but of delay. In addition, verses 13-35 constitute a unit, a conscious work of the storyteller's art, literarily and theologically complete. For a preacher to deal with this story along with something else seems not only impractical but also insensitive.

The story is set on resurrection day (verse 13) and is placed between the account of the disciples' unbelief ("these words seemed to them an idle tale," verse 11) and that of their cautious belief ("they still disbelieved for joy," verse 41). This narrative had no parallel in the other Gospels, and the appearance of the Risen Christ to Cleopas and his companion (man or woman?) is not listed among the appearances recorded in I Corinthians 15:3-8. However, the list mentions an appearance to Peter (I Cor. 15:5) which has its only Gospel reference in this passage (Luke 24:34). A few ancient manuscripts add after 24:11 a line about Peter coming to the tomb, but this is obviously borrowed from John 20:1-10. Whatever may have been the source of this story, it is available to us as clearly Lukan, not only in its aesthetic qualities but in its theological thrust. As a story it reminds the reader of certain Old Testament accounts of God's appearances incognito (Gen. 18:1-15). As a Lukan story, it recalls for the reader two themes vital to this Evangelist: the centrality of the Hebrew Scriptures for Christian faith and the experience of breaking bread together as an experience with Christ. At the risk of inflicting the harm that analysis can do to a story, let us isolate these two themes for special attention.

The Risen Christ joins two dejected disciples, "And beginning with Moses and all the prophets, he interpreted to them in all the scriptures the things concerning himself" (verse 27). At this point Christ is to them a stranger. Just as at the Transfiguration and the Ascension, "clouds" and "sleep" preserve the revealed/concealed quality of God's revelation (Luke 9:28-31; Acts 1:6-11), so here Luke says, "But their eyes were kept from recognizing him" (verse 16). Why? Because faith is not generated by the experience of being overwhelmed but by gaining clarity about the true meaning of Scripture. Later, as the two reflected on the experience they said, "Did not our hearts burn within us while he talked to us on the road, *while he opened to us the scriptures?*" (verse 32, italics added). Nothing is more repeatedly clear in Luke: "If they do not hear Moses and the prophets, neither will they be convinced if some one should rise from the dead" (16:31). This proper understanding of Scripture is the substance of the church's preaching in Acts. The hold of ignorance is broken and now it can be seen that God's purpose with Israel and with the church is one and the same: to offer repentance and forgiveness to all people (24:47).

The second theme in the story has to do with the meal and how Jesus "was known to them in the breaking of the bread" (verse 35). The meal was nothing unusual at the outset; the two disciples shared their bread with a tired and hungry traveler. They prepared supper, and his presence made it a sacrament. Luke clearly has the Eucharist in mind: "When he was at table with them, he took the bread and blessed, and broke it, and gave it to them" (verse 30). This text may provide the occasion for recalling for the listeners the theological significance of the table for this Evangelist, or at least to sense the cumulative effect of the variety and number of table stories: in the home of Martha and Mary; as guest of Simon the Pharisee; observing the behavior of hosts and guests at a banquet; responding to attacks that he ate with sinners; in a parable about a rich man who refused to share bread with Lazarus. In these and many other stories, Luke makes table fellowship the evidence of full acceptance of sinners by Jesus and of one another by us. So also in Acts, story after story points to the conclusion that eating together is the mark of full accord in the church. For Luke, the question to the church is not so much, Would you baptize them? but, Would you eat with them? (Acts 11:3).

But even if this enlargement of the theme of breaking bread is not pursued, the Emmaus story alone is enough for today. What could be a more appropriate act for Easter Evening than to sit at table with one another, and with Him?

Second Sunday of Easter

Acts 4:32-35; Psalm 133; I John 1:1–2:2; John 20:19-31

Acts 4:32-35

This is one of several summaries placed at crucial points in the narrative of Acts (cf. also 2:42-47; 5:12-16; also summaries of the church's growth, 2:47; 6:7; 9:31; 11:21; 12:24; 16:5; 19:20; 28:31). With these vignettes, in which certain motifs are repeated, Luke highlights significant aspects of the early Christian community.

This summary occurs after a major triumph. Peter and John have been arrested for healing a lame man and preaching the Gospel (3:1-26). They were brought before the authorities, but were released (4:1-31). As confirmation that God had been at work in these events, there was an outpouring of the Spirit, which gave new vitality to the apostolic ministry of the Word (4:31).

Before recording the second major crisis faced by the Christian movement, the second arrest of the apostles (5:12-42), Luke pauses to summarize the state of affairs within the community of faith, calling attention to several features of its life.

1. It was a unified movement. "The company of those who believed were of one heart and soul" (verse 32). "Heart and soul," a phrase reminiscent of the Old Testament (Deut. 6:5; 10:12; 11:13; 13:3; 26:16; 30:2, 6, 10; also I Chron. 12:38), suggests that the level of unity among believers was deep and genuine, penetrating to their innermost being. Not every church in the first century exhibited this degree of unity, although it remained an ideal (cf. I Cor. 1:10-17).

2. The community shared its possessions. "No one said that any of the things which he possessed was his own, but

they had everything in common" (verse 32*b*). Here we see Christian unity being translated into Christian charity. Their willingness to dispossess themselves of those things which they owned became a concrete expression of the solidarity of their fellowship. Of the Gospel writers, Luke in particular lays heavy stress on the sharing of possessions as an earmark of Christian discipleship (cf. Luke 8:3; 12:33; Acts 2:45). In this instance, Christian charity took the form of community of goods (cf. 2:44), but this is not the only way in which responsible use of possessions is presented in the New Testament, particularly Luke-Acts. At least two other possibilities are presented: (1) the complete renunciation of possessions as a prerequisite of discipleship (Luke 5:11, 28; 14:25-33; 18:18-23), and (2) the giving of alms (Luke 11:41; 21:1-4).

If we realize that Luke's portrait of the early church at this point is but one of several mandates that he gives for the responsible use of possessions, then "Christian communism" cannot be presented as the single ideal toward which the church should strive. It may be an appropriate response, given the right time and place, but should not be seen as the only, or even the most laudable, form of Christian charity.

The important thing to notice is that "there was not a needy person among them" (verse 34). By seeing to it that the needy are cared for, the early church came to embody the Old Testament ideal (cf. Deut. 15:4). Yet, by sharing their goods in common, they also came to embody the Greek ideal which held that "for friends all things are common." Clearly Luke is presenting the early church as the embodiment of both the Jewish and Greek ideal community in which unity and charity thrive.

3. It continued its proclamation of the resurrection of Christ. "And with great power the apostles gave their testimony to the resurrection of the Lord Jesus" (verse 33). The phrase "great power" doubtless implies the continued demonstration of power through signs and wonders (cf. 4:30; also 2:22; 3:12; 4:7; 6:8; 8:13; 10:38; I Thess. 1:5; I Cor. 2:4-5). Bearing witness to the resurrection lay at the heart of early Christian proclamation (Acts 1:22; 2:32; 3:15; 5:32; 10:41; 13:31; I Cor. 15:1-11, 15; also Luke 24:46-47). It is worth noting that the ministry of the word was carried on along with the ministry of goods. In this respect,

Luke's portrait is exemplary, for it suggests a worthwhile paradigm for the modern church. The concern to proclaim must be balanced with concern for the needy.

One should also be cautious in trying to replicate this image of the ideal church in a modern setting. For one thing, it is the needy *among the church* who are cared for here. At this juncture, Christianity was not of sufficient strength to reach out beyond its own circle and administer assistance, although this need was soon recognized (cf. Gal. 6:10).

In using this text on the Second Sunday of Easter, the preacher should notice, first of all, that it sketches the image of a church empowered and emboldened by the Easter faith. Central to its life was the proclamation of the Risen Lord, and this message was accompanied with powerful signs and wonders. Luke wishes to leave no doubt that it was a Spirit-filled community and that its capacity to preach boldly arose from the power of the Spirit. Second, the text shows that the Easter faith came to expression in the community of faith. Concretely, this was seen in the unity that existed among believers and the love and concern they had for one another. It is Luke's conviction that the messianic community embodies both the Jewish and Greek ideal of life together.

Psalm 133

This psalm has been selected for this Sunday because it stresses fraternal harmony and brotherhood, themes found especially in the reading from Acts.

Psalm 133 belongs to a group of psalms (120–134) which bear the heading, "Psalms of Ascent," or perhaps better "Pilgrim Psalms." These psalms were probably sung as pilgrims made their way to Jerusalem to worship. The emphasis in Psalm 133, in such a context, would be in praise of the fellowship enjoyed in the city of Jerusalem during festival occasions. Such an interpretation fits harmoniously with the description of the early church in the opening chapters of the book of Acts.

Brothers dwelling (or worshiping, as NEB footnote indicates) together are praised in verse 1. Although the psalmist probably did not have this in mind in composing the psalm, it is interesting to note how frequently trouble between brothers is used as a theme in the Old Testament (Cain and Abel, Jacob and Esau, Joseph and his brothers, Absalom and Amnon, Solomon and Adonijah). The lack of brotherly unity and peace so often tears at the fabric of a family that one can sense the reason the psalmist might focus on this universal motif. When Jerusalem was overrun by pilgrim-worshipers during the great festivals of passover and tabernacles, it was necessary for the people to coexist in peace in order to enjoy and benefit from the occasion.

Brotherhood and fraternal unity are described metaphorically in verses 2-3. One image speaks of the precious oil poured on the head of Aaron which runs down the beard and onto his clothes. This picture is probably derived from the ordination ritual of the high priests in which anointing oil was used (see Exod. 29:7; Lev. 8:10-13). For us the imagery seems slightly less than stupendous but what is probably emphasized are the extravagance of the act and the joy that characterized the occasion. The ordination of a new high priest in Israel would have been something like the inauguration of a president, especially in post-exilic days when there was no king and the high priest was the chief official in the community.

Brotherhood is also compared to the "dew of Hermon." Mt. Hermon, standing over nine thousand feet in elevation, was the tallest mountain in Syria-Palestine and the source of much of the headwaters of the Jordan River. Towering over the region, the mountain may have given its name to the dew that falls in late summer to nourish late crops toward maturity.

A secondary theme of this psalm is the greatness of Zion—the goal of pilgrims. The centrality of Zion for the life of the people is found in numerous psalms (46, 48, 76, and so forth). Zion is described in verse 3 as the place which God has blessed and where the blessing is bestowed for abundant life.

I John 1:1–2:2

Many of the themes celebrated in the Easter Season come to expression in this passage: life (1:1-2), light (1:5, 7), and joy (1:4). The themes are played out in the distinctive Johannine key and naturally recall similar themes in the Fourth Gospel.

Let us look first at the overall structure. The first section (1:1-4) constitutes the preface of the epistle and introduces themes and motifs that are more fully exploited elsewhere in the epistle. These verses look quite different when compared with other opening sections of the New Testament, in that they contain no personal greetings (cf. II John 1-3; III John 1-4). They look much more like the opening words of a homily, and may suggest that the epistle as a whole should be read more as a sermon than as a letter. The address is couched in terms of endearment, seen by the way in which the readers are addressed (2:1, 7, 12, 18, 28; 3:13; 4:1, 4, 7; 5:21).

The second section (1:5-10) begins the sermon proper, with its emphasis on light, fellowship, and the life of faith as walking in the light.

The third section (2:1-2) is a self-contained unit, and is so rendered in NEB and JB, although RSV extends the paragraph unit through 2:6. In this section, the author urges his readers to break with the life of sin.

The opening words are reminiscent of the Gospel accounts of the Easter appearances, with their emphasis on "seeing and touching" the Risen Lord (John 20:20, 25; Luke 24:39). This directly links the epistolary lection with today's Gospel lesson. The apostles' proclamation was based on what they had seen and heard (Acts 4:20; cf. also John 1:14). We should note the extent to which the senses are being activated here. This is doubtless prompted by the Gnostic threat which denied the humanity of Christ (cf. I John 4:1-3). The author thus emphasizes that the testimony being proclaimed has been experienced at multiple levels: audible, visual, and tactile. All of these have informed the verbal or oral proclamation. Here we see how the entry of the Logos into the world had palpable effects on those encountered by it. Hence, the claim that "the life was made manifest" (verse 2; also cf. I John 4:9; John 1:14; Rom. 3:21).

But our text does more than anchor the Christian message in Easter faith and experience, for the opening words push back to "the beginning." We think immediately of the opening words of the Fourth Gospel, "In the beginning was the Word" (John 1:1), and the author of this epistle shares this conviction that the Christian story actually begins with Christ who was "from the beginning" (I John 2:13). This interpretation of the opening verses assumes that "the word of life" (verse 1) refers to Christ, the Logos of life, and that it is Christ who is the antecedent of verse 1. It is Christ, the Logos, who "was from the beginning, which we have heard, . . . seen, . . . and touched." Another way of construing it, however, is to understand "word of life" as the "message of life," or the gospel itself. If this is the case, then "beginning" may not refer to the primordial beginning of time, but to the beginning of the Christian witness (cf. II John 6).

Also central to today's text is the fellowship (*koinōnia*) created among those who have accepted the Christian testimony of faith. The word "fellowship" actually does injustice to the dynamic content of *koinōnia* and is better rendered participially, for example, "sharing." The life shared together has two dimensions: it is with each other as well as with "the Father [and] his Son Jesus Christ" (1:3). The later verses show, however, that such mutual fellowship can only be sustained through moral renewal (I John 1:7; cf. also I Cor. 1:9; Phil. 1:5). It is also nurtured by love for one another (I John 2:10; 4:7-12) and is typified by joy (cf. John 3:29; 15:11; 16:24; 17:13; II John 12; II Cor. 1:24).

The fellowship envisioned here is understood in strongly dualistic terms, characteristic of the Johannine outlook, but not uncommon in first-century Judaism, for example, within the Qumran community. There is a strong polarity between light and darkness, predicated on the conviction that "God is light and in him is no darkness at all" (1:5; cf. James 1:17). Similarly, Christ is understood as the bringer and embodiment of light (John 1:4-5; 9:5; 11:10; 12:35, 46). This way of understanding itself may also have been informed by Old Testament passages (cf. Isa. 9:2; 42:7; 49:6; 60:1, 3). It was not, however, a uniquely Johannine outlook (cf. Matt. 5:14; I Thess. 5:5; Phil. 2:15). To define moral conduct in terms of conformity to light and darkness represents a continuation of the Johannine understanding of the mission of Christ (John 8:12).

Even though the author of the epistle strongly enjoins his readers not to have truck with the ways of darkness, he nevertheless fully recognizes that Christians can and do sin (I John 2:8, 10). What is called for is the willingness to confess (1:9) and to recognize that the blood of Christ continues to have the power to cleanse us from sin (1:7; cf. Heb. 9:14; Rev. 1:5; 7:14). Also called for is the willingness to recognize our human shortcomings and the refusal to practice deception, either of others or of ourselves (cf. Prov. 28:12-13; 29:5). We can live in the assurance that God is both "faithful and just" (I Cor. 1:9; 10:13; II Cor. 1:18; I Thess. 5:24; II Thess. 3:3; II Tim. 2:13; Heb. 10:23; 11:11; Rev. 1:5; Deut. 32:4).

Besides a faithful God, members of the Christian fellowship possess an "advocate" (*paraklētos*, I John 2:1) who, in this case is Christ himself, although in the Fourth Gospel it is the Holy Spirit (cf. John 14:16, 26; 15:26; 16:7; Luke 24:49). In addition, Christ is the "expiation" for our sins, a very controversial term (cf. I John 4:10; Rom. 3:25; Heb. 2:17). The issue is whether the sacrifice of Christ should be understood as that which placates an angry God or that which removes defilement (NEB). In either case, the effects of his atoning death are universal—"for the sins of the whole world" (John 11:51-52; II Cor. 5:19).

This text is obviously rich with possibilities for the preacher, with its many themes that continue the joyous celebration of Easter. One might choose to focus exclusively on the christological aspects of the passage, such as Christ the Logos of life (1:1), our advocate with the Father (2:1), or the expiation for our sins (2:2). Or, another direction worth exploring might be the nature of Christian "fellowship" and what this entails in the Johannine understanding, and whether this still serves as a viable way for modern Christian churches to define themselves. Still another possibility might be moral renewal and the Christian's need for open confession and reliance on a faithful God.

John 20:19-31

The Easter Season provides opportunities for the church to reflect the biblical witness concerning the disciples' experiences of the Risen Christ and to appropriate anew the blessing upon those who have not seen and yet who believe (verse 29). As stated in comments on the Gospel for Easter Day (John 20:1-18), the Fourth Evangelist provides testimony to the resurrection in the form of parallel "double-stories": two disciples and Mary Magdalene (verses 1-18) and ten disciples and Thomas (verses 19-29). Each double-story speaks of faith (the beloved disciple, verse 8; the ten disciples, verse 20) and of doubt overcome by a special appearance of Christ (Mary Magdalene, verses 11-18; Thomas, verses 24-29). These four experiences of the Risen Christ are certainly not random examples by the writer; they are recounted as further testimony to a central conviction in this Gospel: there are different types and levels of faith. Throughout the book, the Evangelist has shown that there is faith based on signs and there is faith that needs none; there is faith weak and faith strong; faith shallow and faith deep; faith growing and faith faltering. In this Gospel faith is not a decision made once but a decision made anew in every situation. As a case in point, notice that the last "convert" in this Gospel is Thomas, already a disciple, even one of the Twelve. This understanding of faith should encourage as well as instruct members of the church who are made to feel guilty that their faith was not born full grown in one dramatic experience.

We focus now upon John 20:19-31 with four observations that grow out of the text. The first concerns Thomas. Even though this Gospel elsewhere portrays him as courageously devoted to Jesus (11:16) and theologically alert (14:5); even though a non-canonical Gospel bears his name; even though tradition associates him with a mission to India, Thomas has been, because of this text, tagged "Doubting Thomas." But see him in the Johannine context. The beloved disciple believed with no evidence but an empty tomb, Mary Magdalene believed because of a word, and the ten disciples believed because they saw the Lord (verse 20). But for the absent Thomas, faith could come only with difficulty; too much was at stake. He could be sure only after physical contact (verse 25), but whether he actually touched Jesus is not clear (verses 27-29). For some, faith is as gentle as a child on grandmother's lap, but for others, it is continual wrestling with doubt.

Our second observation concerns Jesus' response to Thomas (verse 29): "Blessed are those who have not seen and yet believe." This statement is most important, for the Evangelist has been concerned throughout the Gospel to assure his readers that faith is no less a possibility for them than for the original disciples. Faith is available to all persons in all places and times with no loss of efficacy due to distance from Jesus of Nazareth. Therefore, having recited different ways faith was generated in the earliest Christian community, the writer pronounces upon the readers the blessing of Jesus Christ. This blessing complements the prayer of Jesus in 17:20: "I do not pray for these only, but also for those who believe in me through their word."

The third observation has to do with the gift of the Holy Spirit. The promise of the Spirit, so repeatedly given by Jesus in the farewell discourses (chapters 14–16) is here fulfilled: "He breathed on them, and said to them, 'Receive the Holy Spirit'" (verse 22). Brief as it is, this is the Johannine Pentecost. While many functions and benefits of the Spirit are stated in chapters 14–16, only here are the apostles given authority to grant or refuse to grant forgiveness of sin (verse 23; Matt. 16:19; 18:18). Through the apostles the church is joined in continuity of mission, authority, and benefit to Jesus Christ.

Finally, a word about verses 30-31. These verses obviously are a conclusion, not to the preceding narrative alone but to the entire Gospel. There may have been a time when the Gospel closed here, before chapter 21 was added as an epilogue. If so, the Evangelist's last word was to state as the purpose of the Gospel the generation of faith. Since the book assumes the readers already have some faith in Jesus Christ, this purpose is clearly to clarify, inform, and deepen faith to the end that it be full and life-giving. The last word to the world that crucified Jesus is not a judging one, but a gracious word: "That believing you may have life in his name" (verse 31). The assurance of 3:16 has not been forgotten: "For God so loved the world."

Third Sunday of Easter

Acts 3:12-19; Psalm 4; I John 3:1-7;
Luke 24:35-48

Acts 3:12-19

The words of today's text come from Peter's sermon, delivered in the precincts of the temple in response to the healing of the lame man at the Gate Beautiful (3:1-10). This was the first "sign and wonder" done through the apostles that Luke chose to record (cf. 2:43). The response of "all the people" (verse 11), that is, the Jews gathered for worship at the hour of prayer, was one of astonishment (verse 11). It was this response that gave rise to Peter's sermon.

The sermon, or more correctly, Luke's summary of Peter's sermon, is given in verses 12-26. Thus, today's first reading actually consists of only the first part of the sermon, and in fact stops in the middle of the sentence in verse 19! If one wishes to abbreviate the text at all, a more appropriate cutoff point would be either at the end of verse 16 or at the end of verse 21. Preferably, the text should include verses 12-26.

The sermon does not stand alone, but is directly related to the preceding narrative which reports the healing of the lame man. This is typical of the way in which the rest of Acts is constructed. At various points in the narrative speeches occur, but they are invariably connected closely with a narrative episode, usually preceding the speech. In this instance, certain parts of the sermon are linked directly with the healing story (cf. verses 12, 16). Perhaps as important is the prominence given in the sermon to the prophets (verses 21-25). This may suggest that Luke understands the work of Peter and John as standing in the prophetic tradition. If this is Luke's intended connection, then the healing of the lame man (verses 1-10) and the sermon that follows (verses 12-26) should be construed as a single episode depicting a prophetic deed and word.

The connection between the sermon and the preceding miracle is made in the opening verse when Peter disclaims personal responsibility for the miracle. "Why do you stare at us, as though by our own power or piety we had made him walk?" (verse 12). It was only natural, when a divine miracle occurred, that onlookers would regard the human agent as the source of divine power rather than its conduit. Interestingly, Peter insists that neither their power nor their piety accounted for the miracle. Rather, it was God who had been at work in what had happened. Even more to the point, it was the God whom the Jewish audience had come to the temple to worship who had been at work here: "The God of Abraham and of Isaac and of Jacob, the God of our fathers" (cf. Exod. 3:6, 15-16; also Luke 20:37; Acts 7:32; IV Macc. 7:19; 16:25). Since Peter is trying to clarify the true source of divine power, the phrase, "God . . . glorified his servant Jesus" (verse 13), should probably be understood as referring to the miracle. To paraphrase, "It was the God of your own fathers Abraham, Isaac, and Jacob who was responsible for this miracle, and in doing so God manifested the glory of his servant Jesus." Luke wants his readers to see that the church is the divinely appointed messianic community through which the God of Israel is now at work in new and decisive ways. What the prophets had spoken of earlier (cf. verses 22-25) has now become a reality. The people are called on to see the work of Peter and John, God's new prophets, as the continuation of the salvation history that they already knew.

The locus of divine activity has now shifted, however. Formerly, the presence of God, the Shekinah, dwelt in the temple. Now, it is focused in "the name of Jesus" (verse 16). The healing of the lame man has shown that God no longer exercises divine power exclusively in the precincts of the temple, but does so where prophetic deeds are performed in the name of Jesus. Already, then, in the narrative of Acts Luke begins to show how the temple is being displaced as the locus of God's presence and action. This becomes progressively more apparent as the narrative unfolds and is explicitly stated by Stephen (7:47-51).

The sermon also points up the fundamental paradox of the death of Christ. This is seen especially in the Lukan antitheses: "Jesus, whom you delivered up . . . denied . . . killed . . . God raised from the dead" (verses 13-15). "You . . . asked for a murderer to be granted to you, and killed the Author of life" (verse 15). In the Lukan passion narrative, the death of Christ is presented as a gross miscarriage of justice. The death of Christ is seen as the death of an innocent martyr (Luke 23:4, 14-15, 20,23) who is finally vindicated through the resurrection. Luke underscores the irony of the situation: given a choice between one who took life (Barabbas, the murderer, Luke 23:18-25) and one who is the very Author of life, the Jews opted for death over life. Now that Easter has righted this injustice, such a horrible choice is seen to have been done "in ignorance" (verse 17; Acts 13:27; 17:20; also Lev. 22:14; Num. 15:22-31). Now, the appropriate action is repentance and reformation of life (verse 19) through which forgiveness is possible. "Times of refreshing" (verse 19) are also promised, that their repentance will enable them to enjoy the Parousia when God's appointed Messiah, Jesus, comes again (verses 20-21).

Some of the themes that might be explored homiletically include the following: (1) the Risen Lord as the locus of God's activity as opposed to supposedly sacred places, in this case the temple; (2) God's messengers as the conduits rather than the source of divine power; (3) the misplacement of emphasis on human "power and piety" in accounting for the work of God in the world; (4) the Easter faith as that which illuminates and overcomes human ignorance as well as offering repentance and the forgiveness of sins; and (5) the messianic community as the continuation of Israel and the place where the prophetic succession continues.

Psalm 4

This psalm was in all probability originally used in worship when a person felt that he/she had been wrongly accused of some deed. Ancient Israelite society recognized the right of persons in this predicament to appeal for a hearing in the temple before God (see Exod. 22:7-8; Deut. 17:8-13; 19:15-21;

I Kings 8:31-32). In such religious adjudication at the temple, both parties in a case might appear and present their arguments, and the priests would render a verdict regarding guilt and innocence or else make both parties swear an oath of self-imprecation.

Something of the legal proceedings can be seen in the structure of the psalm which switches back and forth between different addressees. The following is a plausible outline of the psalm: address and plea to God (verse 1), worshiper's address to the opponents (verses 2-3), priest's address to parties in the dispute (verses 4-5), and the worshiper's address to God manifesting confidence and trust (verses 6-8).

One factor of interest about this psalm is the possibility it raises that people, in this case litigants in a case, spent the night in the precincts of the sanctuary. Verses 4-5, if these can be related to the ritual in the temple, bring together sleeping and the offering of sacrifice. Verse 8 has the worshiper speak about lying down to sleep in peace. Sleeping in the sanctuary in order to receive dreams, revelations, or priestly interpretations about one's condition—called incubation—was widely known in antiquity. The priests may have observed the worshipers during this period and drawn conclusions about guilt and innocence on the basis of the person's activity and sleeping patterns. Reference to sleeping has been the basis for considering this text to be an evening psalm.

Two features of this psalm are worthy of special note and can be related at least indirectly to the reading from Acts which has the disciples defend themselves against false charges.

First of all, it is clear that the supplicant lamenting a case before God considers him/herself to be falsely accused. The person's honor has been challenged and vain words and lies have produced shame (see verse 2). Thus the worshiper has undergone the turmoil and pain of accusation and felt the psychic blows of opposition.

At the same time, a second emphasis in the psalm is the person's sense of innocence and firm reliance on God to act for the worshiper's vindication. Such assurance can be seen in verse 1 which appeals to past relations ("thou hast given me room when I was in distress"), in verse 3 where the worshiper expresses confidence ("the Lord hears when I call to him"), and in verse 7 where God is seen as the cause for rejoicing ("thou hast put mere joy in my heart"). The apex of confidence is expressed, however, in verse 7 where the worshiper speaks of the ability to lie down and sleep peacefully confessing that God alone is the source of peace and tranquility. The guilty soul may frequently find sleep to be lacking but an innocent conscience is a blessing when one seeks rest in sleep.

I John 3:1-7

To conclude today's epistolary reading with verse 7 seems slightly arbitrary, since the sentence begun in verse 7 appears not to end until verse 8 (so, Nestle, 26th ed.; JB, NEB). Still, it is not at all clear where the thought-unit ends (cf. RSV, JB, NEB). The preacher would do well to consult several translations before deciding on the limits of the pericope.

Taking verses 1-7 as the lection, we may analyze the text thematically: (1) being children of God (verses 1-3), and (2) living as children of God (verses 4-7).

First, the text treats our status as children of God, which is introduced with an air of incredulity: "Think of the love that the Father has lavished on us, by letting us be called God's children!" (JB). To be sure, enabling us to become children of God is understood in the Johannine writings as part of the mission of the incarnate Logos (John 1:12; 11:52). The Gospel tradition represents Jesus speaking of this as a possibility (Matt. 5:9, 45; cf. Luke 20:36), as does Paul (Rom. 8:16; Gal. 3:26-27; Eph. 1:5). But today's text emphasizes especially that we are God's children not by nature, but by gift ("what love the Father has *given* us"). In one sense, of course, all humans are God's children in that we have been created by him (Acts 17:28-29), but the relationship spoken of in First John is more specific than this. It is childhood brought about by divine regeneration (2:29; 3:9; 5:1, 4, 18; cf. John 1:13; 3:1-15) and explainable only in terms of divine love (John 3:16).

Being children of God is an existential reality for us ("and so we are," verse 1), but not necessarily a visible reality, especially to those who do not share our experience and understanding of God—the "world" in Johannine terms (John 1:9-11, *passim*). Our true identity and self-understanding may be veiled to the world (cf. II Cor. 4:3-4), but so did Christ's true identity and mission elude the world (John 7:28-29; 8:19, 55; 14:7; 15:21; 16:3; Matt. 11:27). The obscurity we experience living our lives within the gospel is but an extension of Christ's own experience. His inscrutability becomes our own.

But our text also points to another ambiguity about being children of God: it is both actual and potential, realized and unrealized. "We are God's children now," yet what this means fully will not be realized until later (verse 2). At the human level, we understand this. Children, in one sense, know that they have parents and experience the benefits of parental love, but full understanding does not occur until much later, when they are no longer children. In a limited way, this enables us to see the eschatological dimension of our text: at the Parousia, our vision of God will be transparent, and only then will we realize our true identity. Children of God live in the knowledge that there is more to come (Col. 3:1-4; Rom. 8:9), and that before they can "see God" they must be transformed (I Cor. 15:43, 49, 53; Rom. 8:29; 12:2; II Cor. 3:18; Eph. 1:19-22). So then, children live in "hope" (verse 3) but this hope produces the desire for moral purity, always a prerequisite for seeing God (Matt. 5:8; Heb. 12:14; John 1:18). Notice that we purify ourselves (it is a volitional act; cf. II Cor. 7:1), and that Christ is our example ("as he is pure").

On this note, the text shifts to the second major theme: living as children of God (verses 4-7). The tone of these remarks is one of hard practicality. The text speaks quite bluntly about "doing righteousness" and does so in black-and-white terms. Committing sin is not a form of lawlessness; it *is* lawlessness (3:8*a*; 5:17; Matt. 7:23; II Thess. 2:3, 8). The ethical outlook is definitely Johannine, with no shades of gray allowed.

Such ethical dualism is directly related to the Johannine understanding of Christ who was not only sinless (John 7:18; 8:46; 18:37; also cf. II Cor. 5:21; Heb. 4:15; I Pet. 2:22; 3:18; also

Isa. 53:9), but whose work was to "take away sins" (John 1:29; cf. I Pet. 2:24; Isa. 53:4-5, 11-12). Presupposed here is the Johannine understanding of Christ as the Paschal Lamb sacrificed for the sins of the world (cf. John 1:29; also I Pet. 1:19; Rev. 5:6, 12; Isa. 53:7; Jer. 11:19; also Matt. 8:17).

So strongly stated is the moral position here that it stands in tension with remarks made earlier in the epistle. Earlier, we are told that no Christian should ever feign sinlessness (1:8-10), and full allowance is made for Christian sinfulness (2:1-2). Here, however, we are told, "No one who abides in him sins" (verse 6); and later, "No one born of God commits sin" (verse 9). The tension here is real, and should not be resolved too easily. One possibility is that in 3:6, 9, the author is speaking of habitual sinfulness on the part of the child of God. Thus, no one who genuinely abides in Christ is habitually inclined toward the life of sin. Rather, being born of God means that one's life inclines toward doing what is right (verse 7). A similar outlook is expressed by Paul (Rom. 6:14), although not in terms as unqualified as this. For the author, (habitual) sinning precludes true vision and knowledge of God (cf. 2:4; III John 11).

As before, Christ himself is the moral imperative. We do what is right, because Christ is righteous (verses 7, 10; 2:29).

Today's text might profitably be explored as illustrating the relationship between the Christian indicative ("being children of God") and the Christian imperative ("living as children of God"). As we have seen, neither of these is as straightforward as it appears. The sermon may address the ambiguity of our status as God's children—by gift not by nature, actual but veiled, realized but not fully. Or, the preacher may wish to pursue the moral implication of the text, asking whether the theology of sin and righteousness expressed in this text is still viable and, if so, how.

Luke 24:35-48

In preparing to explore the meaning of today's Gospel, the reader is urged to review Luke 24:13-35 and the comments made about those verses for the Easter Evening service. Those earlier verses bear upon these for today, not only because of the overlap of one line (verse 35), but also because the narrative pattern of verses 13-35 is repeated in verses 36-48. That pattern consists of: the appearance of the Risen Christ, the failure to recognize him, the reprimand for their doubt, the sharing of food, the opening of the meaning of Scriptures, and the response of wonder and joy. Because these resurrection narratives and those in other Gospels bear clear resemblances to one another, it is quite understandable that in the process of transmission details of one account would bleed into another. Footnotes in the RSV indicate that at the close of verse 36 and after verse 39 some manuscripts carry borrowings from John 20:21-27. However, neither variation in the text materially affects the story.

In Luke's telling of the resurrection narratives, several themes are recurrent and vital to the whole message of the early Christian writer. One of them, the centrality of the Jewish Scriptures for the ministry of Jesus and the message of the church (verses 44-47), was discussed in the comments about Luke 24:13-35 for Easter Evening and need not be repeated here. A second theme considered at that time was the importance of eating together for Jesus' work (Gospel) and the mission of the church (Acts). However, in verses 39-43, another dimension of eating is added. Here Jesus' act of eating fish joined with his offering of his hands and feet for examination says something about the resurrection. By insisting on the corporeality of the Risen Christ, Luke is saying no to those forms of Christology that said Jesus only "seemed" (docetism) to be human. Even the resurrected Jesus says, "Handle me, and see; for a spirit has not flesh and bones as you see that I have" (verse 39). Luke is also saying no to those doctrines of resurrection that were really pagan notions of the immortality of the spirit. Christians believe in the resurrection of the dead, not escape into a spirit world. And Luke is saying no to those notions of spirituality that view the body and all things physical as inherently inferior or evil. Those who view themselves as just passing through this evil world tend to neglect the physical, economic, and political needs of other human beings. Luke reminds us that the Risen Christ said, "Look at my wounds," and, "Do you have anything to eat?" No one can follow this Christ and say that discipleship means being only concerned with "souls."

A third theme in this resurrection account, only implicit in the Emmaus story (verses 13-35), here takes the form of an injunction of Scripture and a command of the Risen Lord. This is Luke's version of the commission to preach the gospel to the nations (verses 46-49). However, since verses 46-53 will be our Gospel lesson for Ascension Day, we will reserve comment for that time.

As we are now leaving the Easter narratives to move to other Gospel texts, a final word about the resurrection stories might be appropriate. In comments on Easter Day we reflected upon the restraint of New Testament writers in the use of this material. Let us add a second word to that description: realism. This may not seem accurate at first, given the appearance of dazzling angels and of Jesus suddenly present and just as suddenly gone. But focus upon the believers to whom Jesus appeared; how realistically they are portrayed! They took resurrection stories as idle tales; they were startled, frightened, and confused; they "disbelieved for joy." Minds and hearts raced. What does this mean? Do we continue where we left off? Do we begin anew? Will Jesus now go to God and leave us here alone? What will happen to us? Will anybody believe this? Will we be resurrected as Jesus was? These are realistic Easter thoughts, and the preacher who lives among these questions is more the pastor than the one who misses the pathos and solemnity of resurrection joy.

Fourth Sunday of Easter

Acts 4:8-12; Psalm 23; I John 3:18-24;
John 10:11-18

Acts 4:8-12

Here we have a capsule summary of the first recorded defense speech given by a Christian before religious authorities. Peter and John had healed a lame beggar at the gate of the temple (3:1-10), and Peter had subsequently proclaimed to the astonished crowd that it was the work of their own God, the God who had raised Jesus from the dead (3:11-26). The temple authorities, most notably the Sadducees, took umbrage at their theology of resurrection, and arrested them (4:1-4). The next day Peter and John were brought before the Sanhedrin for a hearing. This provides the setting for Peter's defense.

The inquiry centered not on their theology of resurrection, but their ministry of healing. They were asked "By what power or by what name do you do this [miracle of healing]?" (verse 7). There was no question about the validity of the miracle itself, since the man who had been healed stood beside them as living testimony (verses 10, 14). This could not be denied. The question was rather in whose name the deed was done.

According to the Gospels, Jesus had warned his disciples that they would be brought before Jewish religious authorities and interrogated. But he had also promised them that they should not be anxious about how they would react or what they would say, for the Holy Spirit would give them the words (Luke 12:11-12; also Matt. 10:19-20). In this, they could have the same reassurance Yahweh had given Moses (Exod. 4:12). Thus, we are told that Peter was "filled with the Holy Spirit" (verse 8), thereby fulfilling the promise of Jesus in the narrative of Acts itself. This is but one of numerous instances in Acts where the Holy Spirit inspires the fledgling church, offering divine confirmation of its work and mission (cf. Acts 2:4; 4:31; 5:32; 9:17; 13:9, 52; cf. 16:7; 19:6). So empowered were Peter and John that their boldness was visible to the Sanhedrin (verse 13). This may also have been the dead giveaway that they had been with Jesus (verse 13).

In response, Peter (typically presented as spokesman) provides the proper context in which to understand the miracle of healing: the power derived from the name of Jesus Christ of Nazareth whom God had raised from the dead (verse 10). Here, he continues the theme he introduced in his public proclamation (3:12, 16). In similar fashion, he introduces the antithesis: the man whom you crucified, God raised from the dead (verse 10). Indirectly, then, the Jewish authorities were responsible for the miracle, but they had been unwitting accessories in the plan of God. To underscore the dramatic turn of events, Peter cites Psalm 118:22, "The stone which the builders rejected has become the head of the corner," but he does so with a crucial difference; he personalizes it, "This is the stone which was rejected by *you* builders" (verse 11, italics added). This passage, which so pointedly expressed the divine reversal that had taken place at Easter, became deeply embedded in early Christian preaching (cf. Matt. 21:42; I Pet. 2:4, 6-8; cf. also Isa. 8:14; 28:16; Rom. 9:33; Eph. 2:20). To their rejection, God had responded with exaltation.

To climax his defense, Peter unambiguously locates salvation in Christ: "And there is salvation in no one else, for there is no other name under heaven given among men by which we must be saved" (verse 12). With this exclusive claim, there is an interesting play on words. Earlier, Peter had asked, "If we are being examined . . . by what means this man has been healed" (verse 9). The word for "heal" is *sōzō*, also translated "saved" in verse 12. The speech operates on two levels: it deals with the "healing," or "making whole," of the lame man, but moves beyond this to the "healing," or "making whole," of everyone under heaven (cf. 2:21). We begin to see that Peter is not merely addressing the

Sanhedrin, but the reader of the narrative for whom the lame man is serving as a mirror.

Out of this simple miracle story there arises proclamation of the Easter faith. "A good deed done to a cripple" (verse 9) has become the occasion for universal proclamation of salvation. Irony pervades the narrative: it is "uneducated, common men" (verse 13) who point out to the religious authorities the connection between "a good deed done to a cripple" and the work of God in which they themselves had unwittingly participated. The literary artistry with which Luke has told the story should itself be instructive for the one who preaches from this text.

One theological question presented by the text, and which may provide the theme for the homily, is the absoluteness of the claim made in verse 12. Especially in the modern world have we become more fully aware of religious pluralism. The study of the history of religions, both Western and Eastern, has pointed up many similarities that cannot easily be ignored. It has certainly become more difficult for proponents of any religion to make absolutist claims as they once did. Perhaps it would be worthwhile to explore this text in the light of the modern dilemma and in the context of history, with attention given to such historical episodes as the Crusades or the Holocaust.

Psalm 23

Psalm 23 with its expressions of confidence in God and its portrayal of overcoming turmoil has been selected as a text suitable to accompany the healing episode read from Acts as well as the text from John concerning sheep and shepherding. Although Psalm 23 probably is the best known and best loved of all the psalms, it provides the interpreter with numerous problems, especially with regard to how it was understood and used in ancient Israelite worship.

With an economy of words but with expressive and descriptive metaphors, Psalm 23 describes the relationship between God and worshiper and the sense of serenity that prevails when troubles have been overcome and resolution and repose prevail.

If we analyze Psalm 23 in terms of speaker and addressee, we find the following pattern: the worshiper confesses confidence in God apparently speaking to some human audience (verses 1-3); the worshiper addresses the Deity, stressing what God has done (verses 4-5); and finally, the worshiper again addresses the audience summarizing the person's assurance of divine favor (verse 5).

It is possible to understand the images of God in this psalm in two different ways. In one, he is the skillful and compassionate Shepherd who leads the worshiper like a good shepherd who cares for his sheep, a widespread view of both gods and kings in the Near East (verses 1-3). If the shepherd imagery in verses 2-4 is applied to verse 5, it can be said that the shepherd looks after the feeding and care of the sheep. Shepherds in the Middle East (Lebanon and Syria) used the expression, "to set the table," when referring to preparing fields for grazing. Such activities included uprooting poisonous weeds and thorns and clearing the area of the sheep's enemies such as snakes and scorpion's nests. In the evening as the sheep were corralled, the injured or sickly ones were separated from the others and treated with oil and a curative drink made of fermented material and herbs sweetened with honey. If one follows this line of interpretation, then the imagery of the shepherd runs throughout the psalm.

It is also possible to look at the psalm as presenting a double image of God, that of shepherd for the sheep (verses 1-3) and that of a human host for a guest (verses 4-5). (Note that this breaks the text between the section spoken to a human audience, verses 1-3, and that spoken to God directly, verses 4-5.) The image of God as host emphasizes not only the sufficiency of the Divine to feed but also the care which he takes to meet the other needs of the guest—anointing oil for the head and soothing cup for the psyche.

To decide between these two alternative interpretations is almost a matter of taste, although the latter is certainly found more widely in literature on the psalms.

If the psalm compares the experience of God and his care to that of a shepherd and/or a human host, then what does the imagery of the person's distresses refer to? That is, what happened to the worshiper? From what straits has he or she been saved? Some possibilities are: (1) one could see the imagery to be that of sheep changing or entering new pastures, thus the psalmist could be describing one of life's points of transition; (2) another view is to see the prayer as one offered by a wandering traveler who has safely returned to Jerusalem; (3) the entire imagery may be simply that of a worshiper who eats a sacrificial meal in the sanctuary; (4) a further alternative is to see all the imagery as merely verbal images without any exact frames of reference; and (5) a final interpretation suggests that this psalm may have been used by a fugitive guilty of manslaughter or accidental killing who took refuge and sought asylum in the temple and lives beyond the reach of the family of the deceased. (See Exod. 21:12-14; Deut. 19:1-13; I Kings 1:49-53; 2:28-35 for this practice.) Dwelling in the temple or house of God would thus be taken literally. There the fugitive could eat in the temple in the presence of his/her enemies.

Regardless of how one interprets the psalm, the general picture of what is stressed is quite clear. One who has known trouble or experienced life-threatening situations has also experienced the protection of the Divine. The psalm exudes confidence that God protects so that whatever life brings to his people, they will not be overwhelmed.

Preaching on this text, one could focus on the diverse expressions of human experience found in the psalm. One set emphasizes the troubles that threaten to overwhelm human life: valley of the shadow of death (or darkness or total darkness), evil, and enemies. Another set stresses the positive instruments and acts of God's care: green pastures, still waters, reviving of the soul, reliable paths, rod and staff, table, oil, and cup. Human life, of course, experiences both the negative and the positive. At times, even the Shepherd must use the rod and staff against his own sheep for their best interests.

This psalm presents the human predicament without any illusion about persons being superhumans and above pain, loneliness, and lostness; yet the symbol of God as protector and even corrector affirms the potential of a tranquil life lived amid adversaries and the harsh realities that are the ingredients of every life.

The closing verse affirms that goodness and mercy, not tribulation or ravenous enemies, shall be a constant companion. To dwell (or to return) to the house of Yahweh in this verse did not refer to immortality but to either residence in the temple (by a priest or a fugitive) or, if read as return, to a visit to the temple.

I John 3:18-24

Even though verse 18 most likely belongs with the preceding paragraph (so, Nestle, 26th ed.; RSV; though, cf. NEB and JB), it is a natural point to begin the pericope since it is the direct antecedent of the remarks in verses 19-24.

Several distinct yet interlocking themes emerge from today's epistolary lection:

1. True love is love exercised rather than love spoken (verse 18). It is one thing for love to be "a matter of words or talk," quite another for it to "show itself in action" (NEB). The supreme paradigm of active as opposed to spoken love is Christ who "laid down his life for us" (verse 16; cf. John 10:15). Somewhat related is the distinction made elsewhere in the New Testament between "hearing" and "doing" (cf. Matt. 7:21; Luke 12:47; Rom. 2:13; James 1:22; 4:11).

2. Active love is the sole basis of Christian assurance (verse 19). By loving "in deed" we come to know that we are "of the truth" (verse 19), or "that we belong to the realm of truth" (NEB), which, of course, is the realm embodied by Christ himself (cf. John 5:33; 8:40, 45; 16:7; 18:37; I John 2:21; II John 4).

3. The life of faith is not without dilemmas of conscience (verses 19-20). There is the recognition that even the Christian heart needs reassurance (verse 19*b*), and that there are times when our own hearts condemn us (verse 20*a*; cf. also 1:8-10; 2:1-2). To speak openly of the tensions of the inner life is merely to recognize what every sincere Christian knows: inward conflict is part and parcel of Christian experience. What sustains us, however, is the knowledge that "God is greater than our hearts, and . . . knows

everything" (verse 20*b*; John 21:17; I John 4:4; Ps. 103:14; cf. also I Cor. 4:4-5; 8:2-3; 13:12). If our love for God is genuine and expresses itself in our love for one another, even with our lapses of faith and their attendant pains of conscience, the omniscient God is able to see that these represent us at our atypical worst.

Before adopting this more positive interpretation of verses 19-20, the preacher should recognize that these verses are very difficult to understand. Closer exegesis will be required before one moves too quickly to proclamation. In a word, these verses may be read in at least two ways: (1) as words of hopeful reassurance, or (2) as a cautious warning against complacence.

4. Along with the conflict, there is also confidence (verses 21-22). These verses speak of the other dimension of Christian existence where the norm is confidence toward God (cf. 2:28; 4:17; 5:14; also Heb. 3:6; 4:16; 10:19, 35; also Rom. 5:1-2), and where such confidence enables us to engage in natural conversation with the God who has begotten us. We ask and God gives (cf. John 11:22; 14:13-14; 15:7, 16; 16:23-24, 26; I John 5:14-15; also cf. Matt. 7:7-11; 18:19; 21:22; Mark 11:24; James 1:5-6; Jer. 29:13-14; Prov. 8:17). Here, again, Jesus' relationship with his own Father becomes the paradigm (cf. John 11:41-42).

5. Reduced to its barest minimum, the Christian life consists of two things: faith and love (verse 23; cf. I Cor. 13:13). Neither of these is conceived as Christian virtues in the broad ethical sense. They are rather understood with specific reference to Jesus Christ. The faith called for here is faith in the name of his Son Jesus Christ (cf. John 1:12; 6:29; 20:31; I John 5:13). The love called for is the "new commandment" required by the Son who embodied self-giving love (cf. John 13:34; 15:12-13, 17; I John 2:7-11; 3:11; 4:7, 11-12; II John 5; also Gal. 6:2; I Pet. 1:22).

6. The prerequisite to sustained mystical union with God is filial obedience (verse 24; John 6:56; 14:20; 15:4-7; 17:23; I John 1:3; 2:24; 4:13-16), the express sign of which is the indwelling of God's own Spirit (John 16:7-15; I John 3:6; 4:13; 5:6-8; also Rom. 8:9; Acts 2:11, 32-33).

Today's epistolary lection, with its emphasis on confidence, directly echoes themes expressed in the reading from Acts. Similarly, its note of reassurance is also sounded in Psalm 23. The Gospel reading focuses on the active love of Christ who voluntarily lays down his "life for the sheep" (John 10:15). Today's readings blend well with one another and suggest various homiletical possibilities.

John 10:11-18

The preacher learns quickly that when dealing with the Fourth Gospel one must be careful not to assume that beautiful imagery means simplicity of thought. The fact is, the converse is more likely true. When Jesus speaks in images or figures (analogies, parables) the message is not clear at all. "I have said this to you in figures; the hour is coming when I shall no longer speak to you in figures but tell you plainly of the Father" (16:25). In John 10:11-18, Jesus refers to himself as the shepherd, which was, says the writer, a figure Jesus used with his listeners (verse 6).

We are, therefore, engaged today with a beautiful, familiar and yet complex passage. The commentaries will provide a discussion of the complexities. One difficulty is chronological. Does 10:1-21 belong with 10:22 ff., and therefore to be located in Jesus' ministry during the Feast of Dedication (10:22) or does 10:22 begin an entirely different episode? Another problem is literary. Does 10:1-21 belong with chapter 9 so that we may assume the same audience? With such uncertainties, it seems wisest not to tie 10:1-21 too closely to what precedes or follows. The passage has its own integrity and probably is best interpreted without drawing upon the larger context.

Our Gospel lesson, John 10:11-18, is the third of four sub-units in 10:1-21. The first, verses 1-6, is replete with images of the shepherd, the door, thieves, and robbers. The second, verses 7-10, seems to be a commentary on verses 1-6. The fourth sub-unit, verses 19-21, is the familiar summary of mixed responses to Jesus' speech. Our text, verses 11-18, is less complex than the first two sub-units, leaving behind the images of thief, robber, shepherd, door, and gatekeeper and focusing on the single contrast between a shepherd and a hireling.

In verses 11-18, Jesus is presented as the model shepherd giving his life as the ultimate act of caring. This act of love stands out impressively against the dark backdrop of hired workers who, at the slightest threat of danger, abandon the sheep. This passage may recall the story of David risking his life against bear and lion in behalf of the sheep (I Sam. 17:34-35). In the early church, this model of Christ as shepherd was held up before pastors, urging them to care for the flock in spite of the dangers of false teachers (Acts 20:28-30) or violent persecution (I Pet. 5:1-2). The Johannine church, facing social and religious ostracism and even death at the hands of fanatics claiming to be God's servants (15:18-25; 16:1-4), was surely challenged and encouraged by this image of Jesus, just as it was warned about pastors-for-pay who resign quickly when difficulties arise. In fact, there has never been a time in the history of the church when there were not faithful shepherds who, like Jesus, gave their lives for the flock. Before Roman sword or Nazi boot, burning cross or constant harassment, economic pressure or political reprisal, they remained with the sheep. And then there are the hirelings.

One note in closing. Scholars are not of one mind in identifying the "other sheep . . . not of this fold" (verse 16). Most interpreters take one of three views. One, this is a reference to the Gentile mission, a concern certainly underscored elsewhere in this Gospel (11:52; 12:19-24). Two, this is an expression of Jesus' desire to have all his followers united as one flock under one shepherd. This view assumes that already at the time of this Gospel there were many circles of Christianity moving apart from one another. Such groups probably formed around various leaders: Peter, Paul, James, Apollos, and others. There is no question but that this passion for the unity of believers is found in this Gospel; in fact, it is a major theme in Jesus' prayer in chapter 17. Three, the "other sheep" may be understood as subsequent generations of believers who were to regard themselves as members of the original body of disciples. These, too, receive this Evangelist's attention elsewhere (17:20; 20:29). The preacher whose sermon moves in any one of these three directions will not violate the love and care of the Good Shepherd.

Fifth Sunday of Easter

Acts 8:26-40; Psalm 22:25-31; I John 4:7-12; John 15:1-8

Acts 8:26-40

This story of the conversion of the Ethiopian eunuch is a superb illustration of Luke's storytelling ability. It is a tightly crafted literary piece, with fine attention to detail. We are given the crucial essentials: time (noon), place (deserted road, chariot), character (the Ethiopian, a eunuch, minister of the queen, god-fearer who had traveled to Jerusalem to worship), and plot (an inquiring searcher has his questions answered and his life changed).

We also see in the story some of the major themes of Luke's theology:

1. The Holy Spirit as the primary catalyst in the extension of the Gospel into the world (Acts 2:4; 4:8, 31; 9:17; 13:9, 52). Here, it is the Spirit who, in the form of an angel of the Lord, speaks directly to Philip, instructing him concerning his mission (cf. 10:19; 11:12; 13:2; 21:11). Throughout Acts we see evidence of the Spirit's direction (11:28; 15:28; 20:23; 21:4). As the story begins with the Spirit, so it ends with the Spirit snatching up Philip for mission work in other parts (cf. Ezek. 11:24; I Kings 18:12; II Kings 2:16; II Cor. 12:2, 4; I Thess. 4:17). The picture painted here is consistent with that seen throughout Acts: even after the Lord ascended, he remained at work through his Spirit, motivating his messengers and extending the frontiers of the kingdom.

2. The universal impact of the Gospel as it breaks through geographical and ethnic barriers, reaching beyond Jerusalem to Samaria, even to Ethiopia (cf. Luke 1:29-32; 24:27; Acts 1:8). This too represents a fulfillment of the Old Testament hope which envisioned a time when foreigners would come to the

house of God to worship (I Kings 8:41-43; also cf. Ps. 68:31; Zeph. 3:10). The story is inclusive in another sense. The primary character is a eunuch who, according to Deuteronomy 23:1, should be excluded from the assembly of the Lord (cf. also Isa. 56:3-7). Here, he has not only joined other God-fearers who were attracted to the worship of the one God of Israel (Acts 10:2, 35; 13:16, 26), but is baptized and incorporated into the people of God and returns home rejoicing (verse 39). This incident becomes one scene in the large tapestry woven by Luke to depict the inclusion of the Gentiles into the people of God (Acts 2:39; 11:18; 13:46-48; 28:26-29).

3. The theme of promise-fulfillment with Jesus as the interpretive key unlocking the meaning of the Old Testament scriptures (Luke 24:27, 44-45). The interpretation of Isaiah 53:7-8 is a central element of the story (verses 32-33), a story that shows both how Jesus serves to make sense of the Old Testament and how the Old Testament serves to make sense of Jesus as well as the disciples' experience of the Easter faith (cf. Acts 17:2, 11; 18:24, 28; I Cor. 15:3). In Luke-Acts, the promise-fulfillment theme is worked out on several levels. On the one hand, Jesus is presented as the fulfillment of the Old Testament promises, as the one of whom Isaiah spoke. On the other hand, at various points in the narrative, e.g., in the Gospel, promises are made and fulfilled at a later point, e.g., in Acts. The preaching of the Gospel to the Ethiopian eunuch, taking place as it does in Samaria, fulfills the promise made earlier by the Risen Lord (Acts 1:8).

One way of appropriating the story homiletically might be to focus on the two central characters, the eunuch and Philip, treating them respectively as paradigms for the earnest inquirer and the faithful messenger of God.

A character sketch of the eunuch might include the following observations: (1) his initial inclination toward faith in God, seen in his status as a god-fearer willing to journey to Jerusalem to worship; (2) his searching in the Scriptures and the commendable trait of his questioning spirit which included not only his willingness to ask searching questions but the ability to ask the right ones; (3) his eagerness for divine guidance (cf. John 16:13; Rom. 10:14); and (4) his

Asking the Right Questions

initiative in following through his quest by requesting baptism.

A complementary sketch of Philip might include the following elements: (1) his responsiveness to the Spirit (verses 26, 29, 39); (2) his forthrightness in asking penetrating questions (verse 30); and (3) his knowledge of the Scripture and skill in interpretation (verse 35).

These are naturally only suggestions, but perhaps they will point to ways in which the modern reader can relive this episode on a deserted road and identify with these ancient figures in whom the Easter faith lived.

Psalm 22:25-31

Portions of this psalm, emphasizing its passages on suffering, humiliation, and passion, comprised one of the readings for Good Friday. The present lection emphasizes those passages in the psalm that speak of vindication and celebration. The break between the two main portions of the psalm comes after verse 22 which comprises the supplicant's vow. From verse 23 on, the psalm is concerned with celebration and praise not humiliation and supplication. How can we account for this radically different content of the psalm and the radical break following verse 22?

One way of reading the psalm in its totality is to see verses 1-22 as a prayer for help which was followed by a priestly oracle assuring the worshiper that God had heard and answered the request. Note that the last line of verse 24 declares that God has heard. Verses 23-31 are thus the psalmist's celebration and fulfillment of the vow made in verse 22.

The material in verses 23-31 falls into the following categories: (1) appeal to a human audience calling upon the people to praise God (verses 23-24), (2) worshiper's prayer of thanks to God (verse 25*a*), and (3) proclamation to the human audience of the consequences of the salvation that has been experienced (verses 25*b*-31).

In verse 25*a*, the worshiper interprets the praise now offered as coming from God. Since this is addressed to the Deity, such a statement represents an indirect form of thanksgiving. The great congregation before whom praise and proclamation are offered would be the worshipers assembled in the temple for a festival or for some royal celebration of victory or recovery if the user of this psalm was the king. In the earlier vow (verse 22), the worshiper promised to "tell of thy name to my brethren; in the midst of the congregation I will praise thee." What is referred to here is the participation in a thanksgiving ritual that included sacrifice and thanksgiving as well as the "offering testimony" concerning God's saving power and his redemption. The offering of testimony plays a significant role in Israelite worship and to some extent parallels types of testimonials frequently heard in churches a generation or so ago.

Two characteristics of offering testimony in the psalms should be noted. First of all, testimony was given in rather stereotyped language which described the distress from which a person had been saved in general rather than specific terms. This style was used so the same psalms, probably written by cultic officials or priests instead of individual worshipers, could be used repeatedly. The use of stereotypical and metaphorical language allowed the worshipers to plumb their misery in great depth and to describe it in more colorful and dramatic language than would have been the case if they merely recited the realistic details of their turmoil.

Second, the testimony offered moved into the realm of what might be called proclamation or preaching. That is, worshipers were allowed and encouraged, even required, to speak about the dire straits from which they had recovered and also to preach to the audience of friends and family at the thanksgiving ceremony.

The fulfillment of vows are spoken of in verses 25*b*-26 where persons are called upon not only to share in the praise but also to eat and be satisfied. Th afflicted or poor in verse 26 may refer to persons of this class or perhaps to those persons who sought asylum in the sanctuary and thus lived off the services of the temple. The sharing of food in lavish form is, as every mother knows, a universal act expressive of well-being and contentment. Note that in the psalm "sharing follows receiving" and is a gesture of the blessed to incorporate others into the blessing. The Old Testament has a special concern for the poor and afflicted so much so that orphans, widows, and others were allowed to share in the tithes and sacrifices of others (see Deut. 14:29; 16:10-14; 26:12).

The consequences of the worshiper's salvation and thanksgiving, given in verses 27-31, suggest that the person involved was the king, since the salvation of a single ordinary individual would not have had the universal implications noted in these verses. These royal features, of course, made it easy to apply this psalm to Christ or to use it for understanding him.

Although the text of verses 27-31 contains many problems and makes translation somewhat difficult, what it suggests is rather clear. First of all, there is reference to the universal impact of the situation. The "ends of the earth" is a way of saying everywhere. The text states that people throughout the world will worship Yahweh, the God of Israel. (This seems to have been a common expectation held in the cult and court of Jerusalem; see Isa. 2:1-4 and Mic. 4:1-4.) As king in Jerusalem, Yahweh was also king over the nations of the world.

Verse 29 seems to imply that perhaps even the dead or at least the dying will also bow down before him (God). This idea may sound farfetched but the Apostles' Creed declares that Jesus descended into hell (see I Pet. 3:18-20).

Not only the present (verses 27-28) and past generations (verse 29) but also generations yet to come shall tell of the redemption of Yahweh and proclaim his deliverance to generations yet to be born. The missionary and universal tone of this psalm is one of its key characteristics.

I John 4:7-12

Endearing terms are used to introduce this poignant exhortation to love, which divides naturally in two parts: verses 7-10, the exhortation itself (note the hortatory subjunctive "let us love"), which may be an early Christian hymn (it is printed strophically in Nestle, 26th ed.); and verses 11-12, further reflections on the exhortation. Both are introduced with "beloved," the form of address frequently used in the epistle; the word itself is expressive of the theme of love.

These verses reflect the utter realism of the author who knows too well that Christian communities need to be encouraged to love one another. As the author's later remarks indicate, he understands that the Christian fellowship can be permeated with hate, and what's more, Christians can make the dubious claim of living in the love of God while at the same time exercising active ill-will toward one another (verses 20-21).

Such an impassioned plea for mutual love within the Christian fellowship may be directly related to his previous remarks, which actually form a digression (verses 1-6). The author has just spoken of the need to be discriminating in listening to prophetic utterances. Earlier, he warned against the Gnostic threat, noting that false teachers had originally been part of the Johannine community, but they had now left (2:18-25, esp. 19). The debilitating effects of doctrinal disputes are well-known, and doubtless the Johannine community had been seared by such disputes. If modern examples of such disputes are any indication of the dynamics at work within the community, we can surmise that members had taken sides, positions had become polarized, and heated debates had characteristically degenerated into *ad hominem* verbal assaults. That we have not exaggerated the situation is suggested by the other two Johannine epistles (cf. esp. III John 10).

The exhortation to love is straightforward and recalls similar teaching by the Johannine Jesus (John 13:34; 15:9, 12-13, 17; also I John 2:7-8; II John 5; cf. also Gal. 6:2; I Pet. 1:22; I Thess. 4:9). Of interest here is the basis given for the exhortation.

1. God is the source of love: "Love is of God" (verse 7). Love as it is presented here, does not, and cannot, derive from our own human capacities. Rather it stems from God's own initiative. It is not "that we loved God but that he loved us" (verse 10). Fundamental to the Johannine outlook is the notion that love is properly understood, not as a universal human emotion inherent within the evolutionary process, but as something that transcends us and originates beyond

us. God must be understood as prior to ourselves, especially in love (4:19; also cf. Deut. 7:8; Wis. 6:16; Matt. 18:33; Rom. 8:31-32; II Thess. 2:16).

2. God is the essence of love: "God is love" (verse 8). We should not understand this to mean that God is an abstract principle, as the Greeks understood it. The proper background here is the Hebrew understanding of Deity as a dynamic personal Force who acts, rather than is. To say that God is love is equivalent to saying that God *loves*, in the sense that all the acts of God through and in history have been directed toward our ultimate well-being. Nor has the love of God been hidden and inscrutable, but has become "manifest among us" in the giving of his Son (verse 9; also I John 1:2; John 1:4; Rom 3:21). Here we hear a direct echo of John 3:16, and perhaps an indirect echo of the sacrifice of Isaac (Gen. 22:12; cf. also John 1:14, 18; Matt. 21:37; Rom. 8:32; Heb. 11:17).

3. Our human capacity to love is derivative not original: "He who loves is born of God" (verse 7). To be able to love as God loved when he sent his Son is possible only through divine regeneration of (cf. I John 2:29; 3:9; 5:1, 4, 18; also John 1:13). When we love, it is only proof that a divine seed has been sown in us.

4. Knowledge of God is properly defined only in terms of love (verse 8). The tendency among Gnostics was to elevate knowledge to an unqualified virtue, so much so that it became essentially an act of the head not of the heart. Paul, for example, reminds gnostically inclined Christians that knowledge should be combined with love (I Cor. 8:1-3), observing that "knowledge puffs up," while "love builds up." Thus, whatever one might claim, this text insists that the one"who does not love does not know God" (verse 8). Closely linked with the knowledge of God is the vision of God, which, in certain mystical traditions, can be achieved largely through human powers of concentration and religious devotion. We are thus reminded that "no one has ever seen God" (cf. Exod. 33:20; John 1:18; 5:37; 6:46; 14:9; 17:24; also I Tim. 1:17). This may be seen as another way of saying that whatever knowledge we have is partial (cf. I Cor. 13:9-13). The way in which true and sustained union with

God occurs is through our love for one another (verse 12). In this way, God's love comes to complete expression (cf. 1:7; 2:5; 4:17-18; 5:3). This too may be an indirect slap at the Gnostics for whom perfection was essentially a mental act.

There are obvious affinities between today's epistolary reading and the Gospel reading from John, especially if the latter is extended through verse 11. The vine and branches metaphor may be fruitfully explored as the means for achieving union with the Father through love.

John 15:1-8

On this and the remaining two Sundays of the Easter Season the Gospel lessons will be drawn from the farewell discourses and prayer of Jesus in the Gospel of John (chapters 14–17). This may be the point at which to comment briefly about the nature of that material and the approach the preacher may take.

Chapters 14–17 address the question, What does the Risen and departing Christ have to say to his church? We can expect, therefore, that this section will be rich in assurances, warnings, instructions, and promises. However, the form of the material presents difficulties for the preacher. There are frequent and lengthy repetitions which may best be handled by gathering the subject matter under themes such as promises, the work of the Spirit, warnings of dangers to come, and so forth. In addition, the task of subdividing the material into clear and meaningful units is difficult because of the absence of the usual transitional signals (shifts of time, place, activity, or audience). Commentaries will differ, but the preacher can usually discover controlling images or governing themes that will enable divisions of the text without violation of its sense.

Creators of the lectionary surely experienced these difficulties in deciding upon 15:1-8 as our reading for today. One could argue for verses 1-6 as a unit since the vine and branches imagery shifts at verse 7 to the categories of love and obedience. The RSV makes paragraphs of verses 1-11 and verses 12-17, the NEB makes units of verses 1-4, 5-6, 7-10, and 11-17. Verse 18 clearly is a transition point. Our lection, verses 1-8, has the double advantage of a controlling image and a central verb. The image is that of the vineyard which, like that of the shepherd in chapter 10, evoked rich associations with the Hebrew Scriptures and with everyday life. The vine image is, in Johannine terms, a "figure" (in contrast to direct speech), a form of speaking which we discussed last Sunday in considering John 10:11-18. The central verb is "abide," one of the most significant words in this Gospel. A concordance will lead the reader to meaningful expressions such as "Teacher, where do you abide?"; "they abode with him that day"; "Jesus abode with them for two days"; "in my Father's house are many abiding places"; "my Father and I will come and abide with you." But here in 15:1-8 the word reaches its peak in frequency of use.

Two messages in this text are inescapable. One has to do with the relationship of Christ to the church. That the relationship is possible, whatever the terms used to characterize it, is a gift of grace and the occasion for gratitude and joy. That the relationship is necessary is evident both in Scripture and in experience. Without it, the church is powerless (verses 4-5), wordless (verses 3, 7), prayerless (verse 7), fruitless (verses 2-8), and hopeless (verses 2, 6). The purpose of the relationship is primarily to bear fruit. What is meant by fruit is not specified. However, the search for a definition would best be pursued not in Paul ("the fruit of the Spirit," Gal. 5:22-23) but within this Gospel. For example, in 12:20-27 fruit-bearing refers to preaching and witnessing to the gospel among all nations. That understanding could hardly be inappropriate here.

The second clear message in this text centers on the often neglected statement, "My Father is the vinedresser" (verse 1). The vinedresser comes into the vineyard with a knife and every plant is severely cut. Some are cut away ("takes away," verse 2) because they are fruitless and some are pruned (verse 2; the Greek words for "take away" and "prune" are variations on the same root word) in order to be more fruitful. But how is the church to know the difference? Both experiences are painful. Is it not the case that pruning (severing of debilitating relationships, loss of burdensome things, cessation of meaningless pursuits) is often understood as being cut away from God, leaving believers hurt, confused, and angry? Perhaps the Johannine church, experiencing such extreme difficulties (16:1-4), needed to be reminded that they could be undergoing pruning for greater fruitfulness. Churches that move through hardships to increased commitment to the mission have, indeed, been pruned. Those that pull back in concern for their own comfort and security have, indeed, been taken away.

Sixth Sunday of Easter

Acts 10:44-48; Psalm 98; I John 5:1-6;
John 15:9-17

Acts 10:44-48

Today's text focuses our attention more directly on the work of the Holy Spirit in the life of the church as we approach the end of the Easter Season and move toward Pentecost.

For Luke, the breakthrough event in the life of the early church was the conversion of Cornelius (10:1–11:18). This is seen not only by the amount of space he devotes to the episode, but also by its placement in the overall narrative. It is genuinely transitional and pivotal in the story line, coming immediately after the conversion of Saul (9:1-30) and setting the stage for his mission work among the Gentiles (cf. 11:25-26; 12:25). It also represents a "double narrative," for the story told in chapter 10 is repeated, in summary form, in chapter 11. It figures prominently in Luke's overall depiction of the incorporation of the Gentiles into the people of God (11:1, 18; 13:48; 14:27; 15:7, 11; 28:23-29). In fact, the episode ends on this triumphant note: "And they [the Jewish Christians in Jerusalem] glorified God, saying, 'Then to the Gentiles also God has granted repentance unto life'" (11:18*b*).

Our passage today occurs at the end of Peter's sermon preached before the house of Cornelius in Caesarea. We are told that during the very course of Peter's sermon (10:34-43), "the Holy Spirit fell on all who heard the word" (verses 44; 11:15). This has puzzled many commentators, because it breaks the pattern. Normally, in Acts believers receive the Holy Spirit *after* they have heard the Word proclaimed, and in conjunction with their baptism (cf. 2:38; 5:32). But, surely the important question is not *when* the Holy Spirit engulfed them, but why. This is at least the question that the text makes central.

As the text suggests, what was significant was that the six Jewish Christians, "the believers from among the circumcised" (verse 45; cf. 11:2; Gal. 2:11), who had accompanied Peter to Caesarea, witnessed this spiritual outpouring. Clearly, its effects were audible: "For they heard them speaking in tongues and extolling God" (verse 46; cf. 2:4, 11; 19:6; Mark 16:17; I Cor. 14). No doubt, we are to understand this as ecstatic utterances and not foreign languages. As the text unfolds, we hear echoes of the account of Pentecost in Acts 2: the coming of the Spirit and the speaking in tongues. For this reason it is often referred to as "the Pentecost of the Gentiles." And it is clear that Luke wants the reader to understand it this way.

From Peter's remarks in chapter 11, it was also a moment of illumination for him. He noticed, too, that the Holy Spirit fell on the Gentiles assembled (11:15), but this triggered his memory. He recalled "the word of the Lord, how he said, 'John baptized with water, but you shall be baptized with the Holy Spirit.'" (verse 16). He could only conclude that what he and the other apostles had experienced at Pentecost, the Gentiles were now experiencing. They were now both witnessing and experiencing the breaking in of the messianic kingdom of God whose earmark, as expected and predicted, was the coming of the Holy Spirit (Joel 2:28-32). To have excluded them from formal initiation into the kingdom of God by preventing their baptism with water would have been tantamount to "withstanding God" (cf. Mark 3:28-30 and parallels).

Worth noting at this point are the ingredients of Peter's own "conversion": (1) he witnessed again the coming of the Holy Spirit, which reminded him of Pentcost; (2) he recalled "the word of the Lord" and interpreted this experience in light of it; (3) he drew the inevitable conclusion: God has been at work among the Gentiles; and (4) he conformed his practice to his newly informed perspective; he instructed the Gentiles to be baptized with water (10:48; cf. 8:36; 11:16; Matt. 3:14; Mark 1:4 and parallels).

We should also note that the believers were baptized in a manner conforming to the new realities of the messianic kingdom which they had experienced; they were "baptized . . . in the name of Jesus Christ" (cf. 2:38; 8:16; 19:5).

This incident is illuminating in several respects, most notably in the way it depicts a shift in perspective, not only for Peter but for the resistant Jewish Christians—a shift from exclusiveness to inclusiveness. At first they were truculent (11:3), but finally they rejoice (11:18). Not surprisingly, Luke stresses the role of the Holy Spirit in enabling these Jewish Christians to transcend their own narrow vision of the kingdom. The sermon based on this text might well address the narrowness of modern conceptions of the church which are more keen to find ways to exclude than to include.

Psalm 98

Psalm 98 is one of a group of psalms (47,93, 96–99) which proclaim the enthronement and kingship of God. Various motifs are found in these psalms: Yahweh as king, the judgment of the world, the stabilization of the created world, and the universal rule of God. The selection of Psalm 98 to be read in conjunction with Acts 10:44-48 was made on the basis of the concern of both texts with the universal aspects of God's salvation.

Verses 1-3 call upon the people to sing to Yahweh a new song to celebrate his victory. What victory is the text concerned with? Different answers have been given to this question: (1) the redemption from Egypt, (2) the return of the Jews from exile, (3) some victory in warfare, (4) the creation of the world, or (5) the annual celebration of God's creation of the world. The latter seems the most likely possibility. Such an interpretation assumes that every year at the fall feast of tabernacles, the people led by the king, celebrated Yahweh's rule as king over history, the nations, and creation. Since this was the time of the new year, the festival celebrated the creation of the world and it was assumed that Yahweh re-created the world and reestablished the orders of creation at this time. (If the idea that God annually created the world sounds unusual, we should compare it with the fact that we sing every Christmas that Christ was born today!) As creator, he thus ruled as king and judge over the whole of creation. The victory would thus be God's triumph over chaos or disorder and his establishment of cosmos or order in the universe. In many ancient cultures, it was assumed that the creation of order involved the victory of the Creator God over the powers of disorder and chaos (see Ps. 89:9-10). Every year, order had to be reestablished, the hostile powers subdued, and a new beginning made. What God did in his victory is related both to Israel and the nations (the Gentiles) and thus has a universal quality about it.

Verses 4-6 call for the whole earth to praise and sing to Yahweh, with various musical instruments, because Yahweh is the universal king. Interpreters of the Bible used to assume that the idea that God ruled over the world developed rather late in Israel. One can assume, however, that this was a very old idea and that God's kingship was celebrated in the Jerusalem temple from the time of David. It is true that Yahweh did not actually rule over the whole world, that is, his worshipers were not universal nor did his people rule the whole world. This did not prevent the cult from proclaiming this fact. In a sense, one might say that such proclamations were "predictions" or facts to be realized.

The final verses of the psalm (7-9) talk about the roaring of the sea and the world, floods clapping their hands and hills singing for joy before Yahweh. Here we are obviously in the realm of metaphorical speech. But it is speech that is right at home when talking about the creation of the world. Thus it is a call for the natural and human world to accept the fact that Yahweh is judge, that is, that Yahweh establishes and upholds order in the world of the universe.

The problem of the particular (the elect, the chosen, the people of God, the Jews) versus the universal (the outsiders, the non-elect, the Gentiles) in religion has always plagued believers. The early church had to struggle with universalization of its faith and the inclusion of Gentiles. Such psalms as 98 demonstrate that the Old Testament itself already had strong universal interests and inclinations incorporated within its pages—a universalism that dares to challenge any totally exclusivistic reading of the work of God in the world.

I John 5:1-6

Favorite Johannine themes are interwoven into this passage, any one of which could be connected with other passages in both the Fourth Gospel and the Epistles and developed in its own right: believing, knowing, loving, obeying, begetting, and overcoming. They are all listed here in their participial form as a way of emphasizing their dynamic quality. John, for example, prefers the verb "believe" *(pisteuō)* to the noun "faith" *(pistis)*, for the former captures the active and dynamic force of the concept in a way the latter does not.

This text opens with the favorite Johannine couplet: "believing and knowing" (verses 1-2; cf. 3:23-24). The object of believing, in this case, is the confesson "that Jesus is the Christ" (cf. 2:2; Acts 5:42; 9:22; 17:3; 18:5, 28). A variation of this confession is repeated in verse 5, the one "who believes that Jesus is the Son of God." So much emphasis is placed on this confession here that we are probably still hearing echoes of the Gnostic denial of the humanity of Christ (cf. 2:18-25; 4:1-6). This likely explains, in part at least, the emphasis on the "water and blood" in verse 6: "This is [the one] who came by water and blood, Jesus Christ, not with the water only but with the water and the blood" (cf. Matt. 3:16 and parallels; John 1:31, 33; 19:34). Once again, the author is insisting on the undeniable humanity of Jesus.

Not merely the content of the confession, but its creative power should be noticed. The one who believes in this confession "is a child of God" (RSV), literally, "has been begotten of God." The notion of divine begetting is, of course, a central Johannine concept (John 3:3; 8:42; I John 2:29; 3:9; 5:4, 18; also John 1:13). For John, coming to believe in Christ can only be understood properly as an act of God (John 6:44). It is that which God initiates rather than that which we come to intuitively.

Closely connected with "believing" is "loving": "every one who loves the parent loves the child," or literally, "every one who loves the begetter also loves the begotten (verse 1*b*). This recalls the exhortation to love given earlier in the letter (4:7; cf. comments on epistolary lection for the Fifth Sunday of Easter), as well as the comments immediately preceding concerning the impossibility of loving an invisible God while hating a visible neighbor.

How, then, may we know that we actually love God's children? (verse 2). By loving God and keeping his commandments, which appear to be one and the same thing. Again, the author's instructions are hard and practical: they lay great stress on commandment keeping (cf. 1:6; 2:3, 9; 4:20; John 14:15; 15:16; 21:23; II John 6; also cf. Titus 1:16; Wis. 6:18). As he goes ahead to say, "This is the love of God," that is, "This is the [way we show the] love we have for God" (objective genitive)—by keeping his commandments. Realizing, perhaps, that this may sound too heavy-handed, he pauses to note that God's commandments are not "burdensome" (RSV, NEB), or "difficult" (JB). (Cf.Deut. 30:11; Matt. 11:25-30.)

At this point, the text moves to another theme: overcoming the world (verses 4-6). The Johannine world is sharply dualistic, with the "world" seen as the major adversary of believers. Similarly, our struggle is with the chief adversary of the world, the Devil himself, and in this respect represents an extension of Jesus' own struggle (cf. John 16:33; I John 2:13; 4:4; also I Cor. 15:57). The believer is promised victory in this cosmic struggle (I John 4:4; also Rom. 8:37; Eph. 6:16), but it is predicated on proper understanding of the identity of Christ, that is, the confession of his humanity (verse 5).

In the final verse, we are introduced to the work of the Spirit: "And the Spirit is the witness, because the Spirit is the truth" (verse 7), and this links directly with the reading from Acts 10:44-47. The Spirit as the one who leads into all truth is traceable to the Johannine Jesus (cf. John 4:23; 14:17; 16:13), and we should note the important distinction in the Fourth Gospel between the promise made by the historical Jesus and the bestowal of the Spirit made by the Risen Lord (John 20:22). The Spirit is promised before Easter but not bestowed until after Easter; this is the Johannine way of showing the distinctive difference the resurrection made for the life of faith.

By linking the work of the Spirit with the Johannine understanding of victorious faith, the preacher can expound this text both looking back to Easter and forward to Pentecost.

John 15:9-17

It may be helpful to the preacher to review the introductory comments on John 15:1-8 for last Sunday before moving to verses 9-17. Again, the difficulty of identifying units without violating the integrity of a passage or wresting it wrongfully from its context is with us. However, it seems safe to say that today's lection consists of two parts: verses 9-11 center in the expression "abide in my love"; verses 12-17 are a distinct unit in that they form an inclusion, a literary form in which the beginning and the ending are the same. In both verse 12 and verse 17 the disciples are commanded to "love one another." A case can be made, however, for treating these two subunits together in that the same key words occur throughout and verses 12-17 seem to be an elaboration upon the theme of verses 9-11. We will approach the passage by attending to the key terms within it: abide, love, joy, commandment, friends.

The departing Christ, who has promised not to leave his disciples orphaned (14:18), bridges the distance between himself glorified in God's presence and the church on earth. The key word is "abide" which we explored in last Sunday's lection. The word characterizes a relationship of trust, knowledge, love, and unity, that exists between Christ and God. While on earth Christ was able to remain or to abide in God from whom he came. In the same way the disciples will be able to abide in Christ even after he has returned to God. Abiding in Christ and in Christ's love (verses 9-10) is similar to Paul's characterization of life "in Christ Jesus" (Phil. 2:5). The love of Christ is the arena, the sphere, the location of Christian living.

To be understood here, "love" *(agapē)* has to overcome the many popular overuses and misuses of the word. The word here does not represent a feeling primarily nor is it a synonym for "like." To love is to be *for* another and to act *for* another, even at cost to oneself. The supreme act of love is the giving of one's life for the other (verse 13). The primary canon by which love for one another is measured is God's love for the world (3:16) and Christ's love which carried out in full and final obedience that love of God.

To live in the world and yet within the constancy of this love is to know the joy (verse 11) of which Christ speaks. This joy has its source in God whose presence is sometimes described as joy. ("Enter into the joy of your [Lord]," Matt. 25:21, 23; "the joy . . . set before him," Heb. 12:2.) Given the hatred and hostility of the world (verses 18-25), this word of assurance enables the church not simply to survive but to flourish in fullness of life.

The word "commandment," frequent in these farewell discourses and also in today's epistle (I John 5:1-6), needs special attention for two reasons.

First, this Gospel actually contains surprisingly little moral or ethical instruction such as we find in Matthew. What are the commandments to which Jesus refers (verse 10)? He kept God's commandments and we are to keep Christ's. It is best not to rush to another Gospel to find a few commandments to put to the people. For this Evangelist it is enough to say that we have the model of Jesus who came to do God's will which he obeyed even to death (verse 10) and that the one clearly stated commandment in the discourse is to love one another. The writer apparently understands that this command includes and fulfills all others. What that means in each given situation can be known by those who abide in God's love and who are taught by the Spirit (14:26).

The second reason the word "commandment" needs attention is that it is repeatedly associated with love, not only as the motivation for keeping the commandment, but as the very content of the commandment. We do not easily associate love or friendship with command (verse 14). For many of us love and friendship lie in the feelings and no one can command feeling; we do not even command our own.

But it is helpful to recall that love in this Gospel is not a feeling, rather it is being for the other person and acting accordingly. Emotions are not absent, of course, but neither are they central.

And what about friends? Do friends obey (verse 14)? Servants obey. In what sense are disciples no longer servants (verse 15)? Certainly not in the sense that they have graduated from doing for others what love dictates. There is no upward mobility in the kingdom; otherwise the footwashing by Jesus and the frequent reminder that a servant is not greater than the master (12:26; 13:16; 15:20) would be meaningless. Followers of Jesus are the friends of Jesus in that they know what he is doing (verse 15). Jesus has made God known to them. From this context, Jesus' followers make their prayers, asking what they will because what they will is bathed in the knowledge and love of God (verses 7, 16). But let the church beware: wherever a strong sense of community ("our church is like a family") prevails, elitism and exclusivism can creep in and make outsiders of everyone else.

A final word. Notice how all these significant terms: love, abiding, obedience, friendship, and joy are set within an order of continuity. The sequence—from God, through Christ, to the church— is clear and vital. In case anyone missed it, Jesus gathers it up in a statement that both assures and warns the church: "You did not choose me, but I chose you and appointed you" (verse 16).

Ascension Day

Acts 1:1-11; Psalm 47; Ephesians 1:15-23;
Luke 24:46-53 or *Mark 16:9-16, 19-20*

Acts 1:1-11

Of the many New Testament passages that speak of Christ's ascension, this narrative account by Luke is the most descriptive. Among the Gospels, Matthew contains no tradition relating to the ascension, nor does Mark in its first edition. A later supplement to Mark notes, "So then the Lord Jesus, after he had spoken to them, was taken up [*anelēmphthē*] into heaven, and sat down at the right hand of God" (Mark 16:19). The Fourth Gospel anticipates the Lord's ascension, but makes no attempt to record it (John 3:13; 6:62; 20:17). The fact that the Risen Lord instructs Thomas to touch him seems to imply that he had already ascended (20:27; cf. 20:17). Luke alone of the Gospel writers provides a narrative account of the Lord's ascension, in fact records it twice, once at the end of the Gospel (Luke 24:50-53; cf. also 9:51) and here at the beginning of Acts (1:2, 6-11, 22).

Oddly, the two Lukan accounts are discrepant. In the Gospel account, the ascension occurs on Easter Sunday, as do all the events recorded in Luke 24, whereas in Acts 1 it appears to occur at the end of a forty-day period of appearances by the Risen Lord (1:3). To be sure, the account in Acts is not clear on this point. It may very well imply that Christ, having ascended on Easter Sunday, at various times appeared *from heaven* to the disciples, though the narrative seems to suggest that *the* ascension took place at the end of the forty-day period. The early church recognized these difficulties, as seen by the complicated textual tradition relating to Luke 24:50-53 and Acts 1:6-11.

Within other strata of the New Testament, the tradition of Christ's ascension is known, though variously conceived. Quite often, the resurrection of Christ and his ascension are conceived as a single "exaltation," with no clear attempt made to differentiate them as separate events (cf. Rom. 1:4; 10:6; Phil. 2:9; Eph. 4:8-10; I Pet. 3:22; Heb. 4:14; 7:26; esp. I Tim. 3:16).

In Lukan theology, however, resurrection and ascension begin to be regarded as separate stages of Christ's exaltation (cf. Acts 2:32-33). Psalm 110 becomes crucial in early Christian interpretations of Christ's exaltation, as do other enthronement psalms (cf. the Psalter reading for today). This theological separation thus is expressed in narrative form in Luke 24 and Acts 1. The historical development of the celebration of Ascension Day as a separate feast day may be regarded as a legitimate liturgical expression of the tendency we already detect within the New Testament itself.

Even though the ascension of Christ is given separate treatment in Luke-Acts, it is striking how restrained Luke's narrative description is. Compared with later apocryphal accounts, such as that found in the apocryphal Gospel of Peter, Luke's account is "unsentimental, almost uncannily austere" (Haenchen).

Today's text falls into two parts: (1) the preface (verses 1-5), which recalls the earlier preface in the Gospel of Luke (Luke 1:1-4), and (2) the account of the ascension (verses 6-11).

The Preface. Several features should be noted here: (1) the reference to the beginning of the ministry of Jesus (cf. Luke 3:23; Acts 1:22; 10:37); (2) the Risen Lord's commandment through the Holy Spirit to the apostles whom he had chosen (cf. Matt. 28:20); (3) the emphasis on the Risen Lord as "living" (*zōnta*, verse 3) after his passion; (4) his appearances during forty days (cf. Acts 13:31) during which he preached the kingdom of God (cf. Acts 28:31); (5) his table fellowship with the disciples (taking verse 4 as "when he had been at table with them," JB, as opposed to "staying," RSV and NEB); cf. Luke 24:30; (6) his charge not to depart from Jerusalem, which was to be the center of the messianic ingathering (cf. Isa. 2:2-4); and (7) his promise of the coming

Holy Spirit (cf. Luke 3:16, parallels; also Acts 11:16), the sign of the dawn of the messianic era (cf. Joel 2:28-32).

The Ascension. The account of the ascension actually includes the previous conversation in verses 6-8, and in a sense the sequel in verses 12-14, where we are told, incidentally, that the ascension occurred on the Mount of Olives (cf. Luke 19:29; 21:37; also Zech. 14:4). Especially noteworthy here are the following: (1) the disciples' question concerning the restoration of the kingdom of Israel (verse 6; cf. Matt. 17:11; Mal. 4:5; also Acts 3:21), indicating their persistent concern with apocalyptic timetables (cf. Luke 9:27; 17:20; 19:11; 21:31; 24:21); (2) the Risen Lord's disallowance of eschatological speculation (verse 7; cf. Matt. 24:36 and parallels); (3) the promise of power (cf. I Thess. 1:5; Rom. 15:19) and the outpouring of the Holy Spirit (cf. Acts 2; also Isa. 32:15); (4) the disciples' future role as witnesses (cf. Luke 24:48; Acts 1:22; 5:32; John 15:26-27; I Pet. 5:1); (5) the prediction of the universal spread of the kingdom, which provides the geographical outline of the book of Acts: Judea (Acts 8:1; 9:31; 11:29; 26:20; 28:21); Samaria (Acts 8:5, 9, 14; 15:3; also Luke 9:52); the ends of the earth (Acts 28; also cf. Isa. 49:6).

The ascension is described in an unadorned fashion, though with some Old Testament reminiscences (cf. II Kings 2:11; also Prov. 30:4; Deut. 30:12; Bar. 3:29; IV Esdras 4:8; Wis. 18:15-19; I Enoch 39:3). We are simply told that a "cloud took him out of their sight" (cf. I Thess. 4:17; Rev. 11:12). Two men (cf. Luke 24:4; also II Macc. 3:26) clad in white (cf. Mark 9:3; 16:5; John 20:12; II Macc. 11:8) calmly provide the proper interpretation: the ascended Lord will return in similar fashion (verse 11; cf. Luke 21-27).

The way in which Luke describes the Lord's ascension is in itself instructive—and suggestive. He is less interested in the event as a personal event the disciples experienced than as an event they witnessed as the church's representatives. It sets the stage for the birth and growth of the church. We should also note the almost matter-of-fact way in which the event is depicted, with special attention to the disallowance of eschatological speculation. The Risen Lord says no to the disciples' eagerness to talk about the restoration of the kingdom and to establish a calendar date for the ways of God. They are instructed instead to wait—then to be empowered by the Holy Spirit and go about their appointed business as witnesses to the Easter faith. The business of eager disciples may be to wait patiently, hope realistically, and learn to live with the long duration begun with the Lord's ascension, knowing that eventually he will return.

Psalm 47

In the church's life Psalm 47 has traditionally been associated with Christ's ascension primarily because of the psalm's emphasis on God's ascension in verse 5 and the reference to exaltation in verse 9. As one of the enthronement psalms, Psalm 47 speaks of Yahweh's enthronement and his rule over the nations of the world. Thus it forms an appropriate lection to be used in conjunction with the opening section of Acts which reports the ascension of Jesus.

This psalm probably had its original usage in the Jerusalem cult when once a year God was reenthroned and proclaimed as king. In this ceremony, probably the ark, representing the Deity, was carried out of the temple and then returned to symbolize God's reentry. During God's absence, the temple underwent ritual cleansing.

This psalm, a hymn sung about God, may be divided into three sections based on the content of the passages. Verses 1-4 are a call to praise God and give reasons for such praise. Emphasis is placed on Yahweh as a great king who rules over the world but who in a special way looks after Israel his chosen people by giving them dominion over others. Verse 4 stresses the special character of Israel, but this emphasis on Israel's particularity and election, however, is clearly set within a context proclaiming Yahweh king of the whole created order and thus places it in perspective. The call for the people to clap and shout refers to the noise and jubilation that accompanied the acclamation of a new king (see II Kings 11:12), in this case, Yahweh as the reenthroned monarch.

The second section, verses 5-7, stresses the actual enthronement of Yahweh. Verse 5 clearly refers to the going up of Yahweh to assume his position as king. The divine ascension to the Holy of Holies where God was enthroned was accompanied by human shouts and the blowing of trumpets at royal coronations. Five times the call goes out "praise him" the king, the king of the earth. Pilgrims and participants in the festival must have celebrated with joy the reestablishment of Yahweh as king and judge over the world.

The third section, verses 8-9, speaks of Yahweh's reign as king. The "princes of the peoples" probably denotes foreign representatives who may have been present in Jerusalem to participate in the official ceremony. Even so, the psalm seems to have an eschatological flavor to it in that it talks about conditions that have not yet been fully attained, such as the universal rule of Yahweh and the participation of leaders from other nations in his worship.

In like manner, the ascension of Jesus is depicted as his exaltation to universal rule but a rule that has not yet been fully realized.

Ephesians 1:15-23

If Luke's narrative description of the Lord's ascension in today's first reading is restrained, this magnificent prayer from the opening chapter of Ephesians bursts through all restraint in its depiction of the exalted status of the Risen Lord. Like the first part of the prayer (verses 3-5), this section has participles piled on top of one another and abounds in superlatives. It is a richly textured passage and should be read magisterially, for this is the tone and mood intended by the author. In keeping with the mood of triumph and glory of Ascension Day, this passage sketches the triumph of Christ's exaltation on a truly cosmic scale, in keeping with the rest of the outlook in the Epistle.

The text opens with a reference by the author to the readers' "faith in the Lord Jesus and . . . love toward all the saints" (verse 15). This couplet is reminiscent of earlier epistolary lections from First John which similarly singles out these two fundamental realities of Christian faith (cf. I John 3:23; 5:1 and comments on the epistolary lections in Fourth and Sixth Sundays of Easter).

The remarks are part of the author's thanksgiving: "I do not cease to give thanks for you" (verse 16). One should compare other epistolary thanksgivings (cf. Col. 1:3-4, 9; also Rom. 1:8-9; Philem. 4-5). What follows in verses 17-23, however, constitute the author's prayer in behalf of the readers.

The prayer resists neat outlining, but does exhibit distinct emphases in its two halves. In the first part (verses 17-19), the focus is on the ways in which God can illuminate and enrich the hearts and minds of the readers. In the second part (verses 20-23), which in one sense is merely a continuation of the first request, the emphasis shifts to the figure of Christ, so that it becomes a majestic statement of his exalted status.

The Prayer for the Readers (verses 17-19). Appropriately, the prayer opens by referring to "the God of our Lord Jesus Christ, the Father of glory" (cf. 1:3; also Acts 7:2; Rom. 6:4). The prayer is that God may give the readers a spirit of wisdom (cf. Isa. 11:2; Wis. 7:7) and a spirit of revelation (cf. I Cor. 14:6), or as the NEB says, "Spiritual powers of wisdom and vision." With these spiritually bestowed gifts, there would come true and full knowledge of Christ (cf. Col. 1:9-10). It is also hoped that this illumination would be genuinely "eye-opening," as in the words of the NEB, "that your inward eyes may be illumined" (cf. Matt. 6:22 and parallels). With such inward illumination will come true knowledge of the Christian hope to which they are called (cf. 4:4; Col. 1:5, 27). This includes realizing the "riches of his glory" (cf. 3:16; also Rom. 9:23; 10:12; 11:33; Col. 1:27; Phil. 4:19), and the nature and extent of their legacy (cf. Col. 1:12; 3:24; also Acts 20:32; 26:18; Heb. 9:15; I Pet. 1:4; Deut. 33:3-4; Wis. 5:5). In addition, they are called on to recognize the vast resources of power at work within them (cf. 3:20; Col. 1:11; 2:12; also II Cor. 13:4; Isa. 40:26; Dan. 4:30). The source of this power at work within believers is, of course, God who has already unleashed this force in raising Jesus from the dead. It is at this point that the focus of the prayer shifts to Christ himself.

The Position of the Exalted Christ (verses 20-23). The supreme demonstration of divine power occurred in Christ's resurrection (cf. Rom. 4:24; 10:9; I Pet. 1:21). As already noted in the comments on today's first reading, we detect the first signs of a two-stage distinction between Christ's resurrection and ascension: (1) he raised him from the dead and (2) made him sit at his right hand (verse 20). The latter stage is being interpreted in the light of the enthronement of Yahweh (Ps. 110:1). Distinctive is the description of the location of his reign: "in the heavenly places" (cf. 2:6), which is reminiscent of the fourfold occurrence of "into heaven" in Acts 1:6-11. But Christ's universal dominion is phenomenally extensive here: "far above all rule and authority and power and dominion" (cf. 2:2; 3:10; 6:12; also Col. 1:13, 16; 2:10, 15; cf. Rom. 8:38; I Cor. 15:24; I Pet. 3:22; Heb. 2:5; II Pet. 2:11). Moreover, it exceeds the authority of every other name before which one might conceivably do homage (cf. Phil. 2:9-10). Not only is the reign cosmic, but eschatological, extending from this age to the coming age (cf. Rom. 8:38, "things present, nor things to come"). Employing the language of Psalm 8:6, the author attributes to God the subjection of "all things" to the dominion of Christ (cf. Matt. 28:18-20; also Dan. 7:14; Rev. 12:10). In this position, Christ is "head" over all things (4:15; 5:23; Col. 1:18; 2:10, 19; also I Cor. 11:3), most notably the church, his body (cf. 4:12; Rom. 12:5; Col. 1:18, 24; 2:19), in which position he embodies the very fullness of God (verse 23; 3:19; 4:10, 13; Col. 1:19; 2:9-10; 3:11; also John 1:16; Jer. 23:24).

This epistolary lection and the reading from Acts give two angles of vision on Christ's ascension, one in narrative form, the other in high theologized form, though no poorer in its imagery. Although this epistolary lection grants the believers unique privileges in understanding the mystery of the faith, it does not extend the language of exaltation to the believers themselves, as is the case in the later verses (2:6-7). Since some traditions of the celebration of Ascension Day emphasize not only Christ's ascension but that of believers as well, it may be that the preacher will wish to juxtapose 1:15-23 and 2:1-10 in order to include this dimension. As Chrysostom said, "Through the mystery of the Ascension we, who seemed unworthy of God's earth, are taken up into heaven. . . . Our very nature, against which Cherubim guarded the gates of Paradise, is enthroned today high above all Cherubim" (*Hom. in Ascens., PG,* 50, 444).

Luke 24:46-53 *or* Mark 16:9-16, 19-20

All the New Testament lections for today join in affirming the ascension of our Lord, a fact which may delight the preacher in the search for unity among the readings, but overwhelm the preacher in the decision as to what to say and what not to say. The New Testament presentations of Christ's ascension provide closure to the story of Jesus' ministry, declare his enthronement at the right hand of God, and announce the Lordship of Christ over his church and over all powers in the created order.

For the Gospel lesson, the preacher has a choice. Luke 24:46-53 has the advantage of being continued in the reading from Acts (1:1-11), Luke and Acts being two volumes from the same writer. Mark 16:9-16, 19-20, has the advantage of taking the preacher and the listeners into a text not often treated because of the dispute over its place in the Gospel. We will look briefly at both passages.

Luke 24:46-53 concludes Luke's resurrection appearance stories, two of which we have already considered. A quick review of the comments on verses 13-35 (Easter Evening) and on verses 35-48 (Third Sunday of Easter) will enable us to move directly to these verses. Brief as it is, this passage gathers up the major concerns of Luke and does so by looking backward, looking forward, and offering a gracious word for the meantime. Luke always looks backward to tie the message and ministry of Jesus and the church to the traditions and institutions of Judaism. Jesus and his followers were not rebels against the law, the synagogue, and the temple. They were true to the intent and practices of Judaism because, says Luke, Christianity continues and fulfills God's purposes in and through Israel. God has not had a change of mind nor does the church represent a radical shift in God's way in the world. Luke joins the new and the old in our text in three ways: by asserting that Jesus' passion and resurrection and the mission of his followers are according to the Scriptures (verses 44-46); by naming Jerusalem as the launching point for the universal spread of the gospel (verses 47, 52; the prophecy of Isa. 2:3 fulfilled); by describing the disciples, after Jesus' ascension, as being continually in the temple (verse 53).

Luke 24:46-53 not only looks to the past for continuity but it also looks forward. The future is viewed in terms of a commission and a promise. The commission is to preach the gospel to all nations (verse 47). For Luke the Gospel is God's offer of repentance and forgiveness of sin to all people (verse 47; Acts 2:38; 3:19; 5:31; 11:18; 17:30). The promise is of power from God, the Holy Spirit, which will enable them to carry out the mission (verse 49; Acts 1:4-8).

But Luke 24:46-53 does not leave the disciples (his church) in a desert between a rich heritage and a future that will fulfill God's purpose in the world. They are not left wondering about what happens in the meantime back at the church. Christ blesses them (verses 50, 51) and they move toward their future in great joy, continually blessing God (verses 52, 53). They are now between Easter and Pentecost and for them it is a time of unbounded joy, ceaseless praise, and constant prayer (Acts 1:14).

Mark 16:9-16, 19-20, is an unusual text, not so much in its content as in its uncertain place in the Gospel. Ancient manuscripts are sufficiently divided as to whether Mark ends at 16:8 as to divide scholars and editors of English translations. Each preacher will want to survey the evidence presented in the commentaries and reach a conclusion firm enough to support preaching and satisfy questions that may arise among parishioners. In comments on Mark 16:1-8 for Easter Vigil, the conviction was stated that Mark properly ends at verse 8. That should not hinder our exploring these verses from the longer ending of Mark, especially since the problematic portion (verses 17-18) is not included in our lesson. As for verses 9-16, 19-20, most of the content is to be found in the resurrection stories of Luke, John, and Matthew.

Mark's resurrection narrative consists of six brief but distinct units. The first, verses 9-11, records the appearance to Mary Magdalene (John 20:1-18), identified as the woman from whom Jesus exorcised seven demons (Luke 8:2). Her report of what she had seen was met with unbelief (Luke 24:11). The second, verses 12-13, is a brief reference to the appearance to two disciples walking in the country, a story told at length by Luke (24:13-35). The third, verse 14, mentions the appearance to the eleven with no details except Jesus' reprimand for their unbelief (Luke 24:33-38). The fourth unit, verses 15-18, is the Markan form of the commission to the disciples. This commission is striking in two respects: it enjoins baptism alongside faith (Matt. 28:18-20), and it promises that miraculous signs (which Jesus himself never provided, according to Mark 8:12) will corroborate the witness of the believers. The fifth unit, verse 19, declares the ascension and enthronement of Jesus. Jesus seated at the right hand of God (Ps. 110) is the New Testament's most frequently used image for testifying to the Lordship of Jesus Christ, but of the Gospels only Mark uses it in a resurrection-ascension account. The final unit, verse 20, is a summary statement about the post-ascension activity of the church. The disciples are pictured as obedient to Christ's commission, preaching everywhere while being aided by Christ and having their message confirmed by signs.

This conclusion (verse 20) differs noticeably from Matthew and Luke, both of whom have charges by Christ to his followers to preach to the nations. Matthew closes with the charge, with no statement as to the disciples' response (28:18-20). Matthew's conclusion thus has the effect of addressing not just the eleven but the reader as well. The open end leaves to the reader the completion of the mission. Luke follows Christ's commission with the command to wait until they are equipped with the power to carry it out. This period of waiting leaves the reader poised and serves as the introduction to Acts and the story of the spread of the gospel from Jerusalem to Rome. But Mark, giving both the commission and a brief summary of its fulfillment, turns the Gospel into history; that is, a description of what happened back then. Even a final "Amen" says clearly, "End of story." The Gospel is in part historical description, to be sure, but it is also direct address, and it is this dimension that is absent here. On this matter the preacher will want to ponder. It is a question of how one punctuates one's sermon. Sometimes a sermon properly ends with a question mark, at other times with an exclamation point, a comma, a dash, or a period. The task in preaching is to know when to do what, to be appropriate to the message and to the listeners. Mark 16:9-20 says Jesus was raised from the dead, appeared to his followers, commanded them to preach to every creature, and ascended into heaven; and his followers carried out his command. Period. In one sense that is the appropriate punctuation; the ascension is the end to a story. Some things have occurred once and for all. But having said that, those who take Mark seriously know that his period is not really a period. The period belongs to God alone.

Seventh Sunday of Easter

Acts 1:15-17, 21-26; Psalm 1; I John 5:9-13;
John 17:11b-19

Acts 1:15-17, 21-26

The omission of verses 18-20 in today's reading from Acts serves to bracket the place of Judas in the larger text; it is unfortunate since this is one of the more intriguing features of the passage. This definition of the pericope serves to direct our attention to the selection of Matthias and the reconstitution of the Apostolate.

Even so, we should note that the tradition of Judas' death preserved by Luke has its own character, differing substantially from Matthew who reports that he died by hanging (Matt. 27:3-10; influenced by Zech. 11:12; Jer. 18:2-3; 19:1-2; 32:6-15). According to the tradition preserved in Luke, Judas died ignominiously: "falling headlong he burst open in the middle and all his bowels gushed out" (verse 18). This version has also been influenced by the Old Testament (cf. Num. 5:21-22, 27; Ps. 109:18; 69:23-24). In this respect, Judas' bitter end is typical of those who in Luke's story vainly sought to obstruct the ways of God (e.g., Herod, Acts 12:2-23; Ananias and Sapphira, Acts 5:1-11).

The behavior of Judas obviously created a major problem for the earliest Christians. The betrayal is a firmly entrenched part of the passion narrative in all the Gospels (cf. Mark 14:43-50; Matt. 26:47-56; 27:3-10; Luke 22:47-53; John 18:2-12), even though the motives for his actions are variously treated. Matthew and Luke connect him with the "potter's field," a cemetery for strangers (cf. Matt. 27:9-10; Acts 1:19). Of all the Gospel writers, Matthew is the kindest to Judas; he confesses his sin ("I have sinned in betraying innocent blood,"

Matt. 27:4), returns the money, and hangs himself—the quintessential expression of remorse (Matt. 27:5). For Luke, Judas' actions were a divine necessity (Acts 1:16), and he was thus an unwitting instrument in bringing God's purposes to fulfillment.

But it is less the fate of Judas than the choice of his successor that accounts for the placement of this episode here, immediately prior to Pentecost. The beginning of the messianic community cannot be told until the nucleus of that community, the Twelve, is reconstituted. Theirs is, after all, an eschatological role (cf. Luke 22:30), and the Apostolate occupies a special place in Luke's theology. He does, of course, use the term "apostle" in a non-technical sense (Acts 14:4, 14), but except for this he mostly confines the role of apostle to the Twelve (cf. Luke 6:12-16). As today's text shows, the Twelve serve as the vital link between the Risen Lord and the church; they guarantee the tradition of the earthly ministry of Jesus "from the baptism of John until the day when he was taken up from us" (Acts 1:22). As such, they become the witnesses to the resurrection (Acts 2:32; 3:15; 4:33; 5:32; 10:41; 13:31).

Because of the theological importance Luke attaches to the reconstitution of the Twelve, he tells the story to make two points especially: (1) Scripture was fulfilled, both with respect to the fate of Judas (verses 16, 20) and the choice of his successor (verse 20); and (2) the choice was God's doing (verses 24-25). Luke thus succeeds in preparing the way for the breaking in of the eschatological age. Events have worked out according to divine necessity, and the omniscient God (verse 24; cf. 15:8; Luke 16:15) has taken the last necessary step in bringing about the divine will. Today's first reading serves as the natural prelude to Pentecost. As such, it continues to illustrate the Lukan outlook, with its emphasis on promise-fulfillment and the importance attached to the Twelve as the witnesses to the faith and the guarantors of the apostolic tradition. As the narrative of Acts unfolds, the Israel of the Jerusalem temple is gradually supplanted by the eschatological Israel that includes both Jews and Gentiles. As Acts shows, such a new reality can only be understood as the work of the Spirit.

Psalm 1

The opening psalm of the Psalter contrasts two types of persons, two ways of life, and two sets of consequences for human behavior. The contrast is between the blessed (verse 1) or the righteous (verse 5) and the wicked. The idea of humans being confronted with two ways or types of life between which one must choose is a very common motif in the literature and wisdom of many cultures.

The blessed person is defined first negatively and then positively (verses 1-2). Negatively, the person does not walk, stand, or sit (note the gradations of action) in the advice (counsel) of the wicked, in the way of sinners, or in the seat of scoffers. Perhaps the writer also expressed gradations in the terms used for the unrighteous: the wicked (guilty of a particular charge), the sinners (those constantly missing the mark and deviating from the acceptable), and the scoffers (the self-sufficient and haughty who ridicule). Positively, the blessed person is one who delights in and meditates on the law of God. That is, the one blessed in life is the one who knows the Torah, the way, the instruction of the Lord and delights in what is found there.

The righteous becomes like a tree transplanted by everflowing streams so that its yield and growth are predictable (verse 3). A similar image is found in Jeremiah 17:5-8. As a tree located by the waters naturally grows and yields so does the person who contemplates and lives by the law which is considered here to be good and beneficial.

The description of the wicked suggests a picture opposite to that of the righteous. Unlike the firmly anchored tree, the wicked are described as chaff which is driven whichever way the wind blows. The imagery is a familiar one used elsewhere in the Bible. The chaff of wheat and other grains is lighter than the grain heads and is blown farther away than the grain when both are tossed into the wind together at the threshing floor. The wicked, like the chaff, are persons without much presence or substance.

Because of the behavior of the wicked they will have no weight, influence, or respect in the place of judgment. When persons meet to decide a course of action or to determine guilt or innocence, the wicked will have no place there (verse 5).

The way of the righteous is said to be known or protected by God, whereas the wicked are simply left to perish.

I John 5:9-13

Standing at the end of Easter, we look back at a period of extended celebration centered in the heart of the Christian faith: the conviction that after Jesus died he came to experience life in an unprecedented and unique manner. This form of renewed, transformed life the New Testament calls "resurrection." This is to be distinguished from the various ways first-century people understood revivification, and certainly it meant far more than that Jesus "lived on" in his deeds and words in the memory of his disciples.

The Johannine way of expressing this utterly new and different reality is "eternal life" *(zoē aiōnios)*. Already in the Fourth Gospel, we are introduced to this understanding of life (3:15-16, 36; 6:40, 47; 10:10, 28; 11:25-26; 20:31). It is that which God, the Father, embodies (5:26*a*), and by extension comes to be embodied in the Son (5:26*b*), who was begotten of the Father. Receiving it, or coming to share in this extraordinary life, is predicated on believing and trusting in the Son (3:15). In no way should this life, so conceived, be understood merely as an extension of biological existence as we know it here; it rather transcends our ordinary experience of life in that it is qualitatively different from human existence as we know it.

Accordingly, experiencing it is not postponed until after we die; by believing fully in the Son we are thrust into this "eternal life" here and now. We may be said to "have" eternal life—now (3:36; 6:47; esp. 5:24). There is, nevertheless, a future aspect. Through faith, we experience "eternal life" now, yet it is our human fate to die. But believing in the Son of God means that we are able to transcend even this form of death: "He who believes in me, though he die, yet shall he live" (11:25).

This is what is presupposed in our text today when it says, "And this is the testimony; that God gave us eternal life, and this life is in his Son. He who has the Son has life; he who has not the son of God has not life" (5:11-12). Earlier in the passage the phrase "the testimony of God" is to be understood as "the testimony that comes from God, or which God has given" (subjective genitive).

As the Fourth Gospel shows, the form of this witness has been channeled through the incarnate Logos, God's Son, whose own words and deeds are themselves God's own revelation to us (cf. John 5:19-47). Were this revelation merely an oracle from heaven, it could little be heeded. But it is more than that, because it is substantiated by the incarnate Logos whose historical existence was seen, heard, and experienced—by John the Baptist, the "testimony of men" (verse 9; cf. John 5:36), by the apostolic witness that became embodied in the confession of faith (cf. 5:5; also 2:22-23; 4:2), and, perhaps as important, by the community of faith: "He who believes in the Son of God has the testimony in himself" (verse 10*a*). In addition to these, or rather through all of these, the Spirit has borne witness, and through this witness truth has been revealed (5:7).

This, then, is what the author is asking his readers to believe and continue to accept: extraordinary, transcendent life given by God in and through the Son to those who believe. The passage ends on a note of reassurance: "I write this . . . that you may *know* that you have eternal life" (verse 13, italics added).

This is the faith of Easter.

John 17:11*b*-19

Today is the last Sunday of Easter prior to Pentecost. Easter is fulfilled in Pentecost. A church without Pentecost cannot shout, "He is risen," loudly enough to sustain Easter week after week. Inevitably there comes the post-Easter slump, the special efforts to keep attendance up, and the growing cynicism of ministers complaining about those who worship only at Christmas and Easter. Luke says Easter is not only shouting but waiting in prayer for the coming Spirit. John says Easter is also listening to Jesus pray for us (chapter 17).

As stated in previous lessons, John 14–17 is farewell material. Jesus is returning to God, leaving behind disciples who are confused, afraid, and forlorn. Chapter 17, although in the form of a prayer, really belongs to the discourses. Prayers of Jesus in this Gospel are sermonic (11:42; 12:30), and therefore the readers of 17:1-26 are as a congregation overhearing a pastoral prayer. We are not directly addressed, but we are very much in the mind of the One who is praying. The prayer is of the Christ who is already ascending (verses 11-13). In this sense it is uttered between earth and heaven, a prayer both of the historical Jesus and the glorified Christ.

The prayer comes to us in a noticeably stylized form with poetic qualities. Although scholars differ as to the transitional points within the prayer, a case can be made for a threefold division: Jesus asks to return to God (verses 1-5); Jesus intercedes for his disciples (verses 6-19); Jesus intercedes for the readers of the Gospel who are believers at least once removed (verses 20-26). Our lection is a portion of Jesus' prayer for his disciples.

At first it may not seem all that important to listen to Jesus pray for the Twelve, for probably by the time this Gospel was written they were all dead. Why not concentrate on prayer for the early church and for our church? The fact is, Jesus' prayer for his disciples *is* in behalf of the church through succeeding generations, for it is vital to the life of the church to know that the revelation, the truth, from Jesus has been faithfully transmitted. In other words, can we trust the tradition we have received? Verses 6-19 say yes. The apostles were given by God to Jesus (verse 6); Jesus gave to them the Word of God (verses 6-8); they received that Word, believed it, and kept it (verses 6-8); they had not been corrupted by the world for they were not of the world which, in fact, hated them (verses 9-16); even though one of them had gone astray, even that was within God's knowledge and according to Scripture (verse 12); just as Jesus had sanctified himself in total dedication to God, so were the apostles set apart (consecrated) for the truth (verses 17-19); and the apostles had as their sole purpose the continuation of the mission which Jesus had from God (verse 18). The Evangelist has left no doubt to plague subsequent generations of believers: the church is not an orphan in the world, the creation of a religious imagination, the frightened child of huddled rumors and popular superstitions. For those who need to examine the credentials of the church's life and message, here is truth's pedigree: from God, to Christ, to the apostles, to the church.

For some of us this line of thinking has not been a formalized part of our faith. We have done most of our singing, praying, and witnessing within a circle of believers who agreed with us before we spoke. But the church which takes seriously Christ's mission, which moves out into a world that is hostile and yet the object of God's gracious love, will be asked, and will ask itself, about the reliability of its tradition. John 17:6-19 is one response to one church which, under heavy pressure (15:18-25; 16:1-4), needed to hear this word. Next Sunday is Pentecost, a time for celebrating the charismatic dimension of the church's life. Spending this time reflecting on the tradition which has come to us from Christ himself is an excellent way to affirm and appropriate Pentecost without being caught up in its excesses.

Pentecost

Acts 2:1-21 or *Ezekiel 37:1-14; Psalm 104:24-34; Romans 8:22-27* or *Acts 2:1-21; John 15:26-27; 16:4b-15*

Acts 2:1-21

With the circle of the Twelve reconstituted through the selection of Matthias (Acts 1:12-26), the nucleus of the newly constituted messianic community is in place. The time is now right for it to be legitimated, and this is done through a divine sign (of which there are many in Luke-Acts), doubly forceful since it is both audible and visible. The prophetic words cited from Joel and attributed to Peter are programmatic not only for the structuring of the Pentecost story as Luke narrates it, but for what follows in the rest of Acts. The opening words of Joel's prophecy have been altered to appropriate fully the prophetic message for Christian readers who were living "in the last days," the final period of salvation history. As God's Spirit had been poured out previously in times of rebirth and renewal, so now the birth of the newly constituted messianic community receives divine inbreathing and legitimation in similar fashion.

The prophetic message is programmatic. Major themes, which are unfolded and developed on a grand literary scale in Luke-Acts, are articulated here.

1. The New Age as the era in which God's Spirit generates new life and expectations, but especially as it launches the rebirth of the prophetic witness. It was widely held that the voice of the prophets had been silenced (I Macc. 4:46). With the coming of Messiah Jesus, however, God had raised a new prophet (Acts 3:22; 7:37). Not only does Luke, throughout the Gospel, especially portray Jesus as God's prophet (Luke 4:18-19, 24-30), but he also portrays the main characters of the formative years of the church as prophetic figures, most

notably Peter (Acts 2–12) and Paul (Acts 13–28). Both are prompted and directed by the Spirit in their words and actions (e.g., 4:8; 9:17; 22:17-21). The gradual spread of the messianic movement, accordingly, is attested by "signs and wonders" (Acts 2:43; 4:30; 5:12; 6:8; 7:36; 8:13; 14:3; 15:12), Luke's way of indicating its divine legitimation.

2. The universality of God's spiritual outpouring in the messianic kingdom. The Spirit is promised to "all flesh" (verse 17). No longer will the messianic community be defined along ethnic lines or national boundaries. That all nations, first the Jews, then the Gentiles, are to become incorporated into the messianic community is a recurrent theme of Luke-Acts, and one that receives special treatment (cf. Acts 2:39). The vivid language of the prophecy signifies that the level of participation will be broad: young and old, men and women will participate in the excitement of the prophetic outpouring.

Quite possibly, the apocalyptic signs of verses 19-20—blood, fire, cosmic eclipses—refer to events accompanying the crucifixion (cf. Luke 22:44-45). If so, the "day of the Lord," great and manifest, most likely refers to the crucifixion itself, not to the final judgment. Consequently, this prominent theme of the eschatological day of the Lord here undergoes a major reinterpretation in light of the Christian conviction that the final, eschatological age was ushered in by the Christ-event. Consequently, with the inauguration of God's New Age through Christ's death and resurrection, the call to salvation becomes truly universal; henceforth, from the dawn of the church onward, whoever cries out to the Lord from the depths of despair will receive salvation—both Jew and Gentile.

How thoroughly the prophetic message has influenced the structure of the Lukan narrative should be noted. The detailed list of "the nations" who were present on Pentecost naturally serves to underscore the universality of the Gospel message. Accordingly, the event of Pentecost is seen to "fulfill" the words of the prophecy, and the way the narrative is structured reinforces this even more. Similarly, the opening words of the narrative which mention the "rush of a mighty wind" and the "tongues as of fire" may be seen as descriptive features that also serve to fulfill the Joel prophecy. The scene as described attests the occurrence of "wonders in the heaven above" and "signs on the earth beneath" (verse 19). The way the narrative is constructed here is typical of how Luke tells the story throughout. His narrative technique becomes an extension of his theological program of prophecy-fulfillment. By the end of the story the attentive reader can hardly remain unconvinced that the account of God's prophet Jesus and God's people, the church, are the inexorable fulfillment of God's promise, beginning in the Old Testament and continuing in the unfolding drama.

Ezekiel 37:1-14

The central reading for this day is, of course, the one which fixes the day as Pentecost, Acts 2:1-21. The other New Testament readings concern the Spirit of God, promised as the Counselor and the Spirit of truth in John 15 and 16, and as the Spirit that helps us in our weakness in Romans 8:22-27. The special note in this regard in Psalm 104:22-27, a hymn of praise, concerns the power of God's Spirit to create and renew. Ezekiel 37:1-14 is also one of the texts for the Easter Vigil, Year B (see commentary under Easter Vigil) and in that context its message is one of life out of death. When the passage is read on the Day of Pentecost the emphasis will fall upon the power of the Spirit of God as a gift which enlivens the people of God.

While the central point of the text is the renewal of the people of Israel, an important aspect of that message concerns the "Spirit of the Lord." The understanding of that Spirit in Ezekiel is by no means the same as the Christian doctrine of the Holy Spirit, or even the New Testament beliefs in the Counselor or the Spirit. However, the Hebraic view is important background for the later ones, and the prophetic text has contributions of its own to make to our reflections on the Day of Pentecost.

The same Hebrew word is used throughout the passage in several different senses. It is appropriately translated both "Spirit" (verses 1, 14) and "breath" (verses 5, 6, 8, 9, 10). In the English translation we miss the deliberate plays on the word. These different uses in Ezekiel only touch the surface of the many ways the word is used throughout the Old Testament. The spirit is associated both with the created world and with God. It is wind or breath (Job 9:18), which gives life to both human beings and animals (Gen. 6:17), or it is the "spirit" of a person in the sense of one's emotions or will (Gen. 41:8). It also refers to God's power, both as a creative force (Gen. 1:2) and as inspiring prophecy (Isa. 61:1 and often in Ezekiel).

Certainly not all these senses are visible in Ezekiel 37, but some are. It is the Spirit of Yahweh that makes the vision possible, the breath comes like the four winds, and brings—under the authority of the prophet's divinely directed words—life to the dead bones. The point of the vision report is that God can and will—through the Spirit—bring to life a community that considers itself dead.

Psalm 104:24-34

Psalm 104 is a hymn which praises God as the Creator of the universe and everything that is in it. In primitive encyclopedia fashion, the orders and elements of creation are paraded forth as the works of God in the psalm.

The selection of this lection for Pentecost Sunday is based on its emphasis on the role of God's spirit in creation (see verse 30) and the psalm's universal perspectives. Verses 24-34, however, should be seen within the overall structure of the psalm.

Six realms of creation, somewhat similar to the six days of creation in Genesis 1, are described in poetic style: sky (verses 2-4), earth (verses 5-9), water (verses 10-13), vegetation (verses 14-18), moon and sun (verses 19-23), and sea (verses 24-26). Each of these realms and their component parts are seen as integral elements in the created order with an existence brought into being by divine power and sustained by the Creator's loving care.

Today's lection contains the descriptive praise of the sea (verses 24-26), a hymnic statement about the dependence of all life upon God (verses 27-30), and a final reflection on God's glory (verses 31-34). (The omission of verse 35 by those producing the lectionary is probably a concession to modern tastes and sensitivities!) Except for the opening line in verse 1 and verses 31-35, all of the psalm is addressed directly to the Deity; this is unusual for hymns that generally are a genre in which the human audience addresses itself.

The section on the sea (verses 24-26) begins with an emphasis on the diversity within the creation yet confesses that God in his wisdom made all and that all are creatures of the divine—a point and a perspective we have come to learn anew in light of the modern ecological crisis. (Should one wish to do so, comparison could be made between the great diversity of the world's creatures—both small and great—and the diversity of languages and backgrounds reflected in the audience present in Jerusalem at Pentecost.)

The sea is presented as a boundless expanse of water teeming with things too numerous to count, with ships moving on its surface, and with giant monsters frolicking in its midst. Leviathan (in verse 26) appears to have been one of the names assigned to the great dragon whose slaughter, in the ancient myth, preceded the formation of the earth (see Job 7:12; 26:12; Ps. 74:13; 89:10; Isa. 51:9). Here the monster is depicted as a mere playful "critter" sporting in the water. In fact, the line mentioning Leviathan could be translated "Leviathan which thou hadst made to play with him." Such an interpretation of the text makes the dragon a toy of play for the Deity. The demon of old mythology has been domesticated to live at home in a world of God's creation. This psalm, like Genesis 1, certainly knows of no realm or creature beyond the reach and touch of the Creator or a realm hostile to God and his purposes. The psalm, in other words, presents a world in which all things—both small and great—are at home. Here is a monotheism which delights in the whole of the created order.

In verses 27-30, the psalmist offers praise to God for the gift of life itself. Life presented here is not simply existence in itself or some possession of beast and humankind but is the consequence of the continuing and constant action of God. All living things look to God for the source of their sustenance. The continuity and character of life are seen as the consequence of God's actions: he gives, they gather; he opens his hand, they receive and are filled.

The psalmist is aware of the fragility and precariousness of life. Life is always at the will of the Divine and always in the shadow of death. Without the presence of God's face (that is, his concern) humans are dismayed, overwhelmed; when God withdraws their breath, they return to the dust from which they were shaped. But in like fashion, the presence of God's Spirit brings creatures into being and changes the face of the ground. Thus both the good and the bad in life and in death are related to the action of the Deity.

In the doxology at the end of the psalm verses 31-35, the psalmist expresses the wish that God may rejoice in his works, that is, that God may delight in and not destroy what his hands have made. Two thoughts, like dark portents, raise their heads and produce some doubt in the psalmist's mind. Earthquakes and volcanoes—the earth trembling and the mountains smoking—appear as the dark side of God's action. But worst of all is human sin and wickedness which the psalmist prays will be consumed from the earth and be no more (verse 35).

Verses 33-34 contain a vow and a request. A vow to sing praise to God as long as life is present. Such a vow comes in the context of the mention of the dark side of creation and thus is an affirmation of faith "in spite of." In spite of the disharmonies that intrude into the created order, the psalmist affirms, "I will sing to the Lord as long as I live . . . . I rejoice." The request is that even the inner being, the meditation, of the poet be pleasing to God.

Romans 8:22-27

Today's epistolary text is one of the most profound New Testament passages dealing with the work of the Spirit within Christians. One might say that in this text Paul personalizes the outpouring of the Spirit that is presented in narrative form in Acts 2:1-21. Certainly, in celebrating the feast of Pentecost, we are able to probe Paul's words here to discern how we might appropriate the Spirit within our own lives; or, to put it more felicitously, how we might understand the way in which the Spirit works within us, even if unconsciously.

The text must be understood in the light of Paul's apocalyptic outlook. As seen earlier in the passage (verses 18-21), and as noted in the opening verse (verse 22), Paul envisions that the "whole creation" *(pasa hē ktisis)* has been experiencing cosmic birth pains ("groaning in travail") as it metamorphoses under the impact of the Christ-event. This text is further illuminated by his remarks in II Corinthians 5:17: "If any one is in Christ, he is a new creation; the old has passed away, behold, the new has come." Seen against the background of Paul's theology of the new creation (II Cor. 4:1-6), in which the Christ-event was understood as an even more dramatic enactment of the creation in Genesis 1–2, this passage from Romans indicates that Paul regarded the whole cosmos as being transformed as part of the eschatological process.

That which is happening on the cosmic scale also goes on within those "in Christ": "we ourselves . . . groan inwardly as we wait for adoption as sons" (verse 23). We do so because we have experienced the "first fruits of the Spirit" (cf. II Cor. 1:22; 5:5; Eph. 1:14). By being incorporated into Christ, we have already received the Spirit (8:9-11), and therefore have already tasted of the eschatological era, the dawning of the reign of God. Through the Spirit, God has reached out to us from the future, the "age to come," and allowed us to share, partially at least, in the resurrection life which Christ already experiences fully. We thus wait for our adoption as sons, that is, our full sonship (cf. 8:15; Gal. 4:5-6; Eph. 1:5) and for the full redemption, or transformation, of our bodies (cf. Rom. 3:24; I Cor. 1:30; Col. 1:14; Eph. 1:7, 14; 4:30; also Ps. 130:7; cf. also II Cor. 5:6-7; 4:18).

Hope is an intrinsic part of existence *en Christō*. We already experience salvation in one sense, but not fully. Hope, after all, has a built-in element of unrealization: "hope that is seen is not hope" (cf. Heb. 11:1). As Paul says elsewhere, "For through the Spirit, by faith, we wait for the hope of righteousness" (Gal. 5:5; also Rom. 8:19; I Cor. 7:19). We nevertheless do so "with patience" (verse 25; also Rom. 5:1-5).

Here Paul exposes the anxiety felt by every Christian who lives in the tension between the "already" and the "not yet." Though we have begun to experience transformation, we continue to experience the agony of human existence (cf. II Cor. 5:2-5). It is in such weakness that our own inability to know ourselves and our own needs becomes most fully exposed: "we do not know how to pray as we ought" (verse 26). At this juncture, the Spirit steps in and "intercedes for us with sighs too deep for words" (verse 26).

Too sharp a distinction between the intercessory work of Christ himself and the Spirit should not be drawn (cf. Rom. 8:34; also Heb. 7:25). The lines are blurred even in Paul's own language, for earlier he spoke of the "Spirit of God" in one breath, and the "Spirit of Christ" in another (8:9). However the presence of the Spirit is conceived, what is significant here is that the very Spirit who knows us even better than we know ourselves (cf. Rev. 2:23; I Cor. 4:5; Ps. 139:1) intercedes for us in our weakness, and on our behalf, conforming our wills to the will of God. As Paul says earlier in this chapter, "When we cry, 'Abba! Father!' it is the Spirit himself bearing witness with our spirit that we are children of God" (8:16). By recalling the very words of Jesus in Gethsemane (Mark 14:36; also Gal. 4:6), Paul suggests that the Spirit who brought about filial obedience in the will of Jesus also works within us to achieve the same quality of filial obedience, enabling us to say, in our own lives, "Abba, Father."

Here, then, we have a profound interpretation of the work of the Spirit within the life of the Christian—the level perhaps at which the true significance of Pentecost should be experienced and understood. True, the text speaks of the cosmic work of the Spirit in bringing about the transformation of the universe as we know it, but it also speaks of the anxieties we all feel and the work of the Spirit in bringing us to genuine filial obedience.

John 15:26-27; 16:4*b*-15

Today is Pentecost, for Jews an early harvest festival which came to be also a commemoration of the giving of the law at Sinai; for Christians a celebration of the outpouring of the

Holy Spirit upon the church. Luke is alone among the Gospel writers in historicizing the events of Easter, Ascension, and Pentecost, placing them on a calendar covering a fifty-day period (Acts 1–2). But Luke is not alone in witnessing to Jesus' promise of the Holy Spirit and in linking the coming of the Spirit to Jesus' departure to God's presence. The Gospel of John speaks clearly and repeatedly on this subject.

According to the Fourth Gospel, the Holy Spirit is associated with Jesus. The Spirit descended upon Jesus at his baptism (1:33) and it is Jesus who baptizes with the Holy Spirit (1:33). But according to this Evangelist, the gift of the Spirit to Jesus' followers had to wait upon Jesus' death and ascension to God (7:39). Even the word to Nicodemus about being born of the Spirit assumes the ascension of Jesus as precondition for this work of the Spirit (3:13). In other words, the resurrected, glorified Jesus would send the Spirit upon his church. This promise occupies a central place in the farewell discourses of Jesus (13:31–16:33), discourses that address the pressing question, What does the departing Christ have to say to the church he is leaving behind?

As Luke says that Easter is completed at Pentecost, so John says that the departure of Christ is relieved in its pain and fulfilled in its joy by the coming of the Holy Spirit. This is the theme of our Gospel lections for today. John 15:26-27 and 16:4*b*-15 contain the last three of the five Holy Spirit sayings in the farewell speeches. In the first saying, Jesus promised that the Spirit as Counselor, Comforter, or Helper would come to his followers and would dwell with them, never leaving them alone (14:16-17). In the second, Jesus promised that the Spirit would be a teacher as he had been and would bring to their remembrance all that Jesus had said to them (14:26). This theme of remembering is important here and elsewhere in the Gospels, for while there is value in rehearsals prior to events, there is also value in reflecting upon what has happened. We should not make fun of hindsight; the Christian life is to a large extent an act of memory.

To these descriptions of the work of the Spirit, today's reading adds three important statements.

1. The Spirit will bear witness to Jesus just as the apostles who shared his earthly life bear witness (15:26-27). Notice the

double attestation to the truth about Jesus: the Spirit and the apostles concur. The importance of this cannot be overstated. The church is not left with only the promptings of the Spirit, opening wide the door to ecstasies, visions, mystic trances, and all sorts of nonverifiable claims by inspired speakers. Neither is it the case that the church is left with just the reports of men of antiquity. Rather the church has both the Spirit and the tradition, and the Gospel is located where these two intersect.

2. The Spirit will convict the world of sin, righteousness (justice), and judgment (16:7-11). "Convict" is probably a better translation than "convince" (verse 8), since the image is of a courtroom trial. Here the function of the Spirit is to provide the church with a true interpretation of the life, death, and significance of Jesus. In the eyes of the world, Jesus was tried, sentenced, and executed as an enemy of the state. But the Spirit, as interpreter of Jesus, enables the church to testify to what "really" was going on: in unbelief the world acted unjustly against the Christ whom God has vindicated as the judge of his judges. As Jesus interprets God, so the Spirit interprets Jesus and provides faith's reading of the story.

3. The Spirit will guide the church into all the truth and declare the things that are to come (16:12-15). This text has been used to bless every fad and notion, but the fear of the new and different must not cause the church to abandon this promise. When the church becomes protective and defensive, the present ceases to be God's time and preachers become curators. The Spirit continually presses the question, What is the meaning of Jesus Christ today? and leads to answers. This is not to say the church is left prey to all who proclaim in the name of the Spirit, "Lo, here," and "Lo, there." The apostolic and biblical witness remains as a canon for testing the spirits, for the Holy Spirit does not speak apart from or contrary to the historical Jesus (verses 12-15). Rather the Spirit keeps the voice of Jesus a living voice in the church.

Annunciation, March 25

Isaiah 7:10-14; Psalm 45 or *40:6-10; Hebrews 10:4-10; Luke 1:26-38*

Isaiah 7:10-14

This day is the liturgical commemoration of the events reported in Luke 1:26-38, the angel Gabriel's announcement to Mary that she will give birth to the Messiah. Though it is not quoted in the Lucan passage, Isaiah's promise of the birth of Immanuel as a sign certainly stands in the background. Messianic themes occur in Psalm 45, a royal psalm on the occasion of a king's wedding. The selection from Psalm 40 meets the Gospel lection at two points: the expression of one who delights in doing the will of God and the proclamation of "the glad news of deliverance" (verse 9).

The New Testament and later Christian interpretations of Isaiah 7:10-14 are so familiar that we need not dwell on them here. Followers of Jesus from the earliest times have seen him as "Immanuel," a human sign that God is with us. Our concern at this point is to allow this text from Isaiah to have its own voice from its historical and literary context.

The historical situation is the Syro-Ephraimitic war of 734-33 B.C., summarized briefly in Isaiah 7:1-2 and reported more fully in II Kings 16:1-20. The Assyrian empire under Tiglath-pileser III was on the move and the small states in Syria and Palestine were organizing in opposition. When Ahaz, the Davidic king in Judah, refused to join the coalition, Rezin of Damascus in Syria and Pekah of Israel headed south to Jerusalem to depose him and set up a new king who would do their will. With that threat on the horizon and Ahaz about to align himself with Assyria, Isaiah appeared to the king with a message from Yahweh. With his son Shear-jashub ("a remnant shall return") in tow he gave a speech which was a promise of the Lord's care and a call to trust (7:3-9). The foundation of his message was the Lord's promise of an everlasting dynasty to David (II Sam. 7). Ahaz as a son of David has nothing to fear from these imposters.

Then follows the passage before us. Isaiah, speaking on behalf of Yahweh, invited the king to ask for a sign, but he refused to "put the Lord to the test" (verse 12). Impatiently the prophet rebuked the king, declaring that the Lord himself will give a sign: "Behold, a young woman shall conceive and bear a son, and shall call his name Immanuel" (verse 14).

The surrounding material in the Book of Isaiah is filled with reports of symbolic actions and signs, many of which concern the names of children (7:3-9; 8:1-4; 8:16-22; 9:1-7). Such accounts are not pieces of prophetic biography or autobiography but powerful messages from Yahweh. Typically there is an account of the divine instructions to perform some act and the interpretation of the action. One also finds the report that the action was performed, but, as here, command and performance often are conflated. The actions may convey good news or bad. Hosea 1 contains a series of symbolic action reports concerning the names of the prophet's children, each one proclaiming judgment upon Israel. A "sign," then, need not be a miraculous deed but some visible—or audible—event that reveals God's will. It is an indication that God will act, and how.

There is hardly a significant question concerning this passage which has not been disputed, partly because interpreters have so much invested in the meaning of the lines and partly because the Hebrew of the succeeding verses (7:15-20) is ambiguous. Is the sign one of salvation or judgment? Who is Immanuel, a distant messiah, the prophet's child, a crown prince, any child at random, or a symbol for the people as a whole? Moreover, Bibles have been burned because one of the key words in verse 14 was translated "young woman" instead of "virgin."

This much seems clear: The Hebrew of verse 14 certainly identifies the mother of Immanuel as a "young woman." One so designated in ancient Israel could have been married or single, virgin or not. It is the Greek translation of the Old Testament—the Septuagint—which prepared the way for the

New Testament understanding of the passage by translating that Hebrew word with the Greek term meaning "virgin." The meaning of the original, then, is not in dispute. Moreover, Isaiah's message concerns the immediate future. He has in view a woman either already pregnant—one could translate "is pregnant and will bear a son"—or about to conceive. In any event, the birth is a sign of events to happen before the child "knows how to refuse the evil and choose the good" (verse 15), a few years at most. Finally, the sign announces good news of deliverance from the present military threat.

In addition to placing us in contact with the traditions that lie behind the early Christian messianic faith, this text from Isaiah calls attention to the historical concreteness of the Word of God. It is also a reminder of the social and political dimensions of faith. For God to be with us may mean deliverance from military oppression and having a just and righteous government. The reign of God will be a new age, a new heaven and a new earth. But it is also in and for this world as well.

Psalm 45

Psalm 45 is clearly a wedding psalm. The references to the king and the bride in the text, however, are the source of differences in interpretation. Four approaches are worthy of note.

1. One line of interpretation is what might be called the metaphorical approach. This assumes that the marriage described is simply a conventional wedding. The normal, everyday groom is described in metaphorical language as a "king" and the bride as a "princess."

2. A second approach can be called the mythological. This assumes that the wedding partners are actually the male deity, played by the king, and the female goddess, played by the queen.

3. A third approach is the allegorical. The king in the text stands for Yahweh and the bride is his chosen people. What is said in the text is not to be taken literally but allegorically.

4. A fourth interpretation is the historical. This assumes that the text was composed for an actual wedding for an actual ancient Israelite or Judean king. Since the text refers to Tyre, it has sometimes been assumed that the psalm was composed for the marriage of King Ahab of Israel to the Phoenician princess Jezebel who hailed from the city of Tyre.

The association of this text with the annunciation strains any reading of the text unless one wants to understand the king in the text as God and the bride as the Virgin Mary. The more common Christian interpretation is to relate the figure of the king to that of Jesus as is already done in Hebrews 1:8-9. If Jesus is identified with the groom, the bride, however, is best understood as the church not as Mary. At any rate, any exegesis of the text that Christianizes the interpretation forces the imagery considerably.

Of the four interpretations noted above, the most likely original reading is that which sees the psalm as a composition from an actual wedding though it is doubtful if we can identify which king was the groom.

The following is the outline of the psalm: (1) a statement about the poet and the purpose of the poem (verse 1), (2) the glorification and praise of the king (verses 2-9), (3) the glorification and praise of the bride (verses 10-15), and (4) a statement to the king which promises him great and famous progeny (verses 16-17). The psalm allows us some insight into the opulence of the royal court and a glimpse at some of the flattery of the king which must have characterized court life.

Although the poet praises and flatters the king, he may also have engaged in some "preaching" to the monarch by making frequent reference to the king's responsibilities. The ruler is described as the fairest of men, one blessed with grace. The king, gloriously garbed in regal splendor with girded sword, can be visualized in the imagery of verse 3. The king is portrayed as the defender of the right and the cause of truth, whose arrows destroy his enemies. The throne of the king is proclaimed as eternal and his rule as one of equity and righteousness. The status and well-being of the king are reflected in the perfumes which scent his royal robes, in the ivory palaces where he is entertained by instrumental music, in the daughters of royalty that inhabit his mansion, and in the golden splendor of his queen.

The bride is addressed and admonished to forget her family and country (Tyre) and to give her affection and attention to her new husband. The bride in her wedding finery and her attendants and ladies-in-waiting are described as being led in procession to the palace of the king.

The psalm concludes, like many modern Near Eastern weddings, with a statement expressing the hope and assurance of numerous offspring. Since fertility—numerous offspring—was considered a blessing from God (see Ps. 127:3-5), such a promise or blessing was especially appropriate for the king whose offspring would share in the rule of the Davidic dynasty to whom God had promised eternal rulership.

Psalm 40:6-10

This lection is excerpted from the thanksgiving portion of a psalm probably originally used by the king. Verses 5-10 comprise the worshiper's thanksgiving spoken directly to the Deity in response to having been redeemed from some great distress (described in verses 1-3). The association of this text with and its appropriateness for the Annunciation are its emphasis on willingly submitting to the divine will (see especially verse 8), as was the case with Mary.

Several statements in the text require explanation. Verse 6 declares that God does not desire sacrifice. Four different types of sacrifice are referred to, some of the free-will type and others mandatory. What the verse intends to emphasize, however, is that what God really requires is a faithful, hearing attitude. The expression, "ears thou hast dug for me," probably was a proverbial way of saying, "I am really hearing you."

The book referred to in verse 7 may have been the Book of the Law especially if this was written for use by the king (see Deut. 17:14-17), perhaps an official record or court document, or maybe a heavenly book in which it was believed were recorded all the activities of a person's life. At least, the book seems to give a favorable opinion of the worshiper (see verse 8).

In verses 9-10, the worshiper testifies to having proclaimed the salvation of God. In these verses the same point is made with two positive affirmations (verses 9*a*, 10*b*) and three denials (verses 9*b*, 10*a*, 10*c*). The psalmist declares that the story he/she made known in public worship in the life of the congregation has thus borne testimony to God's salvation.

Hebrews 10:4-10

The Feast of the Annunciation of the Lord occurs on March 25, nine months prior to the celebration of his birth at Christmas on December 25. When the feast first began to be celebrated in the fifth century, it was done in close connection with Christmas, but eventually it was shifted to the spring. It was variously celebrated as a feast of the Lord and as a feast of Mary, as its different names attest: "The Annunciation of the Lord," "Conception of Christ," "Incarnation of Christ," "The Annunciation of Mary." Since it is observed on a fixed date, it may occur during the Season of Lent when the mood is somber and penitential. But it may occur as late as Easter Week, when the joy of resurrection life is the central focus. Thus, it can become an occasion of joy that breaks the penitential mood of Lent, or one that complements the joyous celebration of the Risen Lord. In either case, when we think of the announcement of Christ's birth, it can only be an occasion of joy.

With its mention of the time "when Christ came into the world" (verse 5), the epistolary reading is especially fitting to the occasion. To elaborate on Christ's incarnation, the writer of Hebrews uses the language of Psalm 40:7-9, where the psalmist speaks of "coming" to do the will of God. This psalm quotation is part of one of the psalm selections for this day, and thus the readings from the Psalm and the Epistle can be related directly to each other. We should note, however, that the author of Hebrews puts the words of the psalm on the lips of Christ himself, and uses them to explain Christ's own vocation. In doing so, he has given the psalm an explicit incarnational interpretation when he has Christ say, "Lo, I have come to do thy will, O God" (verse 7). This emphasis on the incarnate Christ coming to the world to do the will of God echoes a major Johannine emphasis (John 4:34; 5:30; 6:38). We may recall that in response to the raising of Lazarus and Christ's discourse concerning the resurrection and the life, Martha confessed, "Yes, Lord; I believe that you are the Christ, the Son of God, he who is coming into the world" (John 11:27). Here we see an explicit connection between Easter and incarnation. Even if we separate them liturgically, they eventually come together in Christian confession.

Because of the prominence of sacrificial language in today's epistolary reading and the emphasis on Christ as the ultimate sacrifice that is to be preferred to that of "bulls and goats" (verse 4; cf. 7:18-19; 9:12, 19), the text may be appropriated within the context of Lenten observance. This is clearly the case in the final verse, "And by that will we have been sanctified through the offering of the body of Jesus Christ once for all" (verse 10; cf. 10:14, 29; 13:12; also I Thess. 4:3; Eph. 5:2).

Like the author of Hebrews, we can only reflect on Christ's incarnation, and more specifically on the announcement of his conception, from a post-Easter perspective. In doing so, we think of it as the moment that began a life of filial obedience committed to doing the will of God. We see it as a life that ended with the ultimate sacrifice, "the offering of the body of Jesus Christ once for all" (verse 10), through which we have been sanctified, or become dedicated to doing the will of the Father.

Luke 1:26-38

The Good News for today is brought by an angel. Angels were not a part of Jewish theology in its earlier stages, apparently entering late as an influence from Persian religions in which angels abounded. In some circles angels were given special assignments as guards or messengers or caretakers, and certain ones had names, such as Michael and Gabriel. Coming out of late Judaism, Christianity was from the start influenced by the widespread belief in angels and demons. And so Luke tells us that the angel Gabriel came twice from God's presence with good news, first to Zechariah to say that he and Elizabeth were to have a child in their old age (1:5-25), and then to Mary to announce that in her virginity she would conceive and bear the child Jesus, son of David and Son of God (1:26-35). The child of Zechariah and Elizabeth would prepare the way for God's coming (1:17), and God's coming would be in the child of Mary conceived of the Holy Spirit (1:35).

Before trying to distill a theme or central message from this text, the preacher would do well to approach the passage in two ways. First, the literary style and quality of Luke's composition are important for understanding what this text says and does. It is well known that the author of the third Gospel was a conscious literary artist and nowhere is that more evident than in the first two chapters. Many believe Luke is here sharing materials used in the worship of the early church. Filled with songs, the liturgical character of the entire narrative is evident. Doxological texts deserve doxological sermons. Of the passage before us now, 1:26-38, two qualities should be noted.

1. The form of the announcement by the visiting angel, here and to Zechariah (1:5-25), is in the pattern of such stories in the Jewish Scriptures.The angel appears (Gen. 16:7; Judg. 13:3), the person visited reacts (Gen. 17:1-3), the person is reassured (Gen. 17:4ff.), the birth is announced (Gen. 16:11; Judg. 13:3), the one to be born is named (Gen. 16:11), the child's future is predicted (Gen. 16:12; Judg. 13:5), an objection is raised (Gen. 15:8; Judg. 6:15), a final reassurance or sign is given (Gen. 17:21; Judg. 6:17ff.), and the word is accepted (Gen. 16:13; Judg. 6:24).

2. The entire narrative is filled with the language of the Jewish Scriptures: "Hail, the Lord is with you"; "you shall conceive and bear a son"; "the Holy Spirit will come upon you"; "let it be to me according to your word"; "with God nothing will be impossible." Unlike Matthew who often tags a citation, "As it is written," in order to prove or authorize his point, Luke weaves the language and phrasing of the Scriptures into his own narrative. Luke is no less filled with Scripture than Matthew but the difference is important for those who communicate the Gospel materials. Matthew

argues, establishes, proves; Luke tells a story. Sermons should reflect the difference.

In addition to approaching the text literarily, the passage calls for theological reflection. A visiting angel dazzles us, an obedient Mary moves us, and a virgin birth rouses our minds, but the chief character in this story is God. God is here portrayed as a God of grace and of power. Grace fills the story because God is sending a gift to the world. The cross speaks of grace, to be sure, but so does the manger. And the power of God? In Genesis 18 Abraham and Sarah receive heavenly messengers who promise they shall have a son. To the bewildered old couple, the messenger says, "Is anything too hard for the Lord?" (verse 14). To the frightened and bewildered Mary, the angel says, "For with God nothing will be impossible" (Luke 1:37). This is the creed behind all other creeds and the church should recite it often.

Scripture Reading Index

SCRIPTURE READING INDEX